SPECIAL NEEDS AND LEGAL ENTITLEMENT

Choosing a School for a Child with Special Needs
Ruth Birnbaum
ISBN 978 1 84310 987 7
eISBN 978 0 85700 208 2

Kids in the Syndrome Mix of ADHD, LD, Autism Spectrum, Tourette's, Anxiety, and More!
The One-stop Guide for Parents, Teachers, and Other Professionals
2nd edition
Martin L. Kutscher MD
With contributions from Tony Attwood PhD and Robert R. Wolff MD
ISBN 978 1 84905 967 1
eISBN 978 0 85700 882 4

Guerrilla Mum
Surviving the Special Educational Needs Jungle
Ellen Power
ISBN 978 1 84310 999 0
eISBN 978 0 85700 392 8

SPECIAL NEEDS AND LEGAL ENTITLEMENT

THE ESSENTIAL GUIDE TO GETTING OUT OF THE MAZE

MELINDA NETTLETON AND JOHN FRIEL

Illustrations by Columb Friel

Jessica Kingsley *Publishers*
London and Philadelphia

First published in 2015
by Jessica Kingsley Publishers
73 Collier Street
London N1 9BE, UK
and
400 Market Street, Suite 400
Philadelphia, PA 19106, USA

www.jkp.com

Library of Congress Cataloging in Publication Data
Nettleton, Melinda, author.
  Special needs and legal entitlement : a practical guide to getting out of the maze / Melinda Nettleton and John Friel.
       pages cm
  Includes bibliographical references and index.
  ISBN 978-1-84905-595-6 (alk. paper)
  1. Special education--Law and legislation--Great Britain.
2. Children with disabilities--Legal status, laws,
etc.--Great Britain. 3. Children with disabilities--Education--Great Britain. I. Friel, John, 1949- author. II.
Title.
  KD3663.N48 2015
  344.41'0791--dc23

                          2014036689

British Library Cataloguing in Publication Data
A CIP catalogue record for this book is available from the British Library

ISBN 978 1 84905 595 6
eISBN 978 1 78450 051 1

Printed and bound in the United States

CONTENTS

INTRODUCTION

Both authors, John Friel and Melinda Nettleton, are lawyers specialising in the field of special educational needs and disability, but we are both also parents of children with statements of special educational needs. Our other children also had learning difficulties, all being dyslexic.

John was actually involved in the field of advising on disability before realising he would be personally involved. In Melinda's case, it was the fact that her second son had severe language disorder, dyspraxia and dyslexia that meant she became involved in this field. We both therefore have a personal commitment and experience.

Originally, John wrote a number of books for Jessica Kingsley Publishers once the 1993 Act, which substantially reformed this field, came into force. They were initially jointly written by a famous educational psychologist, Dr Harry Chasty, who is credited by the British Psychological Society with achieving the legal recognition of dyslexia in this country. He retired some time ago. These books have always been intended to be used by parents, special educational needs co-ordinators, advisers and any interested professional. It is hoped that they would be of some use to the legal profession, although they are not the books' major target.

John's involvement started whilst he campaigned, together with Dr Chasty, to change the 1981 Education Act, which became the 1993 Education Act Part 4, setting up Special Educational Needs and Disability Tribunal and substantially increasing parents' rights. When the recent Government issued a Green Paper, John and Melinda were involved with many people and charities, together with a large spectrum of political views, in campaigning to make sure that parents did not lose rights. The Green Paper issued by Sarah Tether, MP, who was the Minister in charge at the time, initially did indicate a reform, making matters simpler and easier. It will be seen from this book that this did not happen. However, when the first Bill was issued in September 2012, there was a clear agenda of local authorities and civil servants that parents' rights should be cut down, and that less should be done for children and young persons with a disability. Happily, protests succeeded. They were among the many who successfully campaigned for a retention of parents' rights and gaining some improvements in the system. Unfortunately, the system is now overcomplicated, and confusing. This is a great disappointment.

This book intends to provide, as far as it possibly can, some basic self-help guidance on the new system. What is thought to be likely is that local authorities will try and contend that the new education and health care plans are something different, and therefore that the law has changed, and fewer children and young persons are entitled to support from EHC plans. That is not so; the law is the same, and the rights of children and parents are still preserved in law.

What we have set out to do therefore is first of all to try and give guidance by way of a comparison of the previous system with the current system. We then deal with how a request for a statutory assessment for an EHC plan works, how the Code of Practice works, how the system develops where parents are seeking to obtain an EHC plan and how to make an appeal, if needed.

Please note, the book does not cover Equality Act rights, particularly in terms of disability discrimination in education. However, there is some mention of how the Equality Act affects expert evidence. While the system is evidence-based, obtaining the right evidence in sufficient time, and dealing with the right issues, is an extremely important part of the process. It is relevant to every stage of the process. The chapter on expert evidence is intended to direct attention to the issues required, the extent of evidence required and how experts should address their reports, and indeed what are the requirements set by the Tribunal for their reports.

We try to give some idea of the Tribunal process, and if necessary, appeals to the Upper Tribunal and enforcement. We do not cover in any detail the full range of possible legal grounds for an appeal to the Upper Tribunal or in relation to the enforcement of decisions of the Tribunal and the enforcement of the EHC plan itself. We do, however, give practical guidance. A book like this, which is intended to be understood by both parents and advisers, is not giving a detailed analysis of the law for lawyers. Some of the law is new, but it is based on old law. We believe, where we have outlined the legal situation, that it is correct.

The book is particularly written from the perspective of a parent, family member or adviser seeking to support a child with special educational needs and a disability. This is the same approach taken by the original book published on the 1993 and 1996 Acts. At that time parents considered, as did the advisers and professionals who used the book, that we gave practical guidance on the system. This approach has been continued, at the expense of a more complicated legal text, but we believe that it is the right approach.

At the end of the day, there is a child or young person with severe or significant difficulties, and who may also have associated complex combined medical needs, surrounding the full picture.

The 1993 Act first set up the Tribunal system, replacing an informal advisory appeal system. The Tribunal system has many defects, but must be described as an overall success, with limited resources. It is also the case that the Tribunal plainly expressed in March 2014, through its now-senior Judge Tudur, a wish for a system that parents would find more parent-friendly, and for parents to be more confident with the fairness and complexity involved in the previous system under the 1996 Act. That undoubtedly was the intention of seeking changes to the law, as was outlined by the Green Paper. This intent was confirmed by the December 2012 Parliamentary Select Committee on Education's report on the reforms suggested. However, that objective has not been achieved, and if this book seems overcomplicated, we can only apologise, but we must point out that the system itself is overcomplicated and essentially flawed in this regard.

We hope we have done our best. There is a consultation process in Wales, and we have not covered Wales for that reason, although the consultation looks as though it is producing very similar changes. In the future, we may be able to consider producing an addendum to this book covering Wales.

John Friel
Melinda Nettleton

A BRIEF DESCRIPTION OF THE NEW SYSTEM FOR CHILDREN AND YOUNG PEOPLE WITH SPECIAL EDUCATIONAL NEEDS AND DISABILITIES

A Comparison with the Old System

Introduction

The Children and Families Bill became law on 13 March 2014, but there remains considerable uncertainty, as matters have been rushed. For example, although a draft Code of Practice was issued for consultation in October 2013, with a view to finalising it, substantial changes were made to it in the House of Lords between January 2014 and the final approval of the Bill itself in Parliament. The UK Government tried to push matters through so that their goal of its coming into force in September 2014 would be realised. As a result, the substantial changes made to the Bill have resulted in an Act that has not been thoroughly thought out.

The regulations for the draft Bill were as follows:

- Clauses 36, 37, 44, 45, Education (Special Educational Needs) (Assessment and plan) Regulations

- Clause 41, Approval of Independent Educational Institutions and Specialist Post-16 Institution Regulations

- Clause 49, Special Educational Needs (Personal budgets and direct payments) Regulations

- Clause 52, Special Educational Needs (Mediation) Regulations

- Clause 54, Special Educational Needs (Children's Rights to Appeal Pilot scheme) Order

- Clause 63, Special Educational Needs (SEN coordinators) Regulations

- Clause 65, Special Educational Needs (Information) Regulations.

Approximately 133 amendments to the Bill were made in the House of Lords, some of which are significant, and probably more than the Government ever intended to concede. The final Code of Practice was issued in July 2014, and the Regulations were finalised in June, largely into one long regulation, The Special Educational Needs and Disability (SEND) Regulations 2014.[1] Consultations are also currently underway regarding changes to the assessment procedures for the Disabled Students' Allowance.

We therefore intend to address the following:

- Where are we now?

- What are the main changes?

- How do they affect processes/practical application?

- How does the new legislation affect children who already have a statement?

- The SEN changes post-16/18 to 25.

- The transitional arrangements.

Where are we now?

In 2012, the Government published a Green Paper setting out proposals for changes in the system of supporting children and families with

---

1   See www.legislation.gov.uk/uksi/2014/1530/made.

special educational needs (SEN) and disabilities.[2] The proposals were primarily aimed at those with SEN, who also often had a disability. As a result of these proposals, the Government set up a number of Pathfinder schemes, which were non-statutory. Although the object of the Pathfinders was to test the proposals, they were actually set out without any assessment or outcome criteria, and the whole process was extremely rushed. Not surprisingly, concerns arose, and a form of assessment for monitoring the Pathfinders was eventually put in place. Despite trying to ensure the Pathfinders developed into a coherent pattern of exploring improvements in the system, controlling and measuring their performance, and ultimately assessing their success, the Government produced a draft Bill to go before Parliament in draft terms in September 2012. It was issued by the then Minister, the Right Honourable Sarah Tether MP, who had sole responsibility for this very important area of both law and social policy. The Bill was nothing short of astonishing in its proposals: in brief, it seemed intent on reducing parental rights, and removing from the system large numbers of children with significant learning needs and disabilities, most of whom were theoretically in the higher bracket of cognitive functioning. It was quite clear that the initial intention was to remove severe and significant dyslexia, high functioning autism, hearing impairment and visual impairment from the new Education, Health and Care (EHC) plans. Parental rights to apply for assessments and appeals were significantly reduced. One of the more astonishing claims made later to justify this proposal was that this was just bad draftsmanship by those responsible.

The Minister lasted, so far as can be recalled, a few days after the Bill was published in 2013. Her replacement, the Right Honourable Edward Timpson MP, when interviewed in September 2013 on Radio 4 on the 'World at One' about this proposed new Act, contended that it was definitely the Government's intention to reduce parents' rights

---

2   Gillie, C. (2012) *The Green Paper on Special Educational Needs and Disability*. London: House of Commons Library. Available at www.parliament.uk/business/publications/research/briefing-papers/SN05917/the-green-paper-on-special-educational-needs-and-disability.

and to restrict access to EHC plans and to the appeals system, relating to the enforcement of rights already existing. This intention did not last long, as the new Minister was able to take stock of the situation, and quickly referred the matter to the Parliamentary Education Select Committee. In the meantime, he announced that he did not intend to reduce parents' rights, and that he would retain rights to specificity of provision.

The Select Committee's report in December 2012 was essentially, in polite terms, a strong criticism of the proposed Bill.[3] Although it recognised a lack of logic between moving the proposed legislation forward without the final Pathfinder reports, together with an assessment of the outcomes of the Pathfinders, it made a number of excellent recommendations, many of which were adopted (although, in fact, the majority were not). One of the recommendations adopted by the Pathfinders was that they were simply too narrow, and particularly needed to look at those children receiving services post-16. The Act has come into force before any proper assessment of the Pathfinders could be made in any cogent or coordinated manner, including how they worked out, and whether, in fact, these proposals were practical.

What is quite clear is that the Government's intention announced in the Green Paper, and put forward in support of this legislation, is that the process of supporting children with SEN, whether currently with a Statement, or in the future with an EHC plan, will be less adversarial, more simplified and user-friendly. As will be appreciated, and it doesn't take very long, just look at the 2014 Regulations and the Special Educational Needs and Disability (SEND) Code of Practice issued in July 2014 to see that what has emerged is a system that is:

- supposedly unified, in that the EHC plan now covers principally health, education and care (input from all three services are required, if applicable to the child or young person);

- in reality, far more complex, particularly for parents and young people with SEN and a disability.

---

3   House of Commons (2012) *Education Committee – Sixth Report, Pre-legislative Scrutiny: Special Educational Needs.* London: The Stationery Office. Available at www.publications. parliament.uk/pa/cm201213/cmselect/cmeduc/631/63102.htm.

Despite the hyperbole, the changes do not move matters forward very much

When all these points are stripped away, it does not, in fact, move matters forward very much. The changes contained in the new legislation could have been achieved by amendments of the current legislation rather than replacing the current system with a process that is more complex and difficult to understand.

The principal outstanding issues are as follows. There was all party support for extending EHC plans to those at university, as well as to those in further education and training, but the Government persuaded Parliament that guidance on this issue would be enough. It is quite clear that although there is all party support for such a reform, if matters continue to be as unsatisfactory as they currently are, a large number of relatively bright disabled students will fail at university because the system does not transfer from school, or adequately support them. Second, the information from the Pathfinder schemes has yet to be completed, analysed and considered. The schemes themselves may throw up significant issues to be addressed. Furthermore, the current provisions include an attempt to force mediation. There is now a new system whereby, save in exceptional circumstances, the parent appealing must apply for a certificate from a mediator to say that they don't want mediation, or through the tribunal, the parents or the young person can obtain permission to proceed, which would certainly be given if the certificate is delayed. Overall mediation itself is likely to be of very limited value. The sole exception is where only the school is at issue. However, no appeal currently involves just the school, and this will not change. It is highly unlikely, and it is hard to believe that any mediator will really issue a certificate within three days, to allow for an appeal.

Current position today

- The Children and Families Act 2014 in force September 2014

- A new complex coded practice

- New regulations

- Implementation September 2014; transition over a number of years.

In a letter to the Parliamentary Group on Dyslexia and Specific Learning Difficulties dated 12 May 2014, the Minister, Mr Timpson, stated that every local authority working with local schools, colleges, early years providers and health partners, would need to set out a local offer of support, and make it clear how children, young people and their families could access such support. From September 2014, local authorities are required to consult with families and providers of services and to publish their offer.

Plainly, the Government is in a rush. We will have to look at a second edition soon. In relation to this, there are two considerations.

First, the Welsh Assembly is consulting on a new system which will be similar but not the same. Second, because the whole system was rushed in, it is likely that a new edition will be needed fairly rapidly, to deal with developments.

What are the main changes?

Statements of SEN have been replaced with EHC plans, and there remain two classes of children: those with an EHC plan and those without.

The current SEND Code of Practice, which is unlikely to change on this issue, proposes that the system of School Action and School Action Plus be abolished and replaced with a single category of assessment beneath an EHC plan, called Additional SEN Support.

The major change that is to be welcomed is what is called the *local offer*.[4] This requires local authorities to publish information about services they expect to be available for children and young people with SEN and a disability. It must include information about the provision that the local authority expects to be available in its own area, and also information about provision outside its area from those who are responsible, regardless of whether an EHC plan is in place or not.

The local offer covers special educational provision, health care and social care provision, other educational provision, training provision, provision to assist in preparing children and young people for adulthood and independent living and the like.

From the above it is clear that there are proposed detailed regulations. It should therefore be possible to identify from a published document what provision is available locally, and how it can be accessed. Although attempts have been made to make the local offer mandatory, and indeed to create an overall national standard, this has not happened. The local offer is purely what is available locally according to the individual local authority.

---

4   See www.thelocaloffer.co.uk.

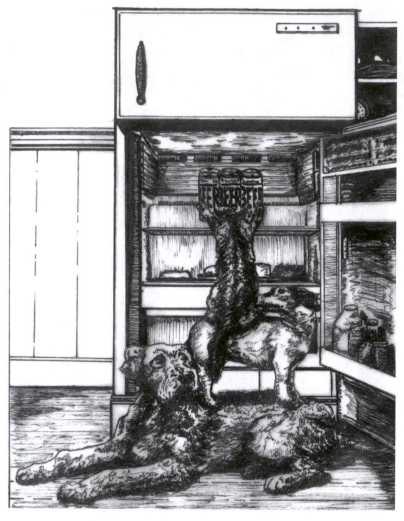

"Joint Commissioning"
(The effectiveness of EHC Plans relies on joint commissioning,
despite criticisms by the Select Committee)

The Children and Families Act 2014 has created a number of duties that are general to public bodies, to improve services working on a multi-professional basis, and relies on joint commissioning in this field. The provisions now also bring in academies.

The Education Select Committee criticised the proposals for joint commissioning in paragraph 4(1) of their December 2012 report, pointing out that the Government was relying too heavily on joint commissioning between local authorities, social care and health to make the reforms work. Although there are additional duties, to include joint commissioning, they essentially tighten up current practice and procedure and statutory provisions, such as Section 322 of the Education Act 1996, whereby local authorities can request support or delivery of provision from health authorities, Section 47 of the National Health Service (NHS) and Community Care Act 1990, and the basic fact that under the Children Acts, children's services (social care and education) should be a joint service.

Duties to individuals

EHC plans are principally still only enforceable against education, although there is now an extended definition of educational provision, which extends the duties of local authorities and the jurisdiction of the Special Educational Needs and Disability Tribunal (SENDIST) (now the First-tier Tribunal).

While an EHC plan involves health, education and care, in some cases only the child or young person subject to the plan requires input from all three services. Sometimes education will be enough on its own. It is to be stressed that the only part of the plan which can be appealed to the Tribunal and is thereby easily enforceable is the education component. Thus, where aspects of health and care which are equally definable as falling within the educational sphere, there is a legal duty to fully deliver it. It is only educational provision, therefore, which is effectively easily enforceable by the appeal process. There is no simple means of redress and appeal of the whole plan, although on the face of it, there is a possible extension of the statutory rights of appeal arising as a result of current changes to the social services legislation just passed, the Care Act 2014. It remains to be seen whether those provisions will be actually put into law.

Regarding duties owed to individuals in relation to education, what has not changed is:

- the definition of SEN and special educational provision, which is no different from the current Section 312 of the Education Act 1996;

- the duty to identify children and young people with SEN – Sections 21/22 of the 2014 Act simply re-enact the sections in the earlier 1996 Act;

- the duty to provide education within mainstream provision, and the right of parents to insist on mainstream education (see Section 33);

- the assessment review and reassessment provisions;

- the duty to specify provision.

Definition of educational provision

Section 21(5) of the Children and Families Act 2014 changes the definition of special educational provision, which is now defined as:

Health care provision or social care provision that educates or trains a child or young person is to be treated as special educational provision (instead of health care provision or social care provision).

The definition of special educational provision in Section 312 of the Education Act 1996 has been extended. Established case law, which excluded social care provision (such as *G. v Wakefield Metropolitan District Council and Another*),[5] is now in the past. Examples of the potential effect of the changes are where, for example, it has been decided that consistency of approach is necessary. This was always considered not to be educational, as opposed to a 'Waking Day' curriculum (residential placement) (see *W. v Leeds City Council*).[6]

In addition, where medical provision is concerned, speech and language therapy, occupational therapy, and where relevant,

5   [1998] 96 LGR 69 (QBD).
6   [2005] EWCA Civ 988 (CA).

physiotherapy, have long been considered special educational provision (see, for example, *Bromley London Borough Council v Special Educational Needs Tribunal*).[7] The situation that now arises is that what was health care provision could be educational provision in specialist environments such as in Young Epilepsy, where there is on-site specialist nursing staff, and, for example, consultant neurologists, who may contribute to either the education or training of the young person. Such provision was previously considered purely medical, but now it may well cross over.

Extension of services to the age of 25

Section 139A Learning Difficulty Assessment (LDA), which relates to the assessment and duty to provide for young people if they leave school and go to college at 16, or leave at 19, has been repealed. EHC plans now continue if appropriate and necessary (the legal test being the same as under the 1996 Act) to the age of 25. This, again, is a welcome extension. There never appeared to be much sense in having two systems, and it unites the whole system bar one, which is higher education, that is, going to university or to apprenticeships (not to be confused with further education, which *is* included within the system). It is, however, relevant to point out that matters are likely to be complicated by the fact that the Disabled Students' Allowance is being reviewed: a much stricter criteria is now proposed without any clear guidance as to the methodology or assessment of needs.

Personal budgets

Another major change is the local authorities' new duty to provide a personal budget that will satisfy its duty to arrange provision. This system is likely to give rise to a number of complex requirements, however, both for the local authority and parents. Initially, the local authority must be satisfied on a number of complex matters, and there are complex monitoring provisions. However, what the system does not deal with satisfactorily is when the personal budget will not

---

7   [1999] ELR 260 (CA).

purchase provision set out in the EHC plan because it is set at too low a level. The local authority does not need to make changes if it doesn't want to, and this leaves the young person stuck until the next annual review if there is a genuine dispute.

Since currently the community care direct payments are, in the majority of cases, unable to secure the correct provision, it is unlikely that personal budgets will be as popular as expected.

There are three options for budgetary control:

- notional arrangement: the local authority retains the funds and the parents direct usage

- third-party arrangements: funds are paid on behalf of the parent or young person

- direct payments.

Appeals and mediation certificates

The Act retains the statutory Right of Appeal in the same terms, which is as follows:

- against a refusal to make a statutory assessment

- refusal to make an EHC plan following an assessment

- appeal against an EHC plan

- refusal to amend an EHC plan or an amended plan

- refusal to change the name of a school in the EHC plan

- decision to cease to maintain an EHC plan

- after an annual review.

The main difference is that SENDIST's powers are now set out in the SEND Regulations 2014. It appears likely that there is some hope in the Department for Education (DfE), that if the Courts continue to come up with decisions that the DfE considers inconvenient, they may be able to change the Tribunal's powers by regulation. This is a worrying aspect, as the full statutory powers were previously set out in Section 326 of the Education Act 1996, and in Schedule 27 of the Act. Nonetheless, the main change is the requirement for either going to mediation or to obtain a mediation certificate.

Regulation 4 of the SEN (Mediation) Regulations require that the mediation adviser *must issue a certificate to the parent or young person under Section 52(4) of the Act within three working days on the date with the parent or young person informing the mediation adviser that he or she does not wish to pursue mediation.*

There is obviously the distinct possibility of parents going through mediation and finding that it doesn't work, and then having to appeal to SENDIST, which increases the complexity of the procedure. Mediation, however, will not deal with cases where a point of law is in dispute. Further, there is no additional funding for mediators, and mediators currently used by local authorities are not the equivalent of mediators used in court cases – a fully trained legally qualified mediator is much better qualified than the mediators generally available under the current system, and this will not be significantly changing.

Regulation 34 does allow a parent or young person to seek an order from SENDIST, and to go ahead in the absence of a mediation certificate.

Nobody considers that the certificate will be provided within three working days – and presumably this is three working days after receipt. In any event, this means a minimum of more than three working days.

Mediation can have a use, however, but only in limited cases, or where it is plainly health care provision or social care provision and not educational provision that would be an issue. There are now possible changes in the ability to appeal in the Care Act, possibly allocating to SENDIST the power to deal with social care issues arising from the current changes in the law that have just passed, concerning social services.

OTHER PROBLEMS WITH APPEALS

Although appeals provide a form of befriender system (although the befriender must be approved by SENDIST) for the child or young person, the current appellate provisions do not provide adequately for those who lack capacity under Section 2 of the Mental Capacity Act 2005. The SEND Code of Practice (July 2014) is frankly wrong about who can appeal. In particular, the issued capacity seems to be assumed, yet it is perfectly obvious that many young people approaching the age of 19, and some beyond 16, will lack the ability to make sense of health and welfare decisions – in other words, decisions about their education, social care and health futures. They often have complex and multiple difficulties, or significant mental health problems. A parent may, of course, become a deputy, via the Court of Protection, and will often take responsibility for the young person once they become adults at the age of 18.

The final point about mediation is that it is unlikely to be of any relevance if an expensive placement is involved. Placements for children and young people with very complex needs, which cost substantial amounts of money (£100,000 and above, possibly even £50,000 and above), are likely to be the subject of an appeal, and are unlikely to be successfully agreed on through mediation.

Format of EHC plans: postcode lotteries

EHC plans do not have to be standardised, and so they may vary between, for example, Lambeth and Yorkshire. However, the plans must include, in separate sections, the following:

- parent(s)'/child or young person's views
- child or young person's SEN
- SEN outcome sought
- SEN provision required (plan should specify)
- health or social care provision (plan should specify)
- school name and type

- details and outcomes intended, if a personal budget

- appendices (professional advice obtained).

As now, the duty to specify and quantify provision is retained in all sections of the EHC plan, according to Section 37(2) of the Children and Families Act 2014.

In practical terms, the EHC plan operates an equivalent of the current Part 2 of the 2014 Act, namely, the needs and all the identified special educational provision must be included to match the needs. Any health and care needs identified through the EHC assessment should also be included so that it is clear how any health and care provision in the plan addresses identified needs, that is, whether it matches. The plan therefore contains the equivalent of Part 3 of the Statement of SEN, but it is basically the education section that is crucially legally enforceable. The plan must specify and quantify, which means that the plan must include:

- All education and training provision, for example, all therapies, a 'Waking Day' curriculum, functional analysis of behaviour with proactive and reactive strategies, delivery by a multi-disciplinary team, input by clinical psychology/speech and language therapy/occupational therapy/physiotherapy/ Applied Behaviour Analysis (ABA) etc.

- More than in the current Part 3 of the 1996 Education Act, due to the broader definition of educational provision. For example, training for respite carers or for the respite care centre, input from speech and language therapists/occupational therapists/ or advice from them or a clinical psychologist.

The section on health and social care in the EHC plan is equivalent to Parts 5 and 6 of the Statement, but there are now also differences, namely, that:

- The plans should specify education, health and care provision. However, the duty to specify health and care provision is a helpful reform.

- In addition, the Care Act 2014 contains an interesting provision in Section 72, which permits the creation of an appeal system by regulation, and it appears that this also permits an appeal to be treated as part of an appeal brought under another procedure, that is, so that all can be brought before SENDIST except for health, for example. However, the Government does not have to put this into force, and, as with the Equality Act 2010, there are still sections that are not in force and indeed unlikely ever to be in force.

There remains, in the EHC plan, a section called 'School name and type', which is the equivalent of Part 4 of the Statement. It is also clear that Section 9 of the Education Act 1996 continues to apply. Following *Haining v Warrington Borough Council*,[8] it is now clear that Section 9 has probably been elevated to a greater status than previously.

The annual review provisions have not changed greatly, and indeed remain as complex as they were before. Currently a teacher who has taught the child is required to provide a report or attend an annual review. This requirement has now been dropped. This is a curious reform, as it is possible that nobody attending the annual review will have taught the child.

Phased transfers

Phased transfers in relation to EHC plans continue to require amended EHC plans before the phased transfer on 15 February in the year of transfer. There is a change with those post-16 – this is now quite clearly a phased transfer. With those post-16, it must now be five months before transfer, to a secondary or post-16 institution. The Regulations in Regulation 18 now provide for post-16 transition from 31st March. In 2015 only, this must be completed before 31 May 2015, and after 2015, before 31 March. In most cases mediation will be impractical, due to the timeframe involved.

Equally, the existing duties on social care services to assess and provide under the Children and Families Act 2014 and adult social

---

8   [2014] EWCA Civ 398 (CA).

care will continue to apply. However, as a statutory power, it is the local authority's choice, and not the parents' or the young person's, to continue to provide for the 18–25 group under children's social care services.

Practical application

The changes in the assessment procedure can be seen in the following table. However, they are more illusory than actual.

STATEMENTS	NEW EHC PLANS
Request for statutory assessment – 6 weeks to decision	Request for EHC plan – 6 weeks to decision
Test – whether it is necessary	Test – whether it is necessary
Advice – 6 weeks	Advice – 6 weeks
Child's parents	Child's parents
Educational	Educational
Medical	Medical
Psychological	Psychological
Social care	Social care
Any other advice LEA considers appropriate including teacher of the deaf/visually impaired	Any other advice LEA considers appropriate including teacher of the deaf/visually impaired
After assessment – if no Statement parents receive Note in Lieu	After assessment – if no EHC plan parents receive nothing
After assessment – if Statement is proposed – 8-week negotiation period with parent giving 15 days for initial response	After assessment – if EHC plan is proposed – parent is given 15 days for comment then finalisation
Total – 26 weeks from request	Total – 20 weeks from request

Note: The difference is that the time for parents' negotiation under the old system has been removed. In fact, nothing is different in relation to the local authority's responsibility on the timescales.

Other major changes indicated by the Code of Practice
Abolition of Individual Education Plans

Individual Education Plans (IEPs) are well understood, and can be traced to measure progress, or indeed measure no progress or inadequate progress. Instead, a graduated approach involving four actions is proposed:

- Assess

- Plan and notify parent

- Do

- Review.

The requirements for parents to be more intimately involved and consulted in relation to IEPs has gone, and there is a clear lack of parental involvement under the current proposed Code of Practice. The new process is not clear, nor is it one that seems to adequately involve parents.

Adequate progress

The current definition of 'adequate progress' for schools is given on page 72, paragraph 6.5 of the July 2014 Code of Practice, and provides a new and more limited definition for parents and advisers to argue from, in that it:

- is similar to that of peers starting from the same baseline;

- matches or betters the child's previous rate of progress;

- closes the attainment gap between the child and peers;

- prevents the attainment gap from growing wider.

The original criteria included a number of criteria that have disappeared, including the following useful criteria. It:

- ensures access to the full curriculum;

- demonstrates an improvement in self-help or personal skills;

- is likely to lead to appropriate accreditation;

- is likely to lead to participation in further education, training and/or employment.

In addition, the SEND Code of Practice currently provides that where progress is not adequate, it will be necessary to take additional different steps to enable pupils to learn more effectively. That rider has disappeared. The current proposals are retrograde.

The role of the Special Educational Needs coordinator

There is now a requirement for a special educational needs coordinator (SENCO) to be professionally qualified within three years of obtaining the post, requiring a National Award for SEN Coordination. This, again, is a welcome change.

In addition, the legislation goes back to the approval of independent schools – previously only schools that had been approved would normally be named in Statements (now EHC plans). This was abolished under the last Labour Government, but has now been reinstated. It is not clear whether the Secretary of State's discretion to give permission for a Statement to be supported outside of approved schools was previously done by the DfE, but it will be reinstated.

CHAPTER 2

IDENTIFYING CHILDREN WITH SPECIAL EDUCATIONAL NEEDS

Part 3 of the Children and Families Act 2014 replaces most of the Education Act 1996 with regard to functions concerning children and young people with SEN and disabilities. It starts with Section 19, which is basically a target duty, meaning that it is not individually enforceable, although it may have an effect in an individual case. The overall target duty is to exercise the functions of a local authority, taking into account the views, wishes and feelings of the child or young person and parent, involving them in the exercise of any decisions. It includes providing the child or young person, or their parents, with the necessary information about the potential decision, and having regard to the need to support them to facilitate their development, or to achieve the best possible educational or other outcome.

The earlier requirement to identify children and young people with SEN has now been replaced by Section 22 of the Act, which requires a local authority to exercise its functions with a view to securing that it identifies:

- all children and young people in their area who have or may have SEN

- all children and young people in their area who have a disability.

The duty to identify all children and young people who have a disability is different from the previous duty, which was confined to SEN; as the definition of disability is different from SEN, it is set out in Section 6 of the Equality Act 2010.

Section 23 creates a new duty on the health authority to bring children with a disability or special needs to the local authority's attention. The health authority forms the opinion that the child has or probably has special educational needs or a disability, the health service (we describe it as the health service because there have been so many changes; it is currently a clinical commissioning group, NHS trust or NHS foundation trust, but obviously this title may change in the future). It is to be noted that the Education Act 1996 was first enacted in 1993, and stayed the same until 2014, for over 20 years; since then, Health Service Acts have changed significantly and more frequently.

The duty imposed in health is to inform the child's parents of the opinion that the child has SEN or a disability. The child's parents then have an opportunity to discuss that opinion, and to draw that opinion to the attention of the local authority.

The local authority itself has a general duty to promote integration in Section 25, to ensure the integration of educational provision, training provision and health care and social provision, to promote the wellbeing of children and young people in the area who have an educational need or a disability, or to improve the quality of the special educational provision.

Local authority responsibility

According to Section 24, a local authority is responsible for a child or young person where:

- he or she resides in a local authority area and has been:
  - » identified by the authority as someone who has or may have SEN
  - » brought to the authority's attention by any person as someone who has or may have SEN.

The Courts have normally interpreted this as where the child is ordinarily resident. Case law, determining ordinary residence, goes back a long time, and is relatively settled.[1] Difficulties arise where a child or young person resides with one parent for some of the time, and with another parent for more of the time, or the young person is residing specifically for the purposes of education in a particular area. Normally the Courts and SENDIST interpret the words of the statute as meaning where the child or young person resides most, although if the child is with their father or mother for more time than the other parent, or the child or young person resides away from home for a substantial period of time to access education or training and the like, this is normally the place of residence (see *R. v Waltham Forest London Borough Council, ex parte Vale*).[2] Therefore the local authority will be responsible. However, it should be noted in law that a person can have two places of residence.

Parents' point of view

Is there a problem? What are Special Educational Needs?

The definition of SEN is unchanged from the Education Act 1996, which is re-enacted in the new Act. There is therefore no change in case law, although there are some significant changes in the duty to provide support under the new 2014 Act. The additional significant change is that the duty to support a child or young person now continues to the age of 25, if it is appropriate to do so.

Does a child or young person have SEN? Section 20 provides as follows:

1. A child or young person has SEN if he or she has a learning difficulty or disability that calls for special educational provision to be made for him or her.

2. A child of compulsory school age or a young person has a learning difficulty or disability if he or she:

    (i) has greater difficulty in learning than the majority of others of the same age, or

---

1   *Levene v Inland Revenue Commissioners* [1928] AC 217 (HL).

2   [1985] *Times*, 25 February (QBD) (Taylor J.).

(ii) has a disability that prevents or hinders him or her from making use of facilities of the kind generally provided for others of the same age in mainstream schools or in mainstream post-16 institutions.

3. A child under compulsory school age has a learning difficulty or disability if he or she is likely to be within subsection (2) when of compulsory school age (or would be likely, if no special educational provision were made).

Those who have a learning disability or disability solely because of the language or because the form of language that they are taught is different from basic English do not count as having a learning difficulty.

Parents who believe that their child has a problem will not normally think, 'Does my child have a special educational need?' Or, it may be more obvious if the child has a visible or established disability. There are, therefore, those who will be identified early, who have obvious disabilities and who have plainly had medical intervention from an early age. For those for whom the process of identification takes place at school at a later age, such disabilities would include dyslexia, or high functioning autism, both of which are often not identified until a much later age. So, too, with mental health difficulties.

In *R. v Hampshire Education Authority, ex parte J.,*[3] Judge Taylor dealt with the difference between a learning difficulty for a child with dyslexia, and a child without dyslexia, and the case is plainly helpful, even in the present day. Judge Taylor drew attention to what was taught in a normal curriculum, and pointed out that specialist provision for a dyslexic child did not fall within the normal provision to be made within schools for children or young people of his or her age.

The SEND Code of Practice, and the 2014 Act itself, now provides that anyone can bring a child or young person who they believe to have SEN to the attention of a local authority. This includes early years provider schools and colleges, together with health authorities.

---

3   [1985] 84 LGR 547 (QBD).

Current legislation includes a number of provisions for joint commissioning and joint planning, parent forums etc. This book, however, is not intended to be a legal analysis of the overall duties of local authorities in this area.

Where health authorities form the opinion that the child has a disability or SEN, or the parents are able to identify that fact due to medical intervention, then, as before, the question is whether the level of intervention requires a statutory assessment, and therefore the equivalent of the old Statement, an EHC plan. With all disabilities, early intervention and early help and prevention are crucial and essential if, of course, it can be pinpointed (see p.37 of the SEND Code of Practice, which states 'Local services should identify needs and offer effective support as soon as possible for children or young people who need it. This will improve children and young people's outcomes, and enable more effective use of resources'). The process of statutory assessment will be considered in this chapter.

For those who have disabilities or SEN that are not so apparent at an early age, the SEND Code of Practice deals with identifying needs in school, and replaces what was in the old Code of Practice with School Action and School Action Plus, an overall approach to monitoring which is more simplified but less detailed. The Code makes it clear that:

- schools should assess each pupil's current skills and levels of attainment on entry;

- class and subject teachers, supported by the senior leadership team, should make regular assessments of the progress of all pupils;

- where pupils are falling behind or making inadequate progress, given their age and starting point, they should be given extra support.

One measurement of extra support is adequate progress, and this is currently defined in the Code as progress that is:

- similar to that of peers starting from the same baseline;

- matches or betters a child's previous rate of progress;

- closes the attainment gap between the child and his or her peers;

- prevents the attainment gap from growing wider.

It is stated that where pupils continue to make inadequate progress, that if this is despite high-quality teaching targeted at their areas of weakness, the class teacher working with the SENCO should assess whether the child has a significant learning difficulty. Where this is the case, there should be agreement about the SEN support, to support the child.

The Code provides for an assessment process that requires the school to:

- Assess

- Plan

- Do

- Review.

The assessment process requires the class teacher working with the SENCO to establish a clear analysis of the pupil's needs. It agrees that parental concerns should be taken seriously, and such concerns should be recorded and compared to the school or college's assessment, and be regularly reviewed. In some cases the Code provides outside professionals from health or social services, who may already be involved. It is not helpful, however, that it doesn't suggest that there should be involvement, where thought appropriate at this point, of outside services if they are not already involved.

A plan should therefore be put in place, which should be implemented and then reviewed. Specialists are suggested to be necessary where *a child continues to make little or no progress despite well-founded support.* This ignores the fact, however, that some children may have previously undetected, unknown or unidentified complex SEN, which require support at an earlier stage or when discovered. It also ignores the fact that class teachers may not have the training and experience, and SENCO training (now mandatory under the 2014 Act) is not specific enough on particular cases.

Further, the definition of 'adequate progress' has omitted the following from the previous Code of Practice, where it should:

- ensure access to the full curriculum;

- demonstrate an improvement in self-help or personal skills;

- be likely to lead to appropriate accreditation;

- be likely to lead to participation in further education, training and/or employment.

It is suggested that the previous definition of 'adequate progress', both at primary and secondary schools, which are in different chapters of the old Code of Practice, should be taken into account by parents, and indeed by parents' experts, when considering the issue of whether there is adequate progress in an individual child's case. The new Code of Practice is less clear.

In Section 30 of the 2014 Act there is provision for a local offer that should set out all available provision for children and young people with disabilities, including health, education and social care. However, it does not answer the question, or certainly not in full terms, as to individual assessments and their identification of needs. For those parents who do have a child with identified needs, whether or not they have an EHC plan or a proposed assessment, the local offer should assist in identifying what is available to support the child. As will be seen later, the 2014 Act deals with children with SEN, and brings into its ambit the issue of social care and health care provision if it falls into the definition of educational provision. There continues to be two categories of children: those children who have SEN or a disability but do not have an EHC plan, and those with an EHC plan.

While it is clear from the DfE guidance on transition issued in May/June of 2014 that the law has not changed as to whether a child needs a Statement of SEN or now, under the new law, an EHC plan, it is a statutory test and the legal considerations, considered later, are the same in the 2014 Act. Where there is no EHC Plan, it is up to the school to provide the necessary support, calling on advice and support from the local authority for a particular child or young person's special educational needs. Guidance on funding arrangements, which currently expect schools to provide the first £6,000 of funding to support a child with a Statement of SEN, indicates quite clearly that it is expected that the school will divert funds to support children with SEN. The fact that a school is expected to provide the first £6,000 in funding has been the subject of recent advice from the Department of Education October 2014 advice to local authorities, which pointed out that the use of £6,000 funding or indeed less for a child, does not mean that the child is *not* entitled to a statutory assessment or an EHC Plan. It is clearly also the intention of the new Code of Practice and the new law, including Ofsted's requirement to assess schools' effectiveness in this area, to ensure that children without EHC plans are supported.

Sections of the SEND Code of Practice are more encouraging in this area. For example, the section dealing with use of data and record keeping makes it clear that provision made for pupils with SEN should be recorded accurately and kept up to date. The Code states that as part of any inspection, Ofsted expects to see evidence of pupil progress, a focus on outcomes, and a rigorous approach to monitoring and evaluation of any SEN provided. Paragraph 6.75 makes it clear that involving parents and pupils in planning and reviewing progress is a requirement, as well as the fact that the school should readily share this information with parents. The Code additionally states in paragraph 6.75 that this information *should be provided in a format that is accessible.*

Governing bodies are also required to publish a SEN information report, and the information that should be published is set out in the Special Educational Needs and Disability (SEND) Regulations 2014.

Schools are required by these regulations to publish information about the kinds of SEN provided for, the schools' policies identifying children and assessing their needs, including the name and contact details of the SENCO in mainstream schools, arrangements for consultation with parents and young people with special needs, and arrangements for assessing and reviewing the implementation of provision. In addition, arrangements for supporting children and young people between phases of education and preparing for adulthood is required, together with details of the approach to teaching children and young people with special needs. Last, details of adaptations to the curriculum, expertise and training and staff, and the evaluation process used to look at the effectiveness of the provision, must be set out. The regulations also require a governing body to publish other information along these lines, but the most essential duties are as listed previously.

"Disappearing Children"
(Para 9.4 of the Code of Practice – No-one should lose their Statement and not have it replaced with an EHC Plan simply because the system is changing)

Statutory assessment

The majority of children with special needs will have their needs met in local mainstream schools, whether in early years settings, schools or colleges. Where an EHC plan is required, as set out below, the test in law has not changed, and this is clearly confirmed by the Secretary of State Circular on Transition Arrangements issued in May/June of 2014.

It is further confirmed in paragraph 9.4 of the Code of Practice, where it is stated that during the transition period, local authorities will transfer children and young people with Statements under the new system, but that 'no one should lose their statement and not have it replaced with an EHC plan simply because the system is changing.' There are concerns here – either a parent requests a statutory assessment or a local authority commences it, as before, where an assessment takes place, it will not always lead to an EHC plan. As the statutory criteria for an assessment is that it is necessary to assess, it is highly likely that most assessments will result in an EHC plan as they did in Statements of SEN previously.

Local authorities can either, based on their own information, assess a child or young person (see Section 36 of the Act), or a parent can request, in Section 36(1), a needs assessment. A request can be made on behalf of a child or a young person; it can be by the parents, or a person acting on behalf of a school or a post-16 institution. As such, the law has widened here, because previously such a request could be made by a school, not by a post-16 institution, and there were some restrictions. The assessment by statute is assessment of the educational health care and social care needs of a child or young person.

However, as will be seen later, the duty to deliver under the Act is quite plainly defined under Section 20 of the Act, as a duty to deliver principally by education, with health and social care a subsidiary to education.

The test of whether or not an assessment is necessary has not changed in law. Section 323 of the 1996 Act, and its statutory predecessor, has been completely re-enacted in Section 36(3) of the 2014 Act.

What does the word 'necessary' mean here? Obviously it is something that the parents, and any experts advising the parents, will have to consider. In relation to the Education Acts, the word 'necessary' was considered in the case of *R. v Devon County Council, ex parte G.*[4] At page 605E-F, Lord Keith of Kinkel defined 'necessary' in terms of the definition of Lord Griffiths in the case *Re. an Inquiry under the Company Securities (Insider Dealing) Act 1985*, where it was defined as 'really needed'.[5] Lord Keith, in *Devon County Council, ex parte G.*, stated that this was the appropriate way of expressing the context. This was in the context of a school transport case, and the test in law is exactly the same. However, most recently in the Upper Tribunal, the test was again considered. What was made clear by the Upper Tribunal was that the authority's case that the child's needs could be met by School Action and School Action Plus was not the test to be applied. The Upper Tribunal stated that the test fell between the words 'really useful' and 'essential' (see *Buckinghamshire County Council v HW (SEN)*).[6] It is also to be noted that the test includes whether it is necessary for the special educational provision to be made for the child, and this is what is to be assessed. So if the health care or social care provision does not fall within that definition, then simply having a health care need or a social care need or both does not come within statutory provisions. It is worth noting, however, that special educational provision has changed in one sense of the word, namely, as in Section 312 of the Education Act 1996, where it is still defined as provision that is additional from that in mainstream schools or post-16 institutions, and now extends up to 25. However, Section 21(5) provides as follows, and adds to the definition:

> Health care provision or social care provision that educates or trains a child or young person, is to be treated as special

---

4   [1989] AC 573 (HL).
5   [1988] AC 660 (HL) 704D.
6   [2013] UKUT 0470 (AAC).

educational provision (instead of health care provision or social care provision).

Thus, the area of what may be necessary to determine special educational provision has undoubtedly expanded. Under previous case law, social care provision alone was not included (see *G. v Wakefield*).[7] Where it is educational or has a training aspect, it now falls into that category, which makes the categories far less clear-cut than before.

What should parents do? The situation for those over the age of 16 or 18

In Section 36 of the Act, a child's parent, a young person over the age of 18 but under the age of 25, or a person acting on behalf of the school or post-16 institution (as the Code of Practice makes clear, ideally with the knowledge and agreement of the parent or young person where possible), can request a statutory assessment. Those over the age of 16 can request a statutory assessment if they have capacity under the Mental Capacity Act 2005, but in practice they will normally do so in conjunction with their parents, or their parents will do it for them. It is unusual for those over 18 to request a statutory assessment at this age, and only likely for those who have basically been missed by the system. In such cases, issues will normally arise under the Mental Capacity Act as to whether they have, in fact, the capacity or the understanding to make such a request. The reality, therefore, is that up to the age of 18, it is likely to be the parent who will make such a request, acting in the interest of and with the child or young person concerned. But after the age of 18, EHC plans are only likely to continue where the child or young person has severe or global learning difficulties, or significant mental health problems. It is rare for those with a disability who require support post-18 or 19 to have a full understanding of their own situation. Nonetheless, the reality is likely to be that, in many cases, they will be supported by, or working with, their parents.

---

7   [1998] 96 LGR 69 (QBD).

Where a local authority considers a statutory assessment necessary, then the issues that are likely to arise are not whether an assessment should take place, but whether the assessment accurately and completely resolves the child's needs and requirements for provision. It is for those young people, who the local authority has not identified, that the parents and the young person, if necessary themselves, will be seeking the statutory assessment. For that reason, a local authority will carefully look at the request, but if it is not accepted, the matter will have to go to an appeal. A request or appeal for statutory assessments where the local authority has not agreed that the criteria for a statutory assessment exists should, if at all possible, be carefully prepared with appropriate expert evidence.

If a parent or young person is making a request for an assessment, it should obviously be in writing, giving good reasons for the assessment, for example. If the child is at school, and the school has not previously reacted to parental requests and/or the parent has already submitted some expert evidence, the parent should consider the following:

- If expert evidence has been submitted, whether it is too old, or whether it is actually adequate.

- If the evidence is not too old and it is adequate, it should accompany the written request.

A parent or young person, in making such a request, should give reasons why an assessment is needed. This may involve stating that the school has not identified the child or young person's needs, and is not meeting their needs. If the child or young person already has an EHC plan, it is strongly advised that the parents or the child or young person should seek additional expert evidence, and that expert evidence should be directed towards why the EHC plan needs to be changed and why it no longer identifies needs and provision. There may be exceptions where the child has been excluded from school, has to leave a particular school at a phased transfer, or whether significant mental health difficulties have emerged.

However, the Code and the Act do not really answer helpfully what happens if we are dealing with a young person who has a lack of ability to make decisions, in particular as defined under Section 2 of the Mental Capacity Act 2005. It is over-complex and wrong in some areas, as will be addressed in the next chapter.

The capacity to decide an appeal is the capacity to make decisions about the child or young person's future. In the case of a young person, particularly post-19, they are either likely to have deep-seated needs, even if they are of average ability or above (and these will be rare cases), or they will have serious and complex difficulties, which generally includes some element of cognitive delay. For those with cognitive delay, they are unlikely to be able to make decisions on their own, and it is strongly advised that parents apply for deputyship of finance, health and welfare from the Court of Protection – they will therefore be able to act on behalf of the young person. But matters are complicated, and the consultation documents available do not really address the point of those with cognitive delay who are unable to manage their own affairs adequately.

On deciding what is necessary, the Code of Practice basically says nothing. Quite plainly, whether the child or young person has made adequate progress is a major issue, and also whether the school has been able to identify all their SEN. As clearly stated by the Court of Appeal in *R. v The Secretary of State for Education and Science, ex parte E.*,[8] a Statement is not necessary if the school can assess and identify all the child's SEN. Although this is the leading case on Statements, it equally applies, as the statutory provisions are exactly the same for EHC plans. This point was further supported by the Upper Tribunal judgment of Judge Jacobs, referred to earlier.[9]

Where there is no agreement that a statutory assessment is necessary, parents would be well advised to put a cogent case together, particularly with the change in law, as local authorities, in the current state of play, are defending budgets; and where a parent thinks a statutory assessment and an EHC plan is necessary, expert evidence is

---

8   [1992] 1 FLR 377 (CA).

9   *Buckinghamshire County Council v HW (SEN)* [2013] UKUT 0470 (AAC).

essential if the child's school has either not supported the request, or it has been rejected, having supported or made a request.

Nature of expert evidence

Chapter 7 looks at what is expected from expert evidence. In relation to a parent or young person looking at requesting a statutory assessment, it is normally essential to obtain an educational psychologist's report. Parents need to seek advice as to an appropriate expert, either from the advisory charities in the field, or if they have consulted specialist lawyers, their own legal advisers. If, for example, you look at educational psychologists advising on independent assessments, a much smaller number provide assessments that are of use in the statutory assessment, which may go to an appeal to SENDIST in relation to an EHC plan. There are a number of psychologists putting themselves forward as capable of providing independent assessments of children and young persons with Special Educational Needs, on issues such as whether or not the child or young person currently has, or qualifies for a Statement, or whether the child currently has or qualifies for an EHC Plan. Many of these independent experts are not prepared to advise, having assessed a child or young person, in more detail, as to the requirements of provision in the form of an EHC Plan, as required under the Statutory Provisions and Regulations, which is essential. Furthermore, they are under no obligation, even if they do provide a report in an acceptable form, to agree to give evidence if a dispute arises and the matter goes to appeal to the Special Educational Needs & Disability Discrimination Tribunal. Advisors, parents and a young person instructing an expert should ensure the expert is prepared to provide a report which covers the requirements of an EHC Plan, to include the criteria for an assessment or the contents and form of the Plan. They should also ensure that they are experienced in giving evidence in a Tribunal or where relevant, a Court, and are willing to give evidence.

EHC plans are still required as a matter of law on the grounds of educational need. If the primary need is either health or social care, where there is no relevant educational need, even allowing for the extended definition of educational need under the new Act, there is no entitlement to an EHC plan. The Parliamentary Education Select Committee considering the initial Bill proposed by Ms Tether, Minister at that time, while advising on major changes to the original Bill (which have been made), also advised that all those with a disability of a sufficiently severe nature should have an EHC plan. The Government did not adopt this recommendation, however sensible it may seem.

CHAPTER 3

HEALTH AND SOCIAL CARE

This chapter provides an overview of the present position in relation to Health and Social Care. An explanation of the procedure for obtaining NHS Continuing Care and NHS Continuing Healthcare has been included. More information is contained in Chapter 4 on the Code of Practice, at the start of each of the sections of the EHC Plan, relating to Health and Social Care.

Where the buck stops

Your local healthcare provider has the legal duty to 'arrange' the healthcare provision specified in the EHC plan. This means your local healthcare provider must make sure the provision set out in these sections is delivered.

If the EHC plan specifies social care provision provided under the Chronically Sick and Disabled Persons Act 1970, the local authority has a legal duty to make that social care provision under the Chronically Sick and Disabled Persons Act 1970.

Unfortunately the local authority does not have any legal duty to deliver any other social care provision in the EHC plan (not resulting from the Chronically Sick and Disabled Persons Act 1970).

It is important to understand what the terms 'healthcare provision' and 'social care provision' mean, because it affects what you receive.

Healthcare provision is defined in **Section 21(3)** of the **Children and Families Act 2014** as follows:

'Healthcare provision' means the provision of healthcare services as part of the comprehensive health service in England contained under Section 1(1) of the National Health Service Act 2006.

Social care provision is defined in **Section 21(4)** of the **Children and Families Act 2014** as follows:

'Social care provision' means the provision made by a local authority in the exercise of its social services functions.

There is a *third* very important legal definition set out in **Section 21(5)** of the **Children and Families Act 2014** which states:

Healthcare provision or social care provision which educates or trains a child or young person is to be treated as special educational provision (instead of healthcare provision or social care provision).

Special Educational Provision, Health or Social Care Provision?

This means that provisions which educate or train children and young people are *not* classified as health or social care provision at all. They are Educational Provision and the Local Authorities Education Department must deliver. Good examples of this are speech therapy, occupational therapy and physiotherapy. They look like they should be health provision, because they are often provided by the health service. However, they must be treated as special educational provision, and not healthcare provision, if they educate or train a child or young person.

Depending on whether a particular element of provision in an EHC plan is healthcare provision, social care provision or special educational provision in the EHC plan, there are different consequences in terms of:

- whether the provision is legally enforceable

- how the provision is legally enforceable

- and if the provision is legally enforceable, who has to provide it.

A joined up system of enforcement is needed with Education Health and Care plans underpinned by a single point of appeal. Without this, too many families will continue to face a long and exhausting process of being passed from pillar to post while they fight for the right support.

One of the main aims of the new legislation is to try and harmonise the Health and Social Care provision for disabled children.

Unfortunately there is no clarity about how social care or health assessments will be part of the new assessments, meaning families may still face parallel processes. This is precisely the challenge that the reforms intended to overcome.

Chapter 4 of this book, under the title 'Code of Practice' sets out the Health and Social Care Sections of the EHC Plan and explains issues that you need to consider when dealing with each of these sections in greater detail.

NHS legislation

Primary legislation governing the Health Service does not use or define the expressions 'NHS Continuing Care', 'NHS Continuing Healthcare' or 'Primary Health Need'.

NHS Continuing Care

NHS Continuing Care is support provided for children and young people under 18 who need a tailored package of care because of their disability, an accident or illness.

It is different from NHS Continuing Healthcare, which can be provided to adults who have very severe or complex health needs.

The main difference is that whilst Continuing Healthcare for adults focuses mainly on health and care needs, Continuing Care for a child or young person should also consider their physical, emotional and intellectual development as they move towards adulthood. Guidance says that the Continuing Care process should focus on the child or young person and their family. As a young person moves towards adulthood, there should be more focus on them as an individual within their family.

There are three phases in the Continuing Care process with children:

1. Assessment Phase

2. Decision-making Phase

3. Arrangement of Provision Phase

There is also a fast-track process to ensure that their care can be put in place as soon as possible.

NHS Continuing Healthcare

To be eligible for NHS Continuing Healthcare, a young person must be over 18, have a complex medical condition and substantial ongoing care needs. The young person must have a 'primary health need' which means that the young person's main or primary need for care must relate to their health.

Eligibility for NHS Continuing Healthcare does not depend on:

- a specific health condition, illness or diagnoses

- who provides the care, or

- where the care is provided.

NHS Continuing Healthcare is free, unlike Social and Community Care Services provided by local authorities.

Procedure

Under 18 or over 18, the procedure is similar. The NHS now has to take reasonable steps to ensure an assessment is carried out in cases where there may be a healthcare need. However, this may not happen automatically and you may need to ask.

The first stage should be the application of the Continuing Health Checklist (also referred to as the Continuing Care Checklist) to decide whether full assessment is necessary. The Continuing Healthcare Checklist is a basic screening tool and may result in a person being told they do not qualify for funding or for a full assessment.

A social care worker or health worker such as a nurse will come and see you. They may also talk to other people like the child or young person's doctor, nurse, social worker and teaching staff and look at the available information. In the first instance a 'Checklist Tool' will be used to make a decision for referral for a full continuing healthcare assessment. The Checklist Tool primarily indicates whether the individual needs a full further assessment called the 'Decision Support Tool'. They will use the checklist to decide if you go on to the next step. You can ask for a copy of the completed checklist.

If an assessment is agreed, a full assessment will be carried out by a Multi-Disciplinary Team which may include health and social care professionals. who have different roles relating to health and social care requirements. It is important to build an overall picture of health and social care needs. A health worker such as a nurse will visit again. They may bring someone else with them, such as another social worker or health worker and there may be more than one visit. There will be further questions and other professionals will again be consulted. At this stage they will fill in a lengthy form called the Decision Support Tool (referred to earlier).

The next step is agreeing what is written. You should see what is written and have the opportunity to say whether or not you agree.

Ask for a copy of the Decision Support Tool document (DST) and look carefully at the paperwork. Check the documents and any supporting evidence to ensure it is an accurate picture of your child or young person's healthcare needs, for instance:

- Does it take into account supervision or specialist mental health requirements?

- Is the need defined as moderate when it should be high, severe or priority?

- Has the Assessor underscored a need because it is well managed by the Carers?

A written record should be made about what you disagree with and why. It is a good idea to put your own comments in writing and ask for them to be presented to the NHS alongside the Decision Support Tool and the Multi-Disciplinary Team's recommendations.

The NHS Clinical Commissioning Group for your geographic area is the group that decides on most health services in your area. They decide how to spend NHS money. The *decision on NHS Continuing Healthcare funding* will normally be made by an NHS panel at a closed meeting. The Health Worker will go back to the local *NHS Clinical Commissioning Group* in your area. The information the health worker collected will be used to make the decision, and you will be told what the decision is.

If the NHS Clinical Commissioning Group says 'no', and you are not happy with that, you can ask them to register a review and look at the information again.

If you do not get NHS Continuing Healthcare, sometimes the NHS will agree to joint funding.

In an emergency situation there is a further tool that is utilised to determine whether individuals are able to access continuing healthcare funds, called Fast Track Pathway Tool for NHS Continuing Healthcare. The Fast Track Pathway is used when a clinician considers an individual to have a rapidly deteriorating condition. The Checklist Tool, Decision Support Tool and the Fast Track Pathway Tool can be accessed on the following website: www.gov.uk/government/publications – National Framework for NHS Continuing Healthcare and NHS Funded Nursing Care.

CHAPTER 4

CODE OF PRACTICE

This chapter covers who the Code of Practice is for, how it works and what in it identifies where the Code of Practice is plain wrong about what the law says. To help, we have also set out the sections of the EHC Plan, which are linked together with pertinent information and advice for readers unfamiliar with Education, Health and Social Care legislation.

The DfE originally claimed that 'the new Code will be significantly shorter, clearer and more concise.' The previous Code of Practice (2001) was 142 pages long, with the relevant statutory regulations and an index totalling 210 pages. The new Code (2014) contains 271 pages, not including a comprehensive index or the relevant regulations.

Officially, the Code of Practice is not intended for parents! Lord Nash, Parliamentary Under-Secretary of State for Schools, stated in the House of Lords on 28 July 2014:

> The Secondary Legislation Scrutiny Committee express concern that the Code may be too long and complex to be of use to families. I should point out that the parents are not the Code's key audience. The chief audience is the range of bodies with statutory duties to fulfil which must have regard to it.[1]

On 15 August 2014 the DfE published *Special Educational Needs and Disability: A Guide for Parents and Carers*, which runs to 59 pages.[2]

---

1   *Hansard*, 28 July 14 Col GC 594.
2   DfE (Department for Education) (2014) *Special Educational Needs and Disability: A Guide for Parents and Carers*. 15 August. London: The Stationery Office.

How does the Code of Practice and Guide for Parents work?

The Code of Practice is issued under Section 77 of the Children and Families Act 2014. This requires a range of publicly funded bodies, such as local authorities, school governors and institutions within the further education sector, academies, pupil referral units, independent special schools registered under Section 41 of the Children and Families Act 2014, providers of relevant early years education, youth offending teams, the NHS Commissioning Board, clinical commissioning groups, NHS trusts, NHS foundation trusts and local health boards, and SENDIST all to have regard to the Code. It does not include independent schools, which are not approved under Section 41. Nevertheless, bearing in mind the disability discrimination provisions of the Equality Act 2010, other independent schools, whether mainstream or special schools, would be unwise to totally disregard it.

The expression to 'have regard' only gives the Code of Practice a limited legal status, however, which is obvious to lawyers, but not necessarily to non-lawyers. This book is for non-lawyers. Acts of Parliament, such as the Children and Families Act 2014 and the Equality Act 2010, are part of the law of this country, and must be obeyed by all, including local authority officers, schools and NHS trusts. The same applies to statutory regulations, and decisions of the Supreme Court, Court of Appeal, High Court and Upper Tribunal. Local authority officers cannot, as a matter of law, say in relation to provisions and Acts of Parliament, statutory regulations or decisions of the Courts, that it is all very well, but here in 'Blankshire' or 'The London Borough of X' we do things differently. No local authority officer, teacher, social worker or representative of an NHS trust is exempt, whatever may be suggested from time to time to the contrary. Legally, the expression to 'have regard' confers discretion. The Code of Practice is discretionary; it is not legally binding. That said, each chapter of the Code of Practice opens with a list of relevant legislation and statutory regulations. The fact that information about a particular provision is referred to in the Code *does not mean that the Act of Parliament/*

statutory regulations or case law is no longer legally binding. Equally, the fact that the Code of Practice misunderstands an Act of Parliament/statutory regulations or case law in a number of places doesn't change the law. The first problem for readers is identifying which parts of the Code are also in Acts of Parliament (primary legislation), statutory regulations, and decisions of the Courts, and which appear only in the Code of Practice. The second problem is identifying the sections in which the Code has got the legal position wrong.

While not unhelpful, *Special Educational Needs and Disability: A Guide for Parents and Carers* carries no legal status at all. That is to say, no one has to even have 'regard' to it.

What's in the Code of Practice?

Two categories of children, those with an EHC Plan and those without

The Code of Practice now creates two classes of children – those with an EHC plan, and those without. It refers to a 'graduated approach' (see para. 6.44), which involves five actions:

- Gathering information (paras 6.38–6.39)

- Assessing (paras 6.45–6.47)

- Planning (and notifying parents) (paras 6.48–6.51)

- Doing (para. 6.52)

- Reviewing (no need for a meeting, but parents' views to be obtained) (paras 6.53–6.56).

Gathering information should include an early discussion with the pupil and their parents, and a high-quality, accurate, formative assessment (para. 6.39). The information gathered should then be considered alongside internal and national data and expectations of progress. This should be readily available to and discussed with the pupil's parents (para. 6.51). If it is not readily available, a formal request under the Data Protection Act 1998 could be made, and if still not provided, then a complaint to the Information Commissioner could follow (the Information Commissioner secures compliance with Data Protection legislation).

Where a pupil is receiving SEN support, schools should talk to parents regularly to set clear outcomes, to review progress and to discuss the activities and support that will help them achieve these outcomes. A school should meet parents at least three times a year (para. 6.65).

The requirement for Individual Education Plans for pupils without an EHC Plan has ended. Nonetheless, there is still an ongoing requirement to properly plan intervention in a less precise manner. Unlike scheduled IEP meetings with the SENCO, these meetings 'should wherever possible, be aligned with the normal cycle of discussions with parents of all pupils. They will however be longer than most parent/teacher meetings' (para. 6.69). A record of the outcomes, action and support agreed through the discussion should be kept and shared with all appropriate school staff. This should be given to the pupil's parents. The school's management information system should also be updated as appropriate (para. 6.71).

Paragraph 6.75 emphasises that the school should readily share information with parents, and that it should be provided in a format that is accessible. Suggestions in paragraph 6.75 are for a note setting out the areas of discussion following a regular SEN support meeting, or tracking data showing a pupil's progress together with highlighted sections of a provision map that enables parents to see the support that has been provided.

Paragraph 6.76 also praises provision maps, although not every parent finds a visual format of this kind readily comprehensible or sufficiently detailed. When a pupil continues to make less than expected progress, despite evidence-based support, the school should consider involving specialists, including those secured by the school itself or from outside agencies. Paragraph 6.59 specifically states that:

> The school should always involve a specialist where a pupil continues to make little or no progress or where they continue to work at levels substantially below those expected of pupils of a similar age despite evidence based SEN support delivered by appropriately trained staff.

Schools are asked to assess each pupil's current skills and level of attainments on entry (para. 8.16), with subsequent regular assessments of progress (para. 6.17). These assessments aim to identify pupils making 'less than expected progress', previously known as 'adequate progress'. Less than adequate progress is said to be characterised by progress which:

- is significantly slower than that of their peers starting from the same attainment baseline;

- fails to match or better the child's previous rate of progress;

- fails to close the attainment gap between the child and their peers;

- widens the attainment gap.

The requirement to take additional and different action if adequate progress is not being made (now less than expected progress) is omitted. Paragraphs 5.41 primary and 6.48 secondary of the former Code of Practice included the following descriptions of adequate progress, now omitted by the current Code. It:

- ensures access to the full curriculum;

- demonstrates an improvement in self-help, social or personal skills;

- demonstrates improvements in the pupil's behaviour;

- is likely to lead to appropriate accreditation;

- is likely to lead to participation in further education, training or employment.

While this is disappointing, paragraph 6.18 of the current Code states that less than expected progress can include progress in areas other than attainment, such as wider development or social needs to make a successful transition to adult life.

Further, paragraph 6.23 states 'It should not be assumed that attainment in line with a pupil's chronological age does not mean that there are no learning difficulties or disability.'

Requesting an Education, Health and Care needs assessment

Paragraph 6.63 advises that:

Where, despite the school having taken relevant and purposeful action to identify, assess and meet the SEN of the child or young person, the child or young person has not made expected progress, the school or parents should consider requesting an Education, Health and Care needs assessment.

The Code then continues, that to inform its decision, the local authority will expect to see evidence of the action taken by the school as part of SEN support. This does not reflect the legal position. The statutory framework contains *no requirement* for any particular form of action or record keeping. The test is the same as previously – is a statutory assessment necessary? This will depend on the critical mass of provision that is in reality required by the individual child.

The EHC Plan Assessment

Paragraph 9.47 adopts a 'tell us once' approach, avoiding the parent having to provide the same information on multiple occasions. The local authority *must not* seek further advice if advice has already been provided (for any purpose), and the local authority, parent and young person are satisfied it is sufficient for the assessment. It remains to be seen how SENDIST now responds to multiple requests for assessment made by local authorities.

Role of the SENCO in school

The role of the SENCO has been enhanced (see paras 6.84–6.94). Indicative of the SENCO's status, the previous Code advised that the SENCO should have 'access to a telephone and an interview room is also desirable where possible.'

Now the SENCO must be a qualified teacher (para. 6.85), and where they have not previously been a SENCO for a total period of more than 12 months, they *must* achieve a National Award for SEN Coordination within three years of appointment. This should bring to an end the practice of appointing unqualified teaching assistants and learning support assistants to this role. The Code of Practice specifically states that the SENCO has day-to-day responsibility for the operation of SEN policy and coordination of specific provision made to support individual pupils with SEN, including those who have EHC plans (para. 6.89). The SENCO's key responsibilities are listed in paragraph 6.90.

The school should ensure that the SENCO has sufficient time and resources to carry out these functions, and it is suggested that smaller schools could share a SENCO, who should not have a significant class teaching commitment.

Funding for SEN support

Paragraph 6.99 is potentially misleading. This explains that 'schools are not expected to meet the costs of more expensive special educational provision from their core funding. They are only expected to provide additional support which costs up to a nationally prescribed threshold per pupil per year.' It continues: 'The responsible local authority… should provide additional top up funding where the cost of the special educational provision required to meet the needs of an individual pupil exceeds the nationally prescribed threshold.'

Arrangements for local authority top-up funding cannot lawfully override the requirement set out in Section 42(2) of the Children and Families Act 2014 for children with an EHC plan (and currently a Statement of SEN, while these remain), which creates an absolute legal obligation to secure the special educational provision for the child or young person set out in the EHC plan. The local SEN funding policy cannot override this statutory duty.

At the time of writing, mainstream schools, academies and further education institutions receive a notional £4,000 per pupil, and are expected to provide up to £6,000 from their budget for a high-need student. Local authority-maintained special schools receive £10,000 per pupil. However, where there is a Statement of SEN or EHC plan, the local authority must make this provision as it is an absolute statutory duty. Schools should note, however, that if the school has the budget and is not spending it on SEN, it is also at risk of a disability discrimination claim under the Equality Act 2010.

Transition to higher education

The provision in an EHC plan (and Statement of SEN, while these exist) enables some students to achieve and fulfil the admission requirements of universities. While the majority of EHC plans go up to the age of 25, they will stop if the young person wants to go to university, although their SEN and requirement for provision will not have disappeared. This brings to an end a provision that has worked so well to date.

The Code of Practice provides, in paragraphs 8.47, 8.48 and 9.211, that the EHC plan should be disclosed by the local authority in connection with the young person's application for a Disabled Students' Allowance and to the principal of the higher education institution (university) the young person is intending to attend. This derives from Regulation 47 of the SEND Regulations 2014. However, neither Student Finance England nor the principal of the higher education institution have any obligation to even have a 'regard' to the EHC plan. Students have been waving their Statements of SEN at principals of higher education institutions and Student Finance England for years, and they have consistently refused to take them into account – it makes no difference whether it is the student who hands over the Statement of SEN/EHC plan or the local authority. The issue is what happens. On this regulation and the Code of Practice they still don't have to take any notice at all, so the existing problematic situation continues. When it has all gone wrong (and the student is now in debt), university complaints procedures and disability discrimination and breach of contract claims in the County Court remain the only remedies. This is very unsatisfactory.

The relationship between a university and a student is basically contractual. A contract for the supply of service broadly means an agreement under which a person (in this case, a university) agrees to provide a service (in this case, education) for payment. Here, the student pays and usually obtains a student loan to do so.

A University Student Handbook and website, together with any documentation, form the terms of the contract. In a contract for the supply of a service there is an implied term about providing the service with reasonable care and skill under Section 13 of the Supply of Goods Act 1982. 'Reasonable care and skill' includes compliance with statutory duties such as those under the disability discrimination provision of the Equality Act 2010.

Right of Appeal to SENDIST post-16–25, as set out in the Code of Practice

Paragraphs 8.15 and 11.44 wrongly suggest that the parents' Right of Appeal to SENDIST ceases at the age of 16. Neither paragraph 8.21, which deals with the Mental Capacity Act 2005, nor Annex 1, which also deals with the issue of mental capacity, make the correct position clear. Section 51 of the Children and Families Act 2014 provides that 'a child's parent or a young person may appeal to the First-tier Tribunal against the matters set out in subsection (2).' Parental responsibility for a child continues until the legal age of 18.

Mental Capacity Act 2005, paragraph 8.21 and Annex 1

The assumption under the Mental Capacity Act 2005 is that at the age of 18, everyone has full capacity and can make their own decisions. Where there is no full capacity post-18, Regulation 64(2) of the SEND Regulations 2014 provides that references to 'young person' in Section 51 of the Children and Families Act 2014 are to be read as references to both the young person and the young person's parent. What this means is that the Code of Practice is legally incorrect in any paragraph where it suggests that in all cases the parental Right of Appeal ceases at the age of 16.

Annex 1 of the Mental Capacity Act 2005 states:

In cases where a person lacks mental capacity to make a particular decision, that decision will be taken by a representative on their behalf. The representative will be a deputy appointed by the Court of Protection, or a person who has Lasting or Enduring Power of Attorney. In the case of a young person who does not have such a representative, the decision will be taken by the young person's parent.

Reference to 'Enduring Power of Attorney' is very misleading. Enduring Powers of Attorney have now been abolished, and to be valid they have to have been made before October 2007. Bearing in mind that at the time of writing it is now 2014, any 18-year-old who granted an Enduring Power of Attorney in 2007 would now be over 25. The Code of Practice only affects those under the age of 25, so it is very difficult to see why these are mentioned at all.

Further, references to Lasting Powers of Attorney are also misleading. In order to grant a Lasting Power of Attorney, a young person (18 or over) must have full understanding. Without full understanding of what is being granted, a Lasting Power of Attorney cannot be made. These were created for able older people, who fear that with advancing age they might not always be able to run their own affairs.

A Lasting Power of Attorney is created before the individual older person loses the understanding to run their own affairs – cases in which 18-year-olds expect their mental capacity to diminish by the age of 25 to a point where they no longer have decision-making capacity will be very rare indeed.

The reality is that a deputyship in the Court of Protection is what Annex 1 should have focused on rather than a provision that has been abolished and is irrelevant, or the extraordinarily tiny minority of 18-year-olds who expect to lose decision-making capacity by the age of 25.

A deputyship in the Court of Protection over both finance and health and welfare gives parents the same rights for their children post-18 as they had prior to the young person becoming 18 to manage their affairs. This is particularly important if a parent is going to be fairly demanding in terms of the provision they wish the young person to receive, both currently and in the future.

The Court of Protection can only make decisions about young people who lack capacity to make decisions themselves on an individual basis. Parents must formally prove that the young person cannot make decisions themself. It is important to note here that officers in the Court of Protection do not routinely deal with developmental disability – the bulk of their work deals with previously able adults with assets who develop dementia and who are no longer able to manage their own affairs.

What the Court of Protection is interested in, in lay terms, is the young person's level of functioning, the sort of decisions they can make. Everyone has a level of decision-making capacity, even if it is a preference for vanilla over chocolate ice cream, or a red t-shirt rather than a yellow t-shirt. What is actually needed is something that explains this very clearly. Sometimes there is a cooperative GP or paediatrician who will write something that is suitable, sign and return the Court of Protection's form 'COP 3', but not everyone is willing to do this. Alternatively an educational or clinical psychologist could be instructed. Something is needed from a suitably qualified professional the Court of Protection will recognise, and it will obviously save a lot of money if the young person's GP, paediatrician or a suitably qualified professional clinical psychologist, from the child's school (assuming the child's school has one) is willing to do so.

In the course of an application to the Court of Protection, social services must be notified of the application and they may choose to become respondents to it. This is rare, but it does seem to happen where there are parental disagreements with social services.

Social services can oppose the parental application. Deputyship is particularly important, because adult social services have been known to refuse to deal with parents who are demanding, whether in terms of an expensive placement, or simply in terms of dealing with a residential setting, where parents do not feel that the standards match those of their own home. The process of applying for a deputyship takes some months to work through the Court of Protection. An early application, when the young person is approaching 18, is therefore advisable, before problems with adult social care can arise.

Mediation

Paragraph 11.38 of the Code of Practice is also extremely misleading. It states, 'The parents or young person may be accompanied by a friend, advisor or advocate and, in the case of parents, the child, where the parent requests this and the local authority has no reasonable objection.' This does not reflect the legal position. Regulation 9 of the

SEN (Mediation) Regulations 2014 reads, 'The following persons may attend a mediation meeting (a) the parent or young person and any advocate or other supporter he or she wishes to attend the mediation.' There is no provision stating that the local authority is entitled to object to the parental or young person's advocate or other supporter.

Form and content of an EHC plan

Structurally the Education Sections B, F and I are interlinked

The previous Code of Practice set out a pro forma for a Statement of SEN in the statutory regulations at the back of the Code of Practice (paras 9.61–9.69). Instead of a pro forma, Regulation 12 of the SEND Regulations 2014, No. 1530, provides a written list A–J of the sections that should be in an EHC plan. The statutory regulations say that each section should be separately identified (i.e., labelled). They can, however, appear in any order or format (which makes life difficult for teaching staff who have EHC plans from a variety of local authorities).

Paragraph 9.62 reproduces the list of 12 sections (as section H is in two parts, and it also includes appendices), which are as follows:

Section A: Parents'/child's views

Section B: Child or young person's SEN

Section C: Health needs relating to their SEN

Section D: Social care needs relating to their SEN

Section E: Outcomes

Section F: SEN provision

Section G: Health provision

Section H1: Social care provision resulting from Section 2 of the Chronically Sick and Disabled Person's Act 1970

Section H2: Social care provision reasonably required

Section I: Educational placement

Section J: Personal budget

Section K: Appendices and advice/information separately identified.

Section 37(2) of the Children and Families Act 2014 requires specification of the child or young person's SEN, the outcomes sought, the special educational provision required, and the health and social care provision required. (The meaning of 'specify' has already been decided by the Courts in a line of cases, starting with *L. v Clarke & Somerset County Council*.)[3]

---

3   [1998] ELR 129 (QBD).

Educational sections of the EHC plan

- Section B (equivalent to Part 2 of a Statement of SEN)

- Section F (equivalent to Part 3 of a Statement of SEN)

- Section I (equivalent to Part 4 of a Statement of SEN).

These are the only sections that can be appealed to SENDIST.

Bearing in mind that previous case law continues to apply, Section B is the equivalent of a medical diagnosis and Section F is the equivalent of a prescription for all of the needs diagnosed in Section B.[4] The Courts have held that the school named in Section I of the EHC plan must be capable of making the provision set out in Section F.[5] The key to Section I (the school) is therefore Section F (the prescription). In turn, the key to Section F (the prescription) is Section B (the diagnosis). The structure is extremely important. Sections B, F and I are interlinked, and case law has not changed, which means that no appeal to SENDIST is really ever simply about Section I (placement or school).

If these sections of an EHC plan are vaguely worded, or omit areas of need in Section B (the diagnosis), then Section F (the prescription) of the EHC plan is likely to be 'light on provision'. If Section F (the prescription) of the EHC plan is light on provision, or is so vaguely worded, there is actually no requirement to provide anything very much at all, which means that the maintained school, academy or further education college may not be adequately funded. If the direct payment option is selected, it may not be properly costed, and the pay-out may in reality be insufficient. It is difficult to say whether the totality of provision required is such that an independent specialist school placement of a parent's choice should be named in Section I.

---

4   *R. v The Secretary of State for Education and Science ex parte E.* [1992] 1 FLR 377 (CA).
5   *R. v Kingston upon Thames and Hunter* [1997] ELR 223 (Admin.) 233C.

SECTION B	Child or young person's SEN	All of the young person's identified learning difficulties/disabilities should be included. This means that all of the young person's health or social care needs that are SEN (because the provision they require to deal with them falls within the definition of educational provision) must be included. This means that speech/social communication/ gross and fine motor and sensory needs/needs for consistency/difficulties with change should be included. As explained above, the Courts have compared this section to a diagnosis (i.e., a list of symptoms), each of which must be responded to by prescription in the form of an item of provision in the list of special educational provision contained in Section F. *Each and every one of a child or young person's SEN should be specifically set out here.*
SECTION F	SEN provision	Provision in this section should also be specific, detailed and quantified, e.g., in terms of the type of provision (e.g., specialist dyslexia teaching, speech and language therapy, occupational therapy, physiotherapy etc.) and the duration and frequency of the provision and skill mix of the person delivering. Where health or social care provision educates or trains a child or young person, this is educational provision and should appear in this section (see the statutory definition in Section 21(5) of the Children and Families Act 2014). This means speech and language therapy, occupational therapy, physiotherapy, a 'Waking Day'curriculum, functional analysis of behaviour with proactive and reactive strategies delivered by a multi-disciplinary team comprising clinical psychology, speech and language therapy and occupational therapy, consistency of approach, cognitive behavioural therapy, ABA and independence skills training should all be in this section if they are required by the young person for their education or training.

		Health authorities and social services cannot veto health or social service provision being included in this section. The Courts have decided that flexibility may only be written into this section of the plan if it is there to meet the needs of the child/young person, and not those of the system (see *R. (on the application of IPSEA Ltd) v Secretary of State for Education and Skills*).[6] Case law has also established that speech and language therapy is normally special educational provision (*R. v Lancashire County Council, ex parte M.*).[7] Once specified in this section, the local authority must 'secure' the provision, i.e., they must ensure that it is made. If the NHS trust fails to deliver the provision set out in the EHC plan, then the duty falls on the local authority. This means, if necessary, the local authority must go out to private practice and buy in the provision for the child/young person (*R. v Harrow LBC, ex parte M.*).[8]
SECTION I	Educational placement: *name* and *type* of the nursery, school, post-16 or other institution to be attended by the child or young person should appear here	These details will not appear in the draft plan sent to the child's parents or young person. They will only appear in the final plan. See paragraph 9.77 of the Code of Practice for more details.It remains the case that the placement identified in Section I only has to be 'man enough' to deliver the provision set out in Section F of the EHC plan.If Section F of the EHC plan is light on provision, then parents may not be able to obtain their chosen specialist placement. No appeal to SENDIST against placement will just be about Section I.

---

6   [2003] ELR 393 (CA).

7   [1989] 2 FLR 279 (CA).

8   [1997] ELR 62 (QBD)

> For those who are seeking a specialist independent placement, there are still two ways of achieving the placement:
>
> - The local authority's placement does not meet need and the parental placement does.
>
> - Section 9 of the Education Act 1996 continues to apply – basically parents' placement prevails if it is cheaper or costs the same as the local authority's chosen place.
>
> On the subject of costs, bear in mind the latest case in Section 9, *Haining v Warrington Borough Council*, in which it was held that public expenditure is any expenditure incurred by a public body. Discussion in this case refers to taking into account not only social services' input but also expenditure from health.

Health sections of the EHC plan

There is no Right of Appeal to SENDIST against these sections. If provision is recorded in these sections rather than in Sections B and F, we suggest an appeal against failure to include Sections B and F if in reality provision is required for educational and training services.

In relation to health provision see:

- *National Framework for Children and Young Persons Continuing Care*

- *Decision Support Tools for NHS Continuing Healthcare*, revised November 2012

- *National Framework for NHS Continuing Healthcare and NHS Funded Nursing Care*, revised November 2012.

SECTION C	Health needs relating to child or young person's SEN	The EHC plan must also specify any health needs identified through the EHC needs assessment which relate to a child or young person's SEN.
		The clinical commissioning group (CCG) may also choose to specify other health care needs that are not related to the young person's SEN, e.g., a long-term condition that might need management.
SECTION G	Health provision reasonably required by the learning difficulties or disabilities which result in the young person having SEN	Provision should also be specific, detailed and quantified. This is useful for *Haining v Warrington Borough Council* costing arguments.
		Where therapies or other provision educate or train a child, they should appear in Section F, although it is not a problem if they appear in both Sections F and G.

Social care provision in the EHC plan

If a service can be provided under both Section 17 of the Children Act 1989 or Section 2 of the Chronically Sick and Disabled Person's Act 1970, then the settled legal provision is that it is provided under the Chronically Sick and Disabled Person's Act 1970 because it is the more enforceable duty. In essence, Section 2 'trumps' the lesser duty under Section 17 (see *R. (Spink) v Wandsworth LBC*).[9]

---

9   [2005] EWCA Civ 302 (CA).

Section 2 provides a list of services that councils must make available to disabled children and adults. This includes home-based domiciliary care services, recreational/educational facilities such as day centres, after-school or holiday clubs, and home adaptations such as ramps, grab handles and accessible washing facilities. This can also extend to major works such as lifts and ground floor extensions. An authority may ask the family to apply for a Disabled Facilities Grant to meet some or all of the cost of this work. It is important, however, to bear in mind that the fact that a grant may be available does not take away from the core duty to assist with the making of adaptations under Section 2. Where a Disabled Facilities Grant is not available or not sufficient to meet the cost of the required adaptations, the local authority may have to fund the work (see *R. (Spink) v Wandsworth LBC* referred to above, concerning funding and adaptations to the home).

No doubt because the Code of Practice does not have parents as its intended audience, it does not make it clear in plain terms that eligibility for other input for social services depends on the threshold test set out in Section 17 of the Children Act 1989. The local authority *must* provide services to children (that is, those under 18) once it has been determined that a child is in need, in accordance with the Section 17 criteria.

The importance of the classification of 'child in need' is it operates as a threshold condition or passport to the services offered by the local authority.

The threshold for eligibility for input from social services is set out in Section 17(10) of the Children Act 1989, which defines a child as being in need if:

- he [sic] is unlikely to achieve or maintain or to have opportunities of achieving or maintaining, a reasonable standard of health or development without the provision for him of services by a local authority under this part;

- his [sic] health or development is likely to be significantly impaired, or further impaired, without provision for him of such services; or

- he [sic] is disabled.

The word 'development' for these purposes includes 'physical, intellectual, emotional, social or behavioural development' and 'health' includes physical or mental health. 'Disabled' means a child who is blind, deaf or dumb, or who suffers from a mental disorder of any kind, or is substantially and permanently handicapped by illness, injury or congenital deformity, or such other disability as may be prescribed (Section 17(11) of the Children Act 1989).

The Courts have decided that the local authority's determination that a child is, or is not, in need is not subject to challenge except through Judicial Review procedure.[10]

Government guidance is not usually legally binding. However, where social services are concerned, the position is quite different, and this is because of Section 7(1) of the local authority Social Services Act 1970. The Courts have decided that social services' guidance is legally binding.

Failure to carry out proper assessments within 45 days, the timeframe from referral in accordance with current statutory guidance issued by the DfE's *Working Together to Safeguard Children 2013*,[11] may be a basis for Judicial Review. This guidance, like its predecessor, contains very little mention of children with SEN.

A particularly difficult issue for families that include children with considerable SEN is the balance struck between providing services focused on families where a child is thought to be at risk and family support services for children with substantial SEN. There is substantial evidence that local authorities have, in the overall context of inadequate funding, prioritised the former to the detriment of the latter (see Aldgate, 2001, p.22, and useful commentary in Masson, Bailey-Harris and Probert Cretney, 2002, pp.721–723).[12]

The SEND Code of Practice also fails to offer help and guidance to those unfortunate parents whose children have such substantial

---

10   *Re. J. (Specific Issue Order: Leave to Apply)* [1995] 1 FLR 669.

11   DfE (Department for Education) (2013) *Working Together to Safeguard Children 2013*. London: The Stationery Office.

12   Aldgate, J. (2001) *The Children Act Now: Messages from Research*. London: The Stationery Office, and useful commentary in J.M. Masson, R. Bailey-Harris and R.J. Probert Cretney (2002) *Principles of Family Law*, 8th edn. London: Sweet & Maxwell.

SEN that they require two-to-one 24-hour support. The situation can become impossible to manage at home, and parents in this situation need to be made aware of Section 20 of the Children Act 1989 under which local authorities must accommodate children in need if 'the person who has been caring for him [is] being prevented (whether or not permanently, and for whatever reason) from providing him with suitable accommodation or care.' Accommodation of children under Section 20 of the Children Act 1989 does not confer parental responsibility on the local authority; the parent may remove the child at any time.

Section 20 on voluntary care applies to all children (that is, up to the age of 18). It is clear from the statutory language and case law that Section 20 is given a broad interpretation. Once it is triggered, the local authority is obliged to provide accommodation to the child. This is an absolute duty. The Section 20 duty to accommodate can be discharged by placing the child in *any* type of accommodation that is suitable to the child's needs.

The leading case in the House of Lords, *R. (G.) v Southwark London Borough Council*,[13] made it clear that local authorities cannot sidestep their duties under Section 20 by labelling accommodation as Housing Act accommodation or Section 17 accommodation.

Residential short breaks provided under Section 17 of the Children Act 1989 do not mean that the child is a looked-after child under Section 20 of the Children Act 1989.

Once accommodated by a local authority the child becomes a 'looked-after' child within the meaning of the Children Act 1989. This status imposes a number of duties on the local authority in respect of the child, which, in some cases, can extend into the accommodated person's adulthood. Accommodation may bring to the child a range of services beyond just a roof over the child's head, and has considerable resource implications for the local authority.

Finally, it would be helpful if the Code of Practice dealt with the growing number of applications to the Family Court made by

---

13   [2009] UKHL 26 (HL).

social services when a parent commences SENDIST proceedings, seeking a potentially expensive placement such as a 52-week 'Waking Day' curriculum. Such applications are ineffective and misguided. The Family Court cannot dictate to SENDIST how to exercise its statutory jurisdiction. Such applications, even if resulting in a full care order, still do not bring a halt to the proceedings in the SENDIST (see *X. County Council v D.W., P.W., S.W.*[14] and *R. (on the application of M.G.) v London Borough of Tower Hamlets and Others*;[15] see also *Fairpo v Humberside County Council*).[16]

Social care post-18 is currently dealt with by adult social care assessment.

Existing duties on social care services to assess children and provide under the Children Act 1989 and adult social care will continue to apply, although there is a statutory power (the local authority's choice, not the parents') to continue to provide for the 18–25 group under children's social services.

Social services have always started from the presumption that parents will care for their now adult children until they become too old and infirm to provide such care.

Social services usually propose a day placement at a further education college with the young person living at home with social services input, which is normally a package of domiciliary care and direct payments at a level well below what is necessary. This situation is likely to continue.

If the provision the young person requires can be defined as an educational or training requirement, then residential accommodation post-18 can be obtained through the educational sections of the EHC plan with an appeal to SENDIST if necessary. If the educational or training provision does not apply, then residential accommodation can be obtained via Section 21 of the National Assistance Act 1948. Most higher-functioning young adults will not be Section 21 cases, however.

---

14   [2005] EWHC 162 (Fam) paras 6–20 (Mumby J.).
15   [2008] EWHC 1577 (Admin) para. 64 (Langstaff J.).
16   [1997] 1 FLR 339 (QBD) (Laws J.).

The powers and duties of adult social services departments to provide residential accommodation arise primarily under Section 21 of the National Assistance Act 1948. Section 21(I) specifies three hurdles that must be overcome:

- The person must be over 18.

- The person must have certain characteristics (such as a disability).

- The person must be in need of care and attention that is not otherwise available.

If a parent is using Section 21 of the National Assistance Act 1948, they have to make it very clear that care and attention from themselves is not available, and that they are not going to provide accommodation post-18. *This is harsh and painful for parents.*

Courts have, however, held that social services' obligation to provide residential accommodation only arises where the care and attention a person requires is not available.[17]

If parents are intending to settle their now-adult disabled children in suitable long-term residential accommodation and need to use Section 21 of the National Assistance Act 1948, then the EHC plan needs to record that parental care, attention and accommodation will not be available.

The long-term future of Section 21 of the National Assistance Act 1948 is unclear, and there has been a recommendation for its repeal.

Finally, it should be noted that Section 72 of the Care Act 2014 permits the creation of an appeal system against adult social care assessment by statutory regulation. Section 72(4) permits an appeal to be treated as an appeal brought under another procedure (for example, SENDIST). Therefore, as a consequence of Section 2 of the Care Act 2014, those approaching 18 and adults under 25 may, in 2016, if this legislation is implemented, have a Right of Appeal to SENDIST against their social care provision. Younger children will have no such Right of Appeal, however.

---

17   *R. (Wahid) v Tower Hamlets London Borough Council* [2002] EWCA Civ 287 (CA).

SECTION D	Social care needs relating to the child or young person's SEN or to a disability	An EHC plan must include an assessment of a child or young person's social care needs. EHC plans are intended to be holistic, with a social care assessment at the same time as the educational assessment. Social care assessment and provision arises from Section 2 of the Chronically Sick and Disabled Person's Act and Section 17 of the Children Act 1989. *Working Together to Safeguard Children 2013* sets out the process with a 45-day time frame from referral. The local authority may also choose to specify other social care needs which are not linked to the child or young person's SEN or to a disability.
SECTION H1	Social care provision resulting from Section 2 of the Chronically Sick and Disabled Person's Act 1970	This relates only to children and young people who are receiving social care provision under Section 2 of the Chronically Sick and Disabled Person's Act 1970. This legislation is now over 40 years old – it refers to provision of a 'wireless' and 'telephone', because it was drafted long before mobile telephones. As in other sections, provision must be specific, detailed and quantified.

SECTION H2	Social care provision reasonably required by the learning difficulties or disabilities that result in a child/young person having SEN	The statutory definition of educational provision contained in Section 21(5) of the Children and Families Act 2014 requires identification of training needs. This would involve the training of respite 'in consistency of approach' or 'postural management' to avoid pain so that the child or young person can learn. If this is the case, the required training should appear in Section F, although it is not a problem if it appears in both sections.
		Section H2 must only include services that are not provided under Section 2 of the Chronically Sick and Disabled Person's Act 1970.
		This section will include adult social care provision under the Care Act 2014. Adult (over the age of 18) social care provision can continue to be assessed by children's services, *but* this is the local authority's choice.
		Provision in this section must be specific and quantified.

Remaining sections of the EHC plan

SECTION A	Parents'/ child's views	The information here should include the child or young person's history, details about their play, health, schooling, independence, friendships, further education and future plans including employment (where appropriate and practical). There should also be details of the child or young person's aspirations and goals.
		It is also suggested that there should be a summary of how to communicate with the child or young person. Bearing in mind that EHC plans may be appropriate for an able dyslexic, such as Walt Disney or Richard Branson, this will not be applicable in every case.

SECTION E	Outcomes sought for the child or young person (including outcomes for life)	This section should also deal with monitoring. The EHC plan should identify the arrangements for the setting of shorter-term targets by the early years provider, school, college or other education. This section should incorporate SMART targets, i.e., specific, measurable, achievable, realistic, and time-bound. Outcomes are not a description of provision (i.e., a service provided, such as therapy).
SECTION J	Personal budget (including arrangements for direct payments)	A personal budget is optional. If this option is chosen, then this section should provide detailed information about the personal budget. Guidance on personal budgets is set out in Chapter 9 of the Code of Practice, paras 9.102–9.111. The amount of money specified in this section should be enough to secure provision set out in the EHC plan. The local authority's duty to provide educational provision is satisfied by providing a personal budget. While personal budgets are optional, the concern here is the likelihood that, like community care direct payments, the budget will be disappointingly inadequate and too little. Although it is said the amount of money specified in this section must be enough to secure the provision specified, there is no SENDIST appeal in the event of legitimate disagreement over the skill mix (i.e., qualifications and experience of specialist teachers and therapists). It therefore follows that it is essential that the provision in Section F (i.e., frequency, duration and skill mix required) is specified so that proper costing is possible.

SECTION K	Advice and information	Copies of all of the advice and information gathered during the statutory assessment process should be attached to the EHC plan as appendices.
		There should be a list of the advice and information gathered during the statutory assessment in this section (i.e., who gave the advice and the date of that advice).

Complaints procedures

From paragraph 11.67 onwards, the Code of Practice lists approximately a dozen different complaints procedures that can be used, although complaints to the Health and Care Professions Council (HCPC) (broadly, therapists, educational and clinical psychologists and social workers) and the General Medical Council (GMC) are omitted from the list.

Complaints procedures are generally unsatisfactory due to a tendency to:

- be over-complex and set up to favour officers or the profession complained about;

- lack independence (bias and prejudice – the department or profession complained about investigating itself);

- be pre-judging;

- have inadequate reasoning;

- delay;

- discourage complainants in genuine cases, creating obstacles for parents who hope to complain. Complaints procedures are inherently inappropriate where a point of law is involved, as discussed earlier in this book, and Judicial Review is to be preferred.

Judicial Review

Paragraph 11.10 deals with Judicial Review (this is considered elsewhere in this book); it should be noted that this paragraph of the Code does not reflect the correct legal position.

Transitions from Statements of SEN to EHC plans

The transfer of Statements of SEN to EHC plans will take place over a three-year period ending 1 April 2018. This means that in practice, the two systems will be running Statements of SEN and EHC plans in tandem until 1 April 2018.

The guidance on transition arrangements states at paragraph 2.3:

It is expected that all children and young people who have a Statement and who will have continued to have one under the current system, will be transferred to an EHC Plan – no child or young person should lose their Statement and not have it replaced with an EHC Plan simply because the system is changing.

In order not to overwhelm the new system in 2014/15, local authorities are expected to concentrate on two groups: those who have a non-statutory EHC plan issued under the Pathfinder schemes, and those who no longer have a Statement of SEN and who receive further education and training provision as a result of a Section 139A Learning Difficulty Assessment (LDA).

The transfer of all young people who receive support as a result of an LDA should have an EHC plan by 1 September 2016. Until that point local authorities remain under a duty to have regard to the statutory LDA guidance.

The DfE's intention is that the transition to the new system will happen at a pace that is achievable. To support the transition, it is advising all local authorities to ensure that momentum is maintained during the transition period.

Local authorities are expected to transfer children and young people from their Statements of SEN and EHC plans in advance of them transferring to the next phase of their education. In the academic year immediately prior to the transfer to the next phase of the child's education, a transfer review will replace the annual review.

During the transition period, the child or young person's Statement of SEN will remain in place until:

- the child or young person has a transfer review and an EHC plan is made;

- the child or young person has a transfer review and the local authority decides that an EHC plan is not required;

- the child or young person has an annual review and the local authority decides to cease to maintain the Statement following the annual review.

The local authority should have published the first version of their Transition Plan by 1 September 2014.

CHAPTER 5

DUTY TO DELIVER EDUCATION AND CHOICE OF SCHOOLS

For children and young people with SEN, as already set out, there are two categories: those without an EHC plan (previously those without a Statement of SEN), and those with an EHC plan (in the same position as they were previously with a Statement of SEN). For those without an EHC plan, but who have learning difficulties, it is clear that the intention of the Children and Families Act 2014 is to make schools accountable for providing for children and young people with learning difficulties but with no EHC plan. Nonetheless, where parents or the young person consider that there is an inadequate provision, this may be, in most cases, a clear indication that there should at least be an assessment or an EHC plan. Where it is the case that the young person or child will not have an EHC plan, the Equality Act 2010, particularly Section 20, the duty to make reasonable adjustments, provides a means of enforcement. It is not the intention of this book to look at the Equality Act in any detail, but the fact that those with a learning difficulty may well fall within the definition of disability under the terms of the Equality Act, means that the test is very different. This was made clear by the Employment Appeal Tribunal in the case of *Paterson v Metropolitan Police Commissioner.*[1] The key issue here was whether under the Act, disability affected day-to-day activity and was long term. The case involved a police officer who needed concessions when taking exams – passing exams for promotion was held to be part of employment and a day-to-day activity. The fact

---

1   [2007] ICR 1522 (EAT).

that the officer's dyslexia might be regarded as mild was completely irrelevant to the test.

General duty

In Section 35 of the 2014 Act, for children and young people attending a maintained nursery or mainstream school, those concerned with making the special educational provision for the child must ensure that the child engages in the school's activities, together with children who do not have SEN, subject to:

- the child receiving the special educational provision called for by his or her SEN so long as it is reasonably practical;

- the provision of efficient education for other children with whom he or she is educated;

- the efficient use of resources.

This duty to provide is plainly restricted by the words 'reasonably practical' and 'efficient use of resources' (see Section 35(3)). If a child's needs cannot be met because it is either not practical or an efficient use of resources, a request for a statutory assessment should be made in most cases.

According to Section 32, in cases where the local authority is responsible, it must arrange for the child or young person, or parents, to be provided with advice and information about matters relating to SEN regarding the child or young person concerned. The duty extends to arranging information for children and young people with a disability. The local authority must take such steps as it thinks appropriate.

While advice and information is therefore something that should be available, and the local offer previously considered should outline all provisions generally for children with disabilities and SEN, Section 35 of the 2014 Act creates a duty, although limited, for those without EHC plans, to ensure that special educational provision is made, but it is subject to the test of efficient use of resources, the provision of efficient education of other children, and what is reasonably practical. However, if read together with the duty under the Equality Act, particularly Section 20, it is actually an improvement on the earlier law.

Children and young people with EHC plans: duty to deliver

Section 42 provides for the duty to secure special educational provision and health care provision in accordance with an EHC plan. It is interesting, however, that it fails to deal with children's services or adult services, and this appears to be a result of the Care Act, which includes better enforcement provision for adult services, but currently not children's services. Nonetheless, the improved definition of special educational provision, which relates to social care provision in Section 21(5), should be borne in mind here, because social care provision that falls within Section 21(5) falls under the statutory duty to deliver.

Section 42 relates to the duty to secure special educational provision and health care provision in accordance with the EHC plan. This applies where a local authority maintains an EHC plan for a child or young person.

1. The local authority must secure the special educational provision for the child or young person.

2. If the plan specifies health care provision, the responsible commissioning body must arrange the specified health care provision for the child or young person.

3. The responsible commissioning body, in relation to any health care provision, means the body (or each body) that is under a duty to arrange health care provision of that kind in respect of the child or young person.

4. Subsections (2) and (3) do not apply if the child's parent or the young person has made suitable alternative arrangements.

5. Specified in relation to an EHC plan means specified in the plan.

In Section 43, a school or other institution that is named in the plan is under a duty to admit the child or young person. This includes maintained schools, maintained nursery schools, academies, an institution within the further education sector, a non-maintained special school and an institution approved by the Secretary of State under Section 41, which allows for the approval of independent special schools.

EHC plans must still specify educational and now other provision, as did Statements of SEN before them. By virtue of the case *R. v The Secretary of State for Education and Science, ex parte E.*,[2] the local education authority is required to determine the special education provision for a child with learning difficulties in respect of each and every educational need identified in the Statement. This now plainly applies to EHC plans. In *L. v Clarke & Somerset County Council*,[3] Mr Justice Laws stated that in relation to Statements, and this now applies to the duty to specify:

> The real question…in relation to any…statement [now EHC plan] is whether it is so specific and so clear as to leave no room for doubt as to what has been decided is necessary in the individual case. Very often a specification of hours per week will no doubt be necessary and there will be a need for it to be done.[4]

This approach was confirmed by the Court of Appeal in *Bromley London Borough Council v Special Educational Needs Tribunal.*[5]

On this issue, it is also to be noted in *E. v Rotherham Metropolitan Borough Council*[6] that the Court set aside a provision which allowed a change in speech therapy support as a result of a formal discussion between a local authority and a local NHS trust. It was not specific as the provision could be reviewed simply on a formal discussion. It allowed for the amendment of a Statement of SEN without an appeal. The Judge decided that it was unlawful to provide a statement which

---

2   [1992] 1 FLR 377 (CA).
3   [1998] ELR 129 (QBD).
4   *L. v Clarke & Somerset County Council* [1998] ELR 129 (QBD) 137 (Laws J.).
5   [1999] ELR 260 (CA) (Sedley L.J.).
6   [2002] ELR 266 (Admin.).

allowed for substantial changes in provision without amendment. The case remains good law. It is also worth mentioning that in *S. v City and County of Swansea*[7] it was accepted that there should be some flexibility, but that this should not have been an excuse for lack of flexibility. Further, Sullivan J. made it quite clear that provision in a Statement should be actually available in that case, and not theoretically available.[8] There must therefore be evidence that provision can actually be delivered under an EHC plan.

However, Statements did not need to be over-specific, and the same law will apply to an EHC plan. They should not, for example, specify every pencil or item in the curriculum. It may well be that when in a special school, because of its organisation and the resources available, the Statement does not need to be so specific as in a mainstream school or in a non-maintained special school or a school in the independent sector (see *E. v Newham London Borough Council and the Special Educational Needs Tribunal*).[9]

The contents or form of an EHC plan are now contained in the SEND Regulations 2014, Statutory Instrument (SI) No. 1530. EHC plans are now extremely complex. Regulation 12 requires them to set out a number of sections to include:

1. The views, interests and aspirations of the child or young person and his or her parents (Section A).

2. The child or young person's SEN (Section B) (*no change here in the law*).

3. The child or young person's *health* (*new, and if it is an educational need, it needs to be in Section B as well as C*).

4. The child or young person's social care needs that relate to their SEN or disability (Section D) (*new; if this amounts to educational provision, it needs to be in Section F*).

---

7   [2000] ELR 315.

8   *S. v City and County of Swansea* [2000] ELR 315 (QBD) 324.

9   [2003] ELR 286 (CA).

5. The outcome sought for the child or young person (Section E) (*no change here*).

6. The special educational provision required by the child or young person (Section F) (*again, no change, but be aware of the expansion of the definition of 'special educational provision', which now covers some health care and some social care*).

7. Any health care provision reasonably required by the learning difficulty or disabilities that result in the child or young person having SEN (*Section G, this is new*).

8. Any social care provision which must be made for the child or young person as a result of Section 2 of the Chronically Sick and Disabled Person's Act 1970 (a) (Section H(1)) (*new*).

9. Any other social care provision reasonably required by the learning difficulty or disability that is the result of a child or young person having educational needs (Section H) (*new, and this section will be far more relevant than the Chronically Sick and Disabled Person's Act section*).

10. The name of the school, maintained school, post-16 institution or other institution attended by the child or young person and the type of that institution, or where the name of the school or other institution is not specified in the EHC plan, the type of school or other institution to be attended by the child or young person (Section I) (*not new*).

11. Where there is any special educational provision, if secured by direct payments, the SEN and outcomes must be met by direct payments (Section J) (*new*).

Health care provision specified in the EHC plan in accordance with paragraph 1(g) must be agreed by the responsible commissioning body. Further, where the child or young person is beyond Year 9 (school year), the EHC plan must include within special educational, health care and social care provision, specified provision to assist the child or young person in preparation for adulthood and independent living.

The advice and information contained in accordance with Regulation 6(1) must be set out in the appendices to the EHC plan (Section K, which is not new, even though the requirements are much more extensive).

However, the exact form of the plan is now not standard and can vary from authority to authority.

Case law on the duty to deliver

It was generally thought to be quite clear that if provision was clearly specified, there was a duty to deliver the provision. Recently, however, the Court of Appeal was faced with a case in which the High Court dismissed an application in relation to the delivery of direct speech therapy, where the decision was plainly wrong. Sedley L.J. in *R. (N.) v North Tyneside*[10] made it quite clear that the duty to deliver provision under a Statement and the law is no different for an EHC plan, that it was a non-delegable duty, and that the provision simply had to be delivered. This would include arranging for the appropriate school, as specified in the EHC plan.

Choice of school

The more one looks at appeals, parents need to be clear about the child's needs and provision if they are in dispute with local authorities. This may leave school as the only issue, where the choice of school is central to both the delivery of provision and any dispute. Whatever the position, parents will ultimately be choosing a school in which provision is to be delivered, or determine that some provision or all of it should not be delivered at school because of the individual circumstances of the child or young person. Such circumstances are not typical, but it is not uncommon for children with significant medical difficulties to be educated at home or in a hospital school, or for children with autism, who are receiving ABA, to start out at home and gradually integrate into school. Significant mental health

---

10   [2010] ELR 312 (CA).

difficulties may mean a child has to be educated outside, or partly outside, of a school environment.

Whether it is a mainstream or a special school, parents may simply agree on a school, and the issue that might go to appeal is not whether the school is appropriate and the right place for the child to be educated, but rather whether the provision to meet those needs should be greater than that on offer by the local authority. This is often the case with therapy. So not every case will involve a dispute about a school or even a dispute about whether a child is to be educated at home, although most cases do. Appeals may simply involve, for example, the provision of appropriate specialist teaching, or the appropriate level of therapies. It is not unusual in ABA cases for parents to seek a gradual integration into a mainstream primary school, or for parents with children in special schools or in mainstream schools to be appealing for more speech therapy or occupational therapy. The school in such cases is sometimes in dispute.

Additionally, for those children and young people who do not have an EHC plan, the choice of school is solely dependent on the normal arrangements for admission, namely, normal admission appeals, for all children and young people, and it is not dependent on the child's SEN. Nonetheless, in relation to an admissions appeal or application for a place, there may be very good reasons why a child or young person ought to go to the school of the parents' choice, arising out of the child's SEN or disability. Some practical examples would be, for example, that the school chosen by the parents is not the normal school the child would go on to at secondary transfer, but one specialising in supporting pupils with dyslexia and that has a particularly good record for dyslexia, where the child has significant dyslexia but not enough to justify an EHC plan. An individual school may have additional facilities or expertise to support a child with a specific type of learning difficulty or disability. It is not the intention of this book to give detailed advice on admissions appeals, but for parents who are without an EHC plan, and who are contemplating an admissions appeal, it is important that the evidence they provide to support the appeal is 'good enough'. They certainly need to establish the level of disability (for example, dyslexia), the ability of the chosen school to support the child, and the fact that the more local school that would normally be chosen and awarded by the local authority does not have the same expertise.

There remain, however, a number of statutory duties imposed on the local authority, which parents can use to support the choice of school where there is an EHC plan.

Relevant statutory framework

Section 9 of the Education Act 1996 provides:

> In exercising or performing all their respective powers and duties under the Education Acts, the Secretary of State and local authorities shall have regard to the general principle that pupils are to be educated in accordance with the wishes of their parents, so far as that is compatible, the provision of efficient instruction and training and the avoidance of unreasonable public expenditure.

This is a general duty but has very specific application in cases of children and young people with SEN and with EHC plans.

Previously, Schedule 27 of the Education Act 1996 gave additional powers to parents to nominate either mainstream schools or maintained special schools. Sections 316 and 316A allowed parents to effectively veto a special school, subject to the proviso that the child or young person's education within a mainstream school did not interfere with the efficient education of other children.

Section 33 of the 2014 Act replaces Section 316. It is subject to a duty to consult institutions that are suggested or nominated, but where no particular school or institution is nominated under Sections 39 and 40, whether a school is nominated or not. Section 33(2) applies, which states:

> In a case within Section 39(5) or 40(2) the local authority must secure that the plan provides for the child or young person to be educated in a maintained nursery school, mainstream school or mainstream post-16 institution unless that is incompatible with:

- The wishes of the child's parent or the young person; or

- The provision of efficient education for others.

Effectively, therefore, Section 33 now achieves what was set out under the 1996 Act, in particular, in Sections 316 and 316A. It goes on to provide that the local authorities or institutions can only state that the child will interfere with the efficient education of others if a local authority can show that, for its area taken as a whole, there are no reasonable steps it could take to prevent the incompatibility. This applies both to schools, nursery or otherwise, and post-16 institutions and to the governing body, proprietor or principal.

It is an effective veto to a special school, subject to the compatibility test. Section 38, while covering the right to make representations about a draft EHC plan, allows the parent or child or young person to request the authority to secure a particular school or institution, which is named in the plan (Section 38(2)(b)(ii)). The request covers the school, whether maintained, a maintained nursery school, an academy, or a further education institution, as defined under the Act, a non-maintained special school, or an institution approved by the Secretary of State in the dependent sector. The local authority can refuse under Section 39(4) if:

1. the school or other institution requested is unsuitable for the age, ability, aptitude or SEN of the young child or person concerned; or

2. the attendance of the child or young person requested at the school or other institution would be incompatible with the provision of efficient education for others or the efficient use of resources.

A request for a particular school or institution can only be approved under Section 39 if it is suitable for the child's ability, aptitude and SEN, and provides the efficient use of resources (this means it is not too costly), and the child or young person's education does not interfere with the education of others. However, if parents insist on a mainstream school, the test of compatibility with SEN and efficient use of resources is removed, as it was in the previous law in Sections 316 and 316A, by Section 33.

There has been considerable case law on this issue recently, and the result of this case law is quite clear. Section 316 before, and now Section 33, subject to the criteria of interference with the efficient education of other children, operate as an effective veto on special schools. This means that the question of the cost of the provision in mainstream schools is irrelevant, and neither does it have to be shown that the school can meet the child's needs. In a recent interesting judgment, Judge Mark of the Upper Tribunal considered that the only way in which the statute could be married up was for the local authority to make the adjustments to the school so that it could ultimately meet needs, even if it did not do so at the beginning.

Case law

In the case of *R. (MH) v Special Educational Needs and Disability Tribunal and London Borough of Hounslow*,[11] the Court of Appeal made it clear that the process under Sections 316 and 316A operated after the process, which is now Section 39, and previously Schedule 27 of the Act. The Court confirmed that the duty imposed on the local authority was a duty for it to educate a child in a mainstream school if the parents wished it, unless the education of the child in a mainstream school was incompatible with provision of efficient education for other children.

In *Bury MBC v S.U.*,[12] an attempt was made to suggest the law was different from the *Hounslow* case, namely, that despite statutory provision making it clear that subject to compatibility with the efficient education of other children, the parents had an effective veto on a special school, irrespective of whether the child's needs would be met, and irrespective of cost. Judge Ward, in the Upper Tribunal, considered the statutory provisions, and made it quite clear that the test of compatibility with meeting needs, and the test of cost, was

---

11   [2004] EWCA Civ 770 (CA).
12   [2011] ELR 14 (AAC).

eliminated by the new provisions, now Section 33 of the 2014 Act. Judge Lane later confirmed this approach again in the Upper Tribunal in the case of *CCC v London Borough of Tower Hamlets*.[13]

Finally, Judge Mark, in *Harrow Council v A.M.*,[14] having considered the earlier law, stated that the removal of the test of compatibility with meeting a child's SEN could only be established by showing that there were no reasonable steps that the local education authority could take in relation to their mainstream schools, but that the local authority was under an absolute obligation to make the particular school suitable, and if there was no suitable school existing, it had to provide for the identified needs. The local authority could say, Judge Mark stated, that it *will* educate the child in a mainstream school without providing for the child. Nor could it rely on any independent resources issues in this respect.

In other words, Parliament intended that local authorities were under a mandatory duty to educate children and young people in a mainstream environment, and that it was only in very exceptional circumstances, where no reasonable steps could be shown, that a local authority could evade that duty.

Role of Section 9 of the Education Act 1966

Statutory provision, Section 39, which replaces Schedule 27(3), gives the right to a parent to nominate a particular school unless it is incompatible with the child's ability and needs, or the cost (efficient use of resources), or the efficient education of other children. If, however, a special school is nominated, and the parents refuse a special school, they can rely on Section 33 to veto a special school subject to the efficient education of other children test. This is wider than simply those in the class, and can affect the whole of the school in general (see Stadlen J. in *Hampshire County Council v R. & SENDIST*).[15] However, Section 9 has a general application in relation to choice of

---

13   [2011] UKUT 393 (AAC).
14   [2013] UKUT 0157 (AAC).
15   [2009] EWHC 626 (Admin.).

school, and operates throughout the process. It is certainly relevant for those parents considering that an independent specialist school is the right choice. However, it applies to all public expenditure in all cases. This is extremely relevant, because if a parent living in Harrow, for example, wants a special school in Bromley (subject only to the cost of transport), the fact that the Harrow school is much cheaper than the Bromley school, and that the local authority will have to spend more money, is irrelevant, because it is all public expenditure (see *C.M. v London Borough of Bexley*[16] and *F.S. (Re. T.) v London Borough of Bromley*,[17] confirmed by the Court of Appeal in *Haining v Warrington Borough Council*).

Thus, public expenditure largely by one local authority, unless there is exceptional additional expenditure that will be incurred, is the same, in law, as another. It is all public money, and the taxpayer pays for it. Thus, if parents want a special school in another authority, and it is much better and obviously more expensive, this doesn't matter. Further, if parents want a local mainstream school in another local authority, subject to the efficient education of other children, the Statement should cost the same in, for example, Richmond, as it does in Westminster. As long as there is no additional expenditure outside the Statement, parents are entitled to choose another school in another borough.

Section 9 itself operates to support parental choice, whether it is in the independent or mainstream sector. Section 9 is considered in more detail in Chapter 9. However, in *Haining v Warrington Borough Council*, Lord Dyson M.R. stated that:

> The starting point is that s9 does not impose a duty on the local authority to act in accordance with parental wishes (provided that to do so would be compatible with the provision of efficient instruction and training for the avoidance of unreasonable public expenditure). It is a duty to have regard to the general principle

---

16   [2011] UKUT 215 (AAC).
17   [2013] UKUT 529 (AAC).

that pupils are to be educated in accordance with the wishes of their parents subject to those qualifications.[18]

In addition, by statute, the local authority must nominate a school or institution that is appropriate for the child or young person, if the request is made under Section 39. Further, parents considering independent schools that are independent special schools or post-16 institutions can request such institutions, which can be the subject of a request to be named in an EHC plan. Such institutions must, in fact, be inspected and then, on the register, be especially organised to make special educational provision. This includes specialist post-16 institutions. The Act provides for regulations in this regard. Previously under the 1996 Act and earlier legislation, where there was provision for approved independent schools or institutions that were abandoned under the last Labour Government, these have now been reinstated.

If the parents' request is refused, the matter will then go to appeal or, if appropriate, mediation. Nonetheless, parents should remember the following:

1. Subject to the efficient education of other children, parents have a right to nominate a mainstream school if a special school is proposed and they object.

2. Subject to the criteria in Section 33, a local authority must nominate the mainstream school proposed by the parent assuming it meets the suitability criteria. This also applies to some independent schools that are approved by the Secretary of State.

3. Where parents are seeking a school out of their area, and there is no additional expenditure, in this regard parents would be well advised to provide the transport arrangements, as this would be additional expenditure; parents can nominate a school even if it is more expensive – whatever type, it is all public expenditure, and therefore it is not an additional cost.

18　[2014] EWCA Civ 398 (CA) para. 31.

CHAPTER 6

PRACTICAL ISSUES IN RELATION TO EHC PLANS

In this chapter we turn briefly to a number of practical issues in dealing with EHC plans, including reviews and reassessments, ceasing to maintain EHC plans, personal budgets and transfers of EHC plans.

Special educational provision outside of school or post-16 institutions

Section 61 of the Children and Families 2014 Act basically re-enacts Section 319 of the Education Act 1996. It provides that the local authority may arrange for any special educational provision to be made that is deemed necessary for a child or young person for whom it is responsible, other than in school or at a post-16 institution at which relevant early years education is provided. The local authority must be satisfied that it would be inappropriate for the provision to be made in the school or at such post-16 institutions.

Section 9 applies equally to Section 61 provision other than at school. The Court of Appeal has made this issue quite clear (see *T.M. v London Borough of Hounslow*).[1]

In Section 62 special educational provision can be arranged at an institution outside England and Wales. This includes a duty to pay the fees, travelling expenses, maintenance at the institution, and the expenses of someone accompanying the child or young person, where that is necessary.

---

1   [2009] EWCA Civ 859 (CA).

Section 63 applies to local authorities' duties where the parents choose or SENDIST has ordered, or the parents agree via mediation or otherwise, a non-maintained school or post-16 institution. If that institution is named in the EHC plan and the local authority must pay any fees in respect of the education or training at the school or institution, the local authority must pay any fees in respect of the special educational provision, and board and lodging (see Section 63, subsections (4) and (5)). Interestingly, however, there is an additional provision, Section 63(3), which allows a local authority to pay for a specialist non-maintained school or institution if the authority is satisfied that:

- it is in the interests of the child or young person that special educational provision be made; and

- it is appropriate for the education or training to be provided to the child or young person at the school, institution or place in question.

Plainly under this provision, children with no EHC plans but SEN can be placed in a non-maintained independent school or post-16 provision.

Annual reviews

As with Statements where statutory provision previously provided for annual reviews, Section 44 also provides for annual reviews and reassessments. There must be an annual review within 12 months of the date on which the plan was made and each of the subsequent 12 months thereafter, following the first annual review (Section 44(1)).

Where a parent or young person requests a review from the local authority or governing body or proprietor or principal of a school or post-16 institution at which the child or young person attends, the local authority may also secure a reassessment of those needs at any other time it thinks necessary.

The SEND Regulations 2014 provide for the circumstances in which a local authority must review an EHC plan. This duty relates to *phased transfers*, where local authorities must review EHC plans irrespective of whether there is a request or not from the parents or the young person:

- by 31 March, prior to transfer from secondary school to a post-16 institution;

- by 15 February, in any other year of the child's transfer, which would include:

  » early years providers

  » infant to primary school

  » primary to middle school

  » secondary transfer

  » transfer from one post-16 institution to another, which is likely to happen at the age of 18 or 19, five months before the transfer is due to take place.

Additionally, when a child or young person is due to transfer from a secondary school to a post-16 institution on 1 September 2015, the local authority must amend the EHC plan before 31 May 2015. This is obviously a special provision that only applies for a temporary period.

How does one justify a request to reassess? If the child or young person is not making adequate progress, this will obviously justify a request. Equally there could be regression, the discovery of unknown needs or the emergence of additional needs. Parents can consider requesting reassessment as an appeal from an annual review, and the local authority is obliged to make a decision following an annual review. As a result of Regulation 20(10), this includes informing the parent or young person of a Right of Appeal under Regulation 20, following an annual review. In fact, parents and young people would be well advised to appeal from an annual review if it takes place around the time the problem emerges. If, of course, the review has only just taken place, a request for a reassessment would be worthwhile, but the attraction of an appeal from an annual review is that it involves one appeal, whereas if you apply for a reassessment, you may have to appeal for a reassessment, and then appeal again.

Where a review recommends and a local authority agrees to amend the plan as a result of a review, this gives rise to a detailed procedure to serve proposed amendments, allowing parents to make representations before ultimately making the plan or giving the parent a Right of Appeal. This is set out in Regulation 22.

The SEND Code of Practice, discussing reviews, refers to Regulations 2.18, 19, 20 and 21 of the SEND Regulations 2014. However, guidance in the Code points out that EHC plans should be used to actively monitor children and young people's progress towards their outcomes and longer-term aspirations. There must be a focus on the child or young person's progress towards achieving outcomes specified in the EHC plan. The review must also consider whether these outcomes and supported targets remain appropriate (para. 9.166).

The Code makes the point that reviews should also:

- gather and access information so that it can be used by early years settings, schools or colleges, to support the child or young person's progress and their access to teaching and learning;

- review the special educational provision for the child or young person to ensure it is being effective and ensuring access to teaching and learning and good progress;

- review the health and social care provision made for the child or young person and its effectiveness in ensuring good progress towards outcomes.

Although the regulations are complicated, they come down to the very basic point that reassessment is required on the same basis as an assessment. There are new requirements, such as if a child or young person under the age of 18 is not receiving education and training, when the authority must review the plan in accordance with Regulations 18, 19 and 22, to ensure the child or young person continues to receive education and training. Under Regulation 30, a very helpful change in the law is made. Where a young person aged 18 or over ceases to attend the educational institution specified in the EHC plan, and is no longer receiving education or training, the local authority may not cease to maintain the plan unless it has reviewed the plan in accordance with regulations, and ascertained that the young person does not wish to return to educational training. If the young person does wish to return to educational training, and it is appropriate to do so, it must amend the plan.

Before ceasing to maintain an EHC plan, which gives rise to a Right of Appeal, the authority must:

- inform the child's parents or young person that it is considering ceasing to maintain the plan (Regulation 31(1A));

- consult the child's parents or young person;

- consult the headteacher, principal or equivalent person at the educational institution named in the plan.

Code of Practice on ceasing EHC plans and legal implications

The Code of Practice in its previous and in its current form gives some very good guidance on ceasing to maintain EHC plans, as it did before, with Statements. It makes it clear that the local authority must take account of whether the educational training outcomes specified in the plan have been achieved. Local authorities must not cease to maintain the plan simply because a young person is 19 or over (set out on page 202, para. 9-200). Tribunals have previously paid careful attention to these requirements.

Where a young person aged 16 or over leaves education to take up employment, or enters higher education, or no longer wishes to engage in further learning, the plan will simply cease.

The Code makes it clear that the focus of support should be to re-engage the young person in education and training as soon as possible. Where the young person is excluded, or leaves voluntarily from the relevant institution or school, they may still need an EHC plan. And if the young person does not wish to return to education and training, and the local authority 'thinks it is appropriate', then the local authority must amend the EHC plan as necessary, and it must maintain it. The Code proposes further advice for those in custody, to be issued at a later date.

Where the young person is approaching their 25th birthday, the plan can be maintained until the end of the academic year in which they reach 25, that is, a continuation of the current and statutory provision contained in the new Act. Even if the plan ceases, the part that deals with non-educational provision continues, save for where it is not needed.

Transfers of EHC plans

When a child or young person moves to another authority, the old authority must transfer the plan to the new authority. The Government has proposed that transfers should be made much easier. Section 47 deals with the transfer of plans and provides for the regulations to deal with it. In essence, the local authority can either review or reassess EHC plans. However, the system is basically no different from the previous system, and obviously how far a plan can be transferred is dependent on practical issues arising from any move. Regulation 15 now provides, under the SEND Regulations 2014, for a transfer of plans, and the authority that takes a plan must decide whether to conduct a new assessment or review the plan (this is exactly the same as before).

If a child can still attend the same school, no difficulty arises – the plan simply transfers. The next local authority could decide to reassess if it thinks it will be able to do better for the child, or save money, but where the plan is not readily transferrable, for example, if the child is in a mainstream or special school in London and moves to Yorkshire, only some of the plan may be implemented.

Personal budgets

In Section 49 of the Act, parents or a child or young person can now ask for a personal budget. There are specific personal budget regulations, however, and a number of problems arise. Those considering asking for a personal budget should consider the following:

- If you agree a personal budget, and difficulties ensue, you cannot then appeal – you either have to wait for an annual review or request a reassessment.

- Although you have requested a personal budget, the local authority doesn't have to agree, and the personal budget regulations give a local authority a great deal of discretion in not granting personal budgets.

"Legitimate Disagreement?"
(You cannot appeal a Personal Budget to the SEND Tribunal)

Reasons for not granting personal budgets

The regulations give a local authority, in fact, a number of reasons for not agreeing a personal budget. Personal budgets may be secured by the following methods:

- Direct payments where individuals receive the cash to contract, purchase and manage services themselves. However, the regulations make it quite clear that the monitoring system and the system for setting up such direct payments is rigorous, complex and difficult.

- An arrangement where the local authority, school or college holds the funds and commissions the support specified in the plan. If so, unless there is a good reason for the school or college to hold the funds, it is little different from the local authority being under an obligation to arrange the provision in the EHC plan (such circumstances are rare).

- Third-party arrangements for funds where direct payments are paid and managed by a third party, individual or organisation on behalf of the child's parent or young person. This could, for example, be a charity such as Barnardo's or SCOPE, or a combination of the above.

The child or young person's parent should be given an indication of the level of funding beforehand. The budget offered and agreed must be able to make the provision required or proposed. Where the payment is proposed for special educational provision, local authorities must secure the agreement of the relevant institution, school or college. It is clear that the regulations require that the personal budget should be capable of purchasing the whole provision relevant in the EHC plan.

The practical difficulty with personal budgets is that, in social care, whether children's services or otherwise, the amount awarded by the local authority is, in many cases, far less than what can be purchased on the open market, that is, you cannot get an experienced carer to carry out the job for the amount awarded. Many parents may find that the personal budget funds, for example, a learning support assistant with no specialist qualifications, at a level where it requires a learning support assistant with a great deal of training and experience, and qualifications in dealing with SEN, for example, autism, or for speech and language, Elklan-trained. For those negotiating personal budgets, they should be very clear that the cost awarded is the cost that will buy the provision. This can include contributions towards the school for those in a mainstream or special school that is not independent, and it can include funding from the school's budget share.

Although the draft Code indicated that the personal budget could not be used to pay for education as such, on the face of it, a personal budget can be used for part funding.

Note that direct payments for special educational provision, which include health care and social care provision, are subject to *separate regulations*. The Code of Practice usefully sets this out in paragraph 9.121:

- Community Care Services for Carers and Children's Services (Direct Payments) Regulations 2009 (to be replaced by new regulations under the Care Act 2014)

- NHS (Direct Payments) Regulations 2013

- SEN (Personal budgets) Regulations 2014.

For those considering direct payments, and where there are complex needs, including social care and health, this is a morass. There are basically three sets of regulations governing EHC plan direct payments: these are regulations governing direct payments in education, health and care.

The attraction of personal budgets is obviously that the parent or those with responsibility for the young person will consider it very attractive. However, it is surprising that having produced EHC plans, although it must be recognised that the key enforceability in relation to EHC plans is currently educational, there remain three different regulations. Appeals may also extend now to care, if the appeal provisions come in, and the Care Act, which would also give to SENDIST possible jurisdiction over both education and care, regardless of the Section 21(5) considerations. Thus, to have personal budgets for EHC plans subject to three separate sets of regulations is, frankly, ridiculous.

Direct Payments: Up to date problems

Difficulties with Direct Payments have been illustrated first by oral reports of those representing a large number of local authorities, at the very early stages in the process, and secondly, more significantly, by the Department for Education publication on the 28 November 2014, the SEND Pathfinder Programme Local Offer.

This was an evaluation of the Special Educational Needs & Disability Pathfinder Programme covering the development of the Local Offer which was preceeded by an evaluation of the Pathfinder Programme.

An explanation of the issue of Direct Payments, the report in relation to the Pathfinders, made it very clear that the ability to put together a personal budget, in particular coming from three sources (i.e. Health, Care and Education) is causing – at least in the initial stages of the new system – substantial practical difficulties. On that basis, Direct Payments appeared, in most cases, to be a non-starter. Also, the Local Offer itself, work in hand, is considerable criticism of the Local Offer (see www.specialneedsjungle.com/how-the-development-of-the-local-offer) so given the way in which the legislation was rapidly put in place, it is likely that save, where Direct Payments are a cheap and easy option for the local authority, an option which does not reflect the reality of support. Direct Payments is a good idea, but one which is flawed in its implementation.

CHAPTER 7

INFORMATION REQUIRED TO PREPARE A CASE AND EXPERT EVIDENCE

If an assessment for an EHC plan takes place the Authority will have obtained the detailed information required by law.

A local authority must conduct an EHC assessment when considering if it may be necessary for special educational provision to be made for a child or young person in accordance with an EHC plan (see SEND Code of Practice, p.142). In such cases, the local authority must obtain by the regulation, particularly Regulations 6, 7 and 8 of the SEND Regulations 2014, advice, which means:

- A report from the child's parents or the young person, to take into account their views, wishes and feelings.

- Educational advice and information from the manager, headteacher or principal in the early years setting, school or post-16 or other institution attended by the young person (where this is not available, the local authority must seek advice from a person with experience of teaching children and young people with SEN or from a person responsible for the educational provision of a child or young person).

- Advice and information from a person qualified to teach pupils where the child or young person is either visual or hearing impaired, or both, must be given by a person qualified to teach pupils or students with these impairments.

- Medical advice and information must be sought from healthcare professionals with a role in relation to the child or young person's health.

- Psychological advice and information from an educational psychologist, who should normally be employed or commissioned by the local authority, should be obtained. Educational psychologists must consult any other psychologist known to be involved with the child or young person.

- Social care advice and information from or on behalf of the local authority, including, if appropriate, children in need of protection assessments, information from a looked-after child's care plan or adult social care assessments.

- From Year 9 onwards, advice and information relating to the provision to assist a child or young person in preparation for adulthood and independent living.

- Advice and information from any person requested by the child's parent or young person where the local authority considers it reasonable to do so, that is, possibly a GP or other health professional involved.

- Any other advice or information that the authority considers appropriate to a satisfactory assessment which will include, for example: early years health; where the military are involved, the children's education advisory service; in the case of a looked-after child from the Virtual School head in the authority who looks after the child and the child's designated teacher, designated doctor or nurse; from the youth offending team.

The authority must disclose all of this advice to parents as part of the assessment process.

However, in practice, if, for example, the child has an established need for speech therapy, advice must also be obtained from a speech and language therapist, or from an occupational therapist if the child has physical or sensory needs, or from a physiotherapist if the child has physical disabilities.

A parent or a young person who wants to challenge the local authority in relation to its decisions requesting an assessment, or in relation to changes to an EHC plan, must bear in mind that all appeals to SENDIST or mediation issues are evidence-based. It is therefore not possible to go to mediation or to SENDIST without appropriate evidence. Any dispute needs expert evidence. The Practice Direction contained in Appendix 6 makes it quite clear what the Tribunal's criteria is for expert witnesses and expert witness reports. The issue arises that expert evidence cannot be old or stale. Therefore, any case requires reports which need to be up to date: while reports on an initial diagnosis such as a diagnosis of autism will have ongoing effect, an initial report of a diagnosis of autism, for example, will not define or explain the child or young person's current needs at the present moment. Reports must be up to date and relevant to the issues raised – they should not be stale.

While this book is principally concerned with children and young people with SEN, and does not, therefore, address the Equality Act 2010 in any detail, Equality Act issues are now often arising against schools, whether the child has a Statement, an EHC plan, or is in a school with additional support for the child's SEN. A claim may arise relating to the failure to make reasonable adjustments or deliver provision to the child. Experts must also therefore consider duties where the case relates to the Equality Act.

An expert report should be from a professional who has an appropriate skill or professional qualification. They must be prepared to give expert evidence, understand the statutory process and therefore the duty of the expert to advise. Every case of this nature will be in relation to:

- the child's needs;

- the educational provision or other required to meet those needs (this means that the expert must specifically advise on the quantity and quality of the provision, as statutory provision case law and regulations require provision to be specific; there is no change in this duty);

- the appropriate school or institution, and its ability to provide for the child or young person.

The expert must conduct appropriate assessments for the child, and for many it is preferable that this is done within the school, institution or relevant environment, so that they can consult with those working with the child, and see the child operating in a real-life non-clinic-based environment.

The expert needs to address the issues in the case. The report needed depends on the type of appeal in hand, the availability of information, considering the information that is currently available. In a request for a statutory assessment, this will normally include the school's views as to whether a statutory assessment is necessary, the local authority's decision to refuse, and consideration of all available expert reports obtained by the school or the local authority.

Where there is an appeal against an EHC plan, the principles are the same. The expert will need to consider the EHC plan, or relevant appendices attached to the plan, and any psychological reports, therapy reports etc., to conduct any assessment based on the relevant information.

The parents or the young person need to establish that the expert is willing to provide a report for the purpose of potential appeal to SENDIST, even if, at the start, they are hoping that the local authority will concede, for example, the statutory assessment. The expert needs to be asked for a commitment to provide support for the appeal, and, if necessary, to give evidence in the appeal. All cases involving EHC plans normally need an educational psychologist's report. If a child has speech and language difficulties, whether it is a delay, a disorder or an impairment, an independent speech therapist report is required. Where there is evidence of physical and sensory issues, an independent occupational therapist report is required, and often where there is physical disability or similar issues, a physiotherapist needs to give a report. There may be a need for a social worker or medical reports. Each case is different.

As the Regulations and SEND Code of Practice indicate, for those with hearing and visual impairments, a specialist teacher of the deaf or a specialist teacher of the visually impaired who can give independent evidence, will almost certainly be required where there is a disagreement in such cases. However, where parents are dealing with the case of a hearing impaired child or a young person, a report on the school environment from an audiologist or an acoustic specialist may well be necessary if it is felt that the school environment is not properly adapted, and classes are simply too large and too noisy.

Where the child has mental health difficulties associated with their condition, a consultant child and adolescent psychiatrist report or a clinical psychologist report, particularly where there are significant behavioural difficulties related to the disability, is normally required. In cases involving, for example, epilepsy or other medical conditions, at least background reports from the treating physician are necessary. For care issues, a social worker's report may be needed.

Content of the reports

Psychologists and other experts will gather evidence in a variety of ways. This will include:

- observations
- questionnaires
- checklists
- consultation
- interviews
- assessment tools.

The expert will often use criterion reference testing, which is normally a measure of individual progress against defined personal targets such as, for example, progress with reading following targeted support. Norm reference testing is used that ranks individuals across the continuum of achievement from high to low achievers, normally referred to as cognitive testing using psychometric assessments. There are two illustrations at the end of this chapter – one is the Bell curve and one is the application to the psychometric assessment standard test IQ scores based on the average of 100.

Cognitive testing involves standard scores, the distance from the mean, measured in standard deviations. IQ scores are presented in this way, that is, IQ100 = average. There are also percentiles or centiles that are a ranking out of 100. A ranking at 10 per cent of the population means that 90 per cent of the population would be expected to achieve a higher score.

Psychologists often use a number of established scores including the British Ability Scales (3rd edn), the Wechsler Intelligence Scale for Children – 4 (WISC – 4), the Wechsler Pre-School and Primary Scale of Intelligence – 4 (WIPPSI – 4), and the Wechsler Individual Achievement Test – 2 (WIAT II). There are other relevant tests, but these are the most common.

Speech and language therapists will often use the Clinical Evaluation of Language Fundamentals, Fourth Edition (CELF-4) or, for example, the Children's Communication Checklist-2 (CCC-2).[1] Psychologists will often use the Gilliam Autism Rating Scale-2 (GARS-2), the Conners Rating Scale Third Edition (Conners 3), or the Beck Youth Inventories (BYI).

These assessments are both standardised and scientifically validated, and provide a representative sample of the measured behaviour that is assessed. Quantitative information is obtained using scores from an overall national or international sample. They are also conducted under standardised conditions. For example, the Wechsler (WISC IV) has a verbal comprehension index, a working memory index, a perceptual reasoning index and a processing speed index. These confine to produce a full-scale IQ score, or a standard score, where possible. Where the variation is too high between the scores, no

---

1   Bishop, D. (2003) *Children's Communication Checklist (CCC-2)*. San Antonio, TX: Pearson.

overall IQ is possible. They produce an analysis of patterns of scoring for strengths and needs. In some cases, where a full-scale IQ score cannot be calculated, a general ability index can be obtained.

WIAT II provides attainment results for word reading/decoding, spelling/word building, reading comprehension/reading for meaning/ pseudo word decoding/reading nonsense words, reading rate and reading speed, numerical operations, and mathematical reasoning/ number problems using words.

An expert's report, in particular an educational psychologist's report or a therapist's report, and a consultant psychiatrist's report, should always include the following:

- summary of the evidence

- interpretation

- advice on the way forward and recommendations (to include specific advice on the issues in the case such as needs, provision, and where the provision should be delivered).

The reports must comply with SENDIST's practice direction which is reproduced on the SENDIST website.[2] The practice direction is virtually the same as Civil Procedure Rule 35, which requires that the experts owe their duty to SENDIST or to the Court and must give impartial advice. However, expert reports should also consider what are appropriate assessments.

Professor Ireland, in her article in *Educational Psychology in Practice*),[3] outlines very loosely the differences between scientifically validated evidence and evidence of opinion. She also outlines the difference between independent experts and experts who are basically in-house, and therefore who have a slightly different status in law. To put it briefly, although independently mediated, National Curriculum levels fall within the category of evidence of opinion. Scientifically validated evidence, such as cognitive testing, includes the British

---

2   See www.justice.gov.uk/tribunals/send/rules-and-legislation.
3   Ireland, J.L. (2008) 'Psychologists as witnesses: background and good practice in the delivery of evidence.' *Educational Psychology in Practice: Theory, Research and Practice in Educational Psychology 24*, 2, 115–127.

Ability Scales 3 and WISC – 4. So, too, is CELF-4 used by speech and language therapists, and the Assessment of Comprehension and Expression (ACE).

Expert evidence also needs to consider whether the progress alleged, for example, by the school, is supported by a scientifically validated test or other evidence, and whether there is independent evidence to back up the scientifically validated testing, that is, a history of educational psychology tests that all point the same way. The reports must clearly outline the needs, whether the child or young person is making adequate progress, whether further needs are being met, what the provision is to meet the needs, and if there are defects or failure to meet these needs.

The questions will obviously be somewhat different, for example, for a consultant child and adolescent psychiatrist – it could be, for example, questions regarding the mental state of the young person, whether their needs, on the face of it, are unmet, the causes of significant behavioural problems, depression, stress or anxiety, and how that is being dealt with. For speech and language therapists, specialist teachers and other therapists, the questions will be similar to that for an educational psychologist – questions regarding the child or young person's needs, whether the child or young person is making adequate progress, whether there is a gap in provision, or if the provision is adequate, and if not, why not, and what provision is actually required.

Due to SENDIST's practice direction, reports must set out the reasons for instruction. If a lawyer or an adviser has given definite instructions to the expert, the expert must set out, as follows:

- the documents considered, either in an appendix or at the front of the report;

- the expert's CV, qualifications and experience;

- background facts and history;

- details of the consultation with the school/school staff as appropriate;

- details of the expert's testing, observation and assessments of the child or young person;

- conclusions regarding the child's needs;

- conclusions about provision to meet the child's needs;

- the expert's overall views.

The expert should also consider the issues in light of the situation that arises, as the statutory appeals will basically involve the issue of whether a statutory assessment for an EHC plan is necessary, and if there is a dispute about the EHC plan, whether the child's needs have been properly identified and provision identified to meet their needs. If the issue is a change in the EHC plan, the question is whether the child has made adequate progress, whether the child or young person's needs have been adequately identified, whether the provision is appropriate, and whether the placement is appropriate.

If the decision is to cease to maintain the EHC plan, the questions that arise are somewhat more complex, and the Code of Practice offers good guidance on the circumstances, which can be summarised as the objectives of the EHC plan being met. Even if they have been met, the question is whether there is a continuing need for support, because if it is withdrawn, is there a risk of regression or lack of progress? If the objectives have not been met, what is the continuing reason to support need and provision? What is the provision required? What is the placement required? Why, overall, is a continued EHC plan required?

Obviously the point is to be emphasised that both parents and experts have recourse to both SENDIST's practice direction, and to the SEND Code of Practice (July 2014) from the DfE. However, such guidance is not available to the same extent for Equality Act cases, although the requirements of the practice direction for experts in SENDIST remain the same.

Finally, the practice direction from the first President of SENDIST, Trevor Aldridge, given in 1994 and reported in education law reports, remains good law, stating that the issue in any case is not what happened in the past, but whether the child's needs at the date of the hearing have been properly identified and properly met.

We now turn to Equality Act issues.

Equality Act 2010

The Children and Families Act 2014 does not affect the Equality Act 2010. As a result of amendments made in 2001, the Disability Discrimination Act 1995 has now entered the area of education, and the Equality Act 2010 has extended that duty. It imposes a duty on the responsible body not to discriminate against the disabled person in the following,

- including arrangements made for determining admission to a school as a pupil:

- the terms on which a pupil is admitted;

- refusing to accept an application;

- very important provision generally, namely, the provision of education or associated services offered to or provided to a pupil;

- an additional duty to ensure that pupils are not substantially disadvantaged;

- the duty to make reasonable adjustments for disabled pupils;

- the responsible body is normally the school or institution, but where there are residential duties or joint responsibility, it may be the local education authority.

As the earlier disability discrimination Code of Practice points out, children with SEN will often be disabled, but won't necessarily be disabled as defined under the Act. However, a recent decision by the Employment Appeal Tribunal, which has the equivalent status to the High Court, has certainly widened the prospective scope of what is thought to be a disability, where it found that a senior police officer who required concessions in exams fell within the definition of disability.[4] The Equality Act has increased the duties on schools and local authorities.

The twin concepts of disability and disabled people are central to the operation of disability discrimination law, and this remains an issue under the Equality Act. A child or young person who can satisfy the definition of a disabled person within the meaning of the Act can enjoy the protection of its framework. A disabled person is defined as a person who has a disability. The person has a disability if he or she has a physical or mental impairment that has a substantial and long-term adverse effect on his or her ability to carry out normal day-to-day activities (see Schedule 1 of the Act). These provisions are supplemented in some areas by regulations.

The apparent intention of the Act was to create a common-sense definition of disability and to avoid vagueness. In general, issues arising under the Equality Act 2010 in disability discrimination fall to be determined eventually by a Tribunal or an employer or an institution in education as follows:

- Does the claimant have an impairment?

- Does the impairment have an adverse effect on the claimant's ability to carry out normal day-to-day activities?

- Is the adverse effect substantial?

- Is the adverse effect long term?

(Where somebody is overcoming a disability, they are also protected for a certain period under the Act).

The issue of disability was more rigidly defined but has been amended by the Equality Act 2010. In 2005, it was amended to be less rigid and not dependent on, for example, World Health Organization (WHO) definitions, or alternatively, International Classification of Diseases (ICD-10) criteria. It should be remembered that WHO, in its 1980 classification of impairment, disability and handicap, defined impairment as 'any loss or abnormality of psychological, physiological or anatomical structure or function.'

---

4   *Paterson v Metropolitan Police Commissioner* [2007] ICR 1522 (EAT).

In relation to the Act, it gives guidance on carrying out day-to-day activities, and refers to the following as being impaired:

- mobility

- manual dexterity

- physical coordination

- continence

- ability to lift, carry or otherwise move everyday objects

- speech, hearing or eyesight

- memory or ability to concentrate, learn or understand

- perception of the risk of physical danger.

Where someone with a disability has a tendency or propensity to commit criminal actions as a result of the disability, which could include, for example, violence or aggression, a tendency to arson or the like, the existence of the Criminal Act is excluded by regulation, but it is possible to make reasonable adjustments to support the person with the disability excluding the act, which is excluded by law, and there is a failure in that to support the disability generally. That failure is not excluded.

It is also clear that it is the effect on the particular person and not people generally that matters. In *J. Goodwin v The Patent Office*,[5] the Employment Appeal Tribunal pointed out that the Act was concerned with an impairment of a person's ability to carry out activities. The fact that that person could carry out such activities does not mean that his or her ability to carry them out has not been impaired. It is not the doing of the act that is the focus of attention, but the ability to do it or not. The focus of the act is on what cannot be done or what can only be done with difficulty rather than what can generally be done by the person.

In *Paterson v Metropolitan Police Commissioner*, in dealing with the definition of disability, the Employment Appeal Tribunal made

---

5   [1999] IRLR 4 (EAT).

it much clearer as to what was classified as a disability. The Court applied the European case of *Chacon Navas v Eurest Colectividades*.[6] In essence, although in this case Mr Paterson's disability was described as mild, even by the psychologist, whose evidence was accepted, it was decided that he was clearly disabled. Carrying out an assessment or an examination was properly to be described as a normal day-to-day activity. The Court pointed out that the act of reading and comprehension was itself a normal day-to-day activity. That gave meaning to day-to-day activities by also encompassing those that were relevant to participation in professional life. As the effect of a disability such as dyslexia might adversely affect promotion prospects, this hinders professional life. A proper basis for establishing a disadvantage was to compare the effect on the individual of the disability that involved how they carried out an activity, and with somebody who carried out the activity not suffering from the impairment. If the difference was more than the kind of difference one might expect, taking a cross-section of the population, then it would be considered substantial whether or not it was described as mild or medium, etc. Concessions in exams were considered an adequate accommodation.

It is a defence to show:

- that it was not known that the person was disabled;

- that the responsible body could not reasonably be expected to know the person was disabled;

- that failure to take a step was attributable to lack of knowledge;

- that the actions taken were justified;

- that the act itself complained of is excluded – this is a rare defence.

---

6   [2007] All ER (EC) 59 (ECJ).

Reference should be made to the Codes of Practice issued by the Equality and Human Rights Commission.[7]

Involvement of experts in both cases

In relation to SEN or Equality Act cases, psychologists or education experts working for local authorities or other similar bodies will generally be involved in:

- providing reports on the initial assessment or at some later stage when the case is being reassessed for the purpose of deciding whether or not a Statement should be made;

- following up on such reports and advising the school generally by regular visits where appropriate;

- looking at the case overall, and the state of the case generally, once an appeal has been lodged and all information exchanged after the case Statement (see below);

- providing independent reports for an appeal that is being contemplated by parents, looking at the child's needs, progress and the effectiveness of provision and advising on the aspects of the case;

- looking at, from either side, the proposed schools and the frame of the proposed provision, that is, special units and some other provision away from the school;

- providing reports on the above;

- sometimes commenting on evidence used as part of an appeal that has produced a new view or a new light on the case;

---

7   Codes of Practice/Guidance by the Human Rights Commission:
- Code of Practice on Further and Higher Education
- Codes of Practice on a Public Sector Equality duty for England, Wales and for Scotland
- Codes of Practice for schools in England, Wales and in Scotland
- Guidance on new age goods, facilities, services and provisions
- Guidance on trade organisations, qualification bodies, general qualification bodies, housing and transport.

- sometimes educational psychologists and not clinical psychologists give evidence in Family Law cases.

Those providing reports in pure education cases and giving evidence should remember that the statutory test is generally what is needed, and to be added to that is probably (although the Courts have not yet worked this out) what is appropriate to the child's potential. Thus, the fact that the parents don't agree is not sufficient reason for why the EHC plan or support and provision proposed or used isn't working. There must be hard evidence as to why a particular Statement or a particular provision is not effective.

Jane Ireland's warning that experts should stay within their area of expertise and defer to other professionals if needed is important.[8]

The difference between an independent expert witness and a professional witness is not so clear in SENDIST and is likely to become more significant as time goes on. The main distinction of a professional witness from an expert witness is that they are employed as a represented party and are therefore not independently instructed.

Further, SENDIST proceedings are less formal than Court proceedings. There isn't the same emphasis on examination-in-chief and cross-examination, as explained by Jane Ireland. However, the formality of such proceedings varies enormously. These Tribunal proceedings are informal, but some can appear more like a Court. The Tribunal itself may ask a number of very searching questions indeed. The fact that it is not a Court does not mean that the competence and expertise of the Tribunal and those before it should be underestimated.

Tribunal procedure rules: the system and further assessments/further reports

The Tribunal is able to order the assessment of a child (Regulation 15(4)). This is because they consider one party can be given adequate

---

8   Ireland, J. (2008). 'Psychologists as witnesses: background and good practice in the delivery of evidence'. *Educational Psychologists in Practice 24*, 2, 115–127.

access to the child or that some exceptional reason has arisen. However, older children who are competent to make a decision can themselves object and refuse. If they are competent to make a decision, they can also limit experts' access or testing. It is therefore not quite so simple as the Tribunal making an order. Further, there is likely to be detailed legal argument on this issue.

If there is a specific reason to request a further assessment, it should be clearly defined and set out, and what is intended to be done. It should also be further remembered that the fact that the particular party to the proceedings wants an assessment, and a psychologist agrees to carry it out, may not comply with the professional duties of the psychologist as recognised by the Health Professionals Council (HPC). Once orders are made to impose assessments, and if the assessment is carried out in a manner that the parents object to, this is likely to result in further complaints.

Finally, all expert reports should contain the Civil Procedure Rules Statement of Truth required in SENDIST cases. This reads as follows, and is relevant to cases in the Family Court, other Courts and Tribunals.

STATEMENT OF TRUTH

I confirm that insofar as the facts stated in my report are within my own knowledge, I have made it clear which they are and I believe them to be true and the opinions I have expressed represent my true and complete professional opinion.

a)   I believe the facts I have stated in this report are true and that the opinions I have expressed are correct.

b)   I understand that my duty in providing written reports, and in giving evidence, is to assist the Tribunal. This duty overrides any obligations to the party who has instructed or engaged me. I have complied with my duty.

c)   I have done my best in preparing this report, to be accurate and complete. I have mentioned all matters which are required relevant to the opinions I have expressed.

d) I have drawn the attention of the Tribunal to all matters of which I am aware, which might adversely affect my opinion. Moreover, I have had no personal knowledge, I have indicated a source of factual information.

I have not included anything in this report which has been suggested to me by anyone, including lawyers instructing me, without forming my own independent view of the matter.

At the time of signing the report, I consider it to be complete and accurate. I will notify those instructing me if, for any reason, I subsequently consider that the report requires any correction or qualification.

Signed

As will be noticed therefore, the requirements by the Courts and Tribunals have significantly tightened up as regards expert evidence. Those working for local authorities do not normally provide a Statement of Truth. However, even now Tribunals are currently ordering Statements of Truth for local authority-employed psychologists.

Know your curve!!

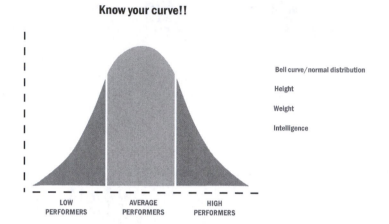

Bell curve/normal distribution

Height

Weight

Intelligence

LOW PERFORMERS   AVERAGE PERFORMERS   HIGH PERFORMERS

Psychometric assessments

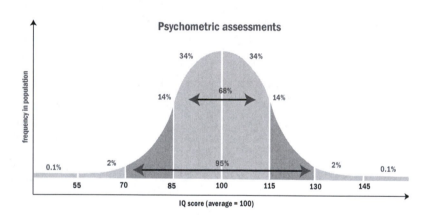

CHAPTER 8

RIGHT OF APPEAL AND MEDIATION

Introduction

Although parents of a child up to the age of 16 can certainly appeal, it is unclear whether the SEND Code of Practice and the Children and Families Act 2014 itself is an attempt to abolish parental rights 'by the back door', which in law exist for children to the age of 18. Section 51 of the Act provides that a child's parent or a young person may appeal to the First-tier Tribunal against the matters set out in Subsection (2), subject to Section 55 mediation.

The Right of Appeal is as follows:

- When the local authority decides not to assess the needs of a child or young person.

- When the decision of any assessment is not to make an EHC plan; although the EHC plan is maintained, the appeal lies against:

  » the child's educational needs set out in the plan;

  » provisions set out in the plan;

  » the type of school or institution set out in the plan; or

  » if no other school or institution is named in the plan, that fact.

- When there is no decision to reassess the child's needs following a request under Section 44 of the Act.

- When there is no decision to secure an amendment or replace the EHC plan it maintains for a child or young person following a review or a reassessment under Section 44 of the Act.

- When there is a decision to cease to maintain the plan.

- When the plan is first finalised or when it is amended.

Section 83 of the Act defines a young person as a person over compulsory school age, that is, aged 16 but under 25. As the Right of Appeal goes to the parent first, the parent remains a parent until the child is 18. It is the authors' view, therefore, that the Right of Appeal to a parent, despite what is said in the SEND Code of Practice, lasts until the age of 18. Obviously, at the age of 16, a young person can appeal themselves; however, to avoid difficulties, for those over 16, the parents may be wise to include the young person. When over 18, if the child or young person has capacity (see below), they will conduct the appeal. They may have legal aid, but even if legal aid is available, the parents may still wish to support the child and pay for additional expert evidence or legal services.

The Code strongly suggests that once 16, only the young person and not the parent appeals. In practice, and certainly for those at school, it is always the parent who appeals, with the young person supporting the parent. This is unlikely to change until the child is 18. Paragraph 11.44 of the Code states that parents can appeal up to the end of compulsory schooling, and young people until the age of 25. Unless it is to be argued that the 2014 Act actually abolished parental rights, the Code must be wrong on this issue. However, local authorities may try to take this point up. In order to avoid silly arguments about the issue of who can appeal, parents are well advised to involve the young person according to the Tribunal Rules that currently exist. The young person will be involved whether they like it or not – as the rules provide for an assessment of that young person under Regulation 15(4) it is invariably used by local authorities.

Mental capacity

The issue of mental capacity is dealt with under Section 2 of the Mental Capacity Act 2005. While a child or young person may have the ability to decide what they want to eat or where to go today, those with moderate or severe learning difficulties may not have the capacity to make a decision. They may not have the ability to understand and conduct their own affairs, or, in fact, to conduct an appeal.

In these circumstances we strongly advise parents to apply to a Court of Protection for deputyship prior to their child turning 18. A deputy can cover financial issues as well as health and welfare. If a parent is already in place as a deputy by the time the child is 18, parents or relatives will deal with any health and welfare decisions. While many local authorities are still happy to deal with parents or carers acting as those responsible for the young person, experience has shown that some local authorities have regarded someone over the age of 18, even if they completely lack capacity, as entitled to conduct their own affairs, and therefore they cut out the parents. There are equally cases when the local authority has applied for deputyship on behalf of the child. It is a relatively simple and cheap procedure, although parents who apply should be warned that there is a very long and complex form to be filled out. Lawyers who normally apply for deputyships are often not experienced in dealing with young people; they are generally more experienced in dealing with the elderly, and some of them have no idea that it is relatively simple to get deputyship for a young person who lacks capacity at 18. It is advisable to use lawyers who have experience of disabled young adults, and to check on their experience of this area.

The Code provides reasonable guidance in Annex 1, in relation to the Mental Capacity Act 2005. Also, where young people do not have parents who have a deputyship or who are willing to support them, or where there are no parents, local authorities are required to ensure that the young person concerned has appropriate support.

In practice, experience has shown that even for young people older than 19, subject to them being able to obtain legal aid, it is effectively the parents, whether or not they have a deputyship, who conduct the appeal and argue for their child's rights. The new law extends, as does the Code, local authorities' duties to provide advice and support, particularly for children either in custody or who are looked-after, who do not have somebody standing by them. This is to be welcomed.

Mediation

Under statutory provisions, a parent or young person can only appeal subject to mediation, but they are entitled to refuse mediation so long as they obtain an information certificate from the mediator. However, Section 55 on mediation does not apply if the appeal concerns only:

- the school or other institution named in the EHC plan;

- the type of school in the EHC plan; or

- the fact that the EHC plan does not name a school.

No appeal against an EHC plan will solely involve a school, save in very exceptional circumstances. Thus, Section 55(3) applies, namely, a parent or young person may make an appeal only if the mediator has issued a certificate under subsections (4) or (5).

The certificate is issued if the adviser has given information about mediation, and the parent has informed the adviser that they do not wish to pursue mediation. If so, according to Section 55(5), the mediator must issue a certificate to that effect.

The time limit for considering mediation or getting a certificate is two months. Under Regulation 34, the mediator must issue a certificate within three working days after being informed by the parent or young person telling them that they do not want mediation. Be warned, however:

- The mediator must be informed either that mediation has been requested, or that it has not been sought, within two months (the current appeal time provided in the Tribunal Regulations).

- Unless exceptional circumstances are shown outside of two months, the appeal goes.

However, the certificate is not issued if the mediator or the young person has failed to comply and to inform the mediator within two months; they may still apply to the First-tier Tribunal, but must show good reason for a late appeal.

Three days to issue a certificate is impracticable. It is difficult to imagine an appointed mediator issuing a certificate within three days, although this is actually three working days. It is highly likely that such a short time limit will not be complied with. In these circumstances, parents are advised simply, that at the expiry of the third working day, they should go straight to the Tribunal and seek permission to appeal. Where a mistake has been made, and somebody has not sought the mediation certificate or pursued mediation within two months, the right to go to the Tribunal and to argue for exceptional circumstances still arises.

Arrangements for mediation, if appropriate, include, under Regulation 39, the right for an advocate or other supporter to attend. If mediation is successful, a certificate must be issued within three working days of the conclusion under Regulation 39.

What is the benefit of mediation?

Mediation has not proved successful, save in a few cases, and is unlikely to prove successful in most appeals to the Tribunal. Mediation does have a role where the Tribunal does not have jurisdiction, principally in health or care, where they are sole issues. It may provide a way of persuading health or children's services or social services to provide greater levels of support. In cases where the Tribunal currently has jurisdiction, it is difficult to see that a mediator would be an appropriate person to decide issues, as provision may cost the local authority a substantial sum. In some very complex cases (provision over £100,000 and above per year for educational placements, that is, 38- or 52-week placements at highly complex provisions), these are very unlikely to be the subject of an agreement in mediation. Either an authority will have reached the conclusion that the needs are so complex that such a provision is justified, or it is to be strongly contested. It is therefore unlikely that mediation will do more than add to the parents' problems and delay the case, except for circumstances where the main issue is already agreed.

What is the benefit of Mediation?

Further, mediators have no jurisdiction over the law, and if there is a dispute in the law, they simply will not resolve it. Many cases will involve legal issues and are unsuited for a mediator to resolve.

The Government imposed this condition, and anybody considering mediation should consider the option very carefully. The Tribunal has, overall, proved to be a very effective body. Under the Act the mediators are not the equivalent of mediators in other legal cases; for example, if there are commercial disputes, mediators are usually highly trained and experienced, as is the case in family law. The requirements here are very different and most cases will not be suitable for mediation, so the parents or young person should consider obtaining or asking for the certificate as fast as possible, and go straight to the Tribunal if it is not sent back in three days, which is highly likely.

There are specific provisions for mediation involving health care issues. In particular, Regulation 35(3) provides where mediation issues relate solely to health care provision, and requires the responsible commissioning bodies to arrange for mediation between them or the child's parent or young person within 30 days of the date on which they are informed of a received notification from the local authority. Where it does not involve health care provision, the authority must arrange for mediation between it and the responsible commissioning body, which would be children's services or education in children's services, within 30 days.

If an agreement is reached in mediation, it is dealt with by Regulation 42, which requires a mediation agreement to be implemented. The object of mediation, therefore, is to obtain a mediation agreement.

A Mediation Certificate will not say what happened in the Mediation, just that mediation has been completed.

Powers of the Tribunal

Regulation 43, unlike the 1996 Act which provided for the powers of the Tribunal within the appeal power, Section 326, this outlines the powers of the First-tier Tribunal when hearing a case to determine the appeal. The Tribunal now has the power, with the agreement of the parties, to correct any deficiencies in the EHC plan which relate to SEN or special educational provision for the young person. The Tribunal may therefore be able to determine obvious points. This is a useful extension to the Tribunal's powers.

When determining an appeal, however, under Regulation 43(2), the Tribunal's powers are to:

- dismiss the appeal;

- order the local authority to arrange an assessment of the child or young person for a reassessment where an assessment for an EHC plan or reassessment has been refused;

- order the authority to make and maintain an EHC plan where the authority has refused to do so;

- refer the case back to the authority for them to reconsider whether having regard to the observations made by the Tribunal is necessary for the authority to determine the special educational provision for the young person, where the appeal is made under Section 51(2)(b) and where the authority has refused to make a plan following an assessment;

- order the authority to continue to maintain the plan in its existing form where it has refused to do so;

- order the authority to maintain the plan with amendments, so far as it relates to the assessment of SEN or special educational provision, and make any consequential amendments the Tribunal thinks fit;

- order the authority to substitute a school or other institution or type of school or institution in the plan where the plan concerns only a specific school or other institution, or the type of school or other institution named in the plan;

- make an order in accordance with Section 51(2)(g), which may include naming a special school or institution, or a mainstream school or institution.

Overall, the Tribunal's powers are effectively the same as they were before.

Parents waiting for the outcome of Mediation, followed by SEND Tribunal

Practice and procedure in the Tribunal

By the time this book is published, the Tribunal will have existed as a specialist Tribunal for 21 years. In 2013, the number of appeals to the Tribunal rose to 3,557. Current reports from the Tribunal are that there has been a reasonably substantial increase over and above that number, and it is to be expected that with the new EHC plans, and with the extension of jurisdiction to the age of 25, it is highly likely that despite the mediation requirement, there will be an increase in appeals.

In 2013, 808 appeals proceeded to a hearing, 24 per cent of the number registered. In her talk in March 2014 at the annual conference held by Jordan's Publishers in relation to the development of the law in Special Educational Needs, Tribunal Judge Tudur, now the senior judge in charge, pointed out that over the last few years a constant number of appeals have gone to a hearing. Appeals allowed in whole or in part made up 84 per cent of the total. Out of 135 disability discrimination claims that were registered, they were a minority; 33 were upheld, and 34 were dismissed to 67 hearings. In March 2014, Judge Tudur reported a 10 per cent increase in workload. The Tribunal has prioritised and developed a fast track appeal for phased transfers. This was subject to a 12-week timetable for registration to hearing. Judge Tudur reported that the arrangement worked very well, and no appeal hearings were postponed due to a shortage in Tribunal time.

In relation to appeals against refusals to assess, the Tribunal has now listed these, before a two-member Tribunal – a normal Tribunal panel is made up of three members, one experienced judge, of at least 10 years' practice, and two lay members, with considerable experience in education. The figures are very interesting. Between 1 October 2013 and 31 January 2104, in relation to refusals to assess, 505 appeals were registered, and 65 hearings conducted. This indicates, and experience indicates as well, that of those 505 appeals, some 440 were conceded by the local authority. The Tribunal also has an ongoing mediation pilot.

The time for appealing to the Tribunal in SEN cases is two months, but the Tribunal judge has judicial discretion to extend the time for making the appeal, but it does require relevant information and facts before making a decision. The Upper Tribunal has considered these issues on a number of occasions, and made it clear that although each case depends on the facts, and there is good reason to extend an appeal, normally the time should be extended.[1]

---

1   CM v Surrey CC (SEN) 2014 UKUT 4 (AAC)

The time for appealing to the SEND Tribunal is normally two months

The time limit for disability discrimination is different, and, it is to be emphasised, it is six months. Judge Tudur, in an address to the March 2014 Jordan's Publisher's conference, stated that throughout its existence the Tribunal has seen only a very small proportion of the decisions made by local authorities about children with SEN, which either reflects a high level of satisfaction and acceptance of decisions made, or lack of guidance and advice about the means of challenging decisions. She considered that access to the relevant information guidance identified by the draft Code of Practice would benefit the families concerned.

The authors do not agree with the judge that the new Code of Practice and the new system will allow families to access justice without incurring significant costs. The imposition of a need for mediation on the requirement of a certificate, and the Code of Practice itself, which has been extended from a short readable volume to, leaving aside appendices and annexes, a document of at least 230 pages, and an EHC plan that contains many new sections and complex sections, cannot improve information.

Judge Tudur would probably be incredibly disappointed to know that the Code of Practice was sent back to the DfE on the basis that it was too long, too complex and too confusing for parents; when it was considered by the Parliamentary Education Select Committee in the House of Lords, it was eventually passed on the basis that it was for professionals, and not parents. Therefore the fact that it was too long, too complex, and not easily understood by parents was not relevant. The record of *Hansard*, relating to the Code of Practice debate moved by Lord Nash, Parliamentary Under-Secretary of State for Schools, stated, after the Legislation Scrutiny Committee of the House of Lords sent it back to the Department, as follows:

> I should point out that parents are not the Code's key audience. The chief audience is the range of bodies with statutory duties to fulfil and which must have regard to it... It was absolutely clear that interested parties did not see shortening as a priority.

So that's all right then. The intention of the Code at first was exactly the opposite from that suggested by Lord Nash, and, of course, the Code of Practice itself was never intended, from its origin, to just be simple advice for statutory bodies.

Appeals process

The appeals process to the Tribunal is set out in the current Civil Procedure Rules, which pre-date the 2014 Act, although there is no particular reason to amend regulations that can be currently determined, and Judge Tudur did not refer to such proposals. However, the regulations probably do need changing to allow for those up to the age of 25. Parents must normally appeal within two months of the decision.

The notice to appeal must be given in writing and the appeal form can be found on the Tribunal's website. All notices and documents required by the regulations should be sent to the Tribunal by post, fax, electronic mail or delivered to the offices of the Tribunal. The appeal should have the relevant documents attached to it, including the EHC plan and appendices, the decision to refuse to amend, assess, reassess, cease to maintain, or following an annual review.

The Tribunal strictly adheres to time limits. Time is calculated in working days, which means, therefore, that Saturdays, Sundays, Bank Holidays and any day from 25 December to 1 January are not included. Additionally, and most importantly, no day in August is included, although hearings can take place in that month; this is because it is an educational appeal.

Once an appeal is lodged, the local authority is obliged to provide a response, which includes their reasons for making the decision and evidence supporting it. The Tribunal has powers under Regulation 6 to order personal additional information or evidence, to extend time limits, and to substitute all the parties.

Additionally, the Tribunal responds to an appeal when received by serving the local authority. It is the Tribunal that in both special needs and Equality Act cases serves the local authority. It will issue a directions notice, requiring information about the witnesses to attend the Tribunal. In English practice this is normally limited to three witnesses, but the Tribunal will allow more if there are exceptional circumstances, and in fact in Wales, it is currently normally limited to two.

Disability discrimination claims require the grounds of claim, and all appeals require the details and name and address of the child and parent. In special needs appeals, guidance given by the judge includes not only a list of witnesses to attend the hearing, but a date for final evidence, and a date for a working document, which is normally issued 10 days before the hearing.

Where there is a particular need because some procedural or other important issue arises, the Tribunal requires a 'Change Request Form'. It normally nominates a date for the final hearing, but often that is not appropriate, and the parties will seek to change the date. Equally, although the Tribunal will set a date for evidence, as long as there is good reason, late evidence is acceptable, and the Upper Tribunal has made it clear that the Tribunal is under an obligation to admit late evidence unless it is procedurally unfair or the hearing is disrupted.

The Tribunal must conduct its affairs under the terms of the overriding objective and its procedural regulations are included. This emphasises fairness to both parties, efficient disposal of the hearing, and consideration of the child or young person's interests.

In relation to costs, these are not normally awarded. However, the Tribunal does have power to award costs ultimately if one party behaves wholly unreasonably (see Regulation 10). There is Upper Tribunal case law on this issue, but most parents or local authorities will get nowhere near to obtaining an order for costs. Such cases are wholly exceptional, and the test in the Tribunal amounts to a test of professional negligence.

Specific issues concerning appeals

The Tribunal does not have jurisdiction in relation to non-educational issues. As an EHC plan now contains a number of sections, issues that are purely medical or social care, for example, are not within the Tribunal's jurisdiction. In addition, the following issues are not within the Tribunal's jurisdiction:

- Failure of the local authority to arrange the special educational provision set out in the Statement (see Chapter 9).

- A refusal to admit a child when the Plan names the child is subject to judicial review or a complaint.

- Failure of the local authority to have regard to its general obligations towards children with SEN.

- Failure of the local authority to comply with the statutory time limits or time limits in regulations.

- Failure of the local authority to carry out the periodic reviews of the EHC plan.

Parents who wish to bring an appeal to the Tribunal must comply with the procedural rules. To lodge an appeal requires the parent and their representative to send to the Tribunal within the two-month period outlined, the following:

- Name and address of the appellant.

- Name and address of the appellant's representative, if any.

- Addresses where documents for the appellant may be sent or delivered.

- Name and address of any respondent local authority.

- Details of the decision or Act to which the proceedings relate.

- Result the appellant is seeking.

- Grounds on which the appellant relies.

The Tribunal has a website that includes the form.[2] However, it is somewhat limited, and in complex cases, detailed grounds of appeal should be attached. Evidence required to be lodged with the appeal is detailed in the *Tribunals and Inquiries, England and Wales, The Tribunal Procedure (First-tier Tribunal), (Health, Education and Social Care Chamber) Rules 2008* SI 2008/2699, and the Tribunal practice direction. An appeal against an EHC plan must therefore have the plan or an amended plan attached, or if there is no amendment, the current plan. If there is a refusal to assess or cease to maintain the plan, the documents should be attached.

The Tribunal registers the appeal and sends out automatic directions. The local authority must respond within 30 working days and the response should set out:

- Name and address of the respondent.

- Name and address of the respondent's representative, if any.

- Address where documents for the respondent may be sent and delivered.

- A statement as to whether the respondent opposes the appeal and if so, grounds for opposition, which are not contained in another document provided with the response.

---

2   This can be found at www.justice.gov.uk/tribunals/send.

- Views of the child or young person about the issues raised by the proceedings, or the reasons why the local authority has not ascertained those views.

- Where the application relates to the contents of the child's Statement.

- Where the application relates to the contents of an EHC plan and the local authority does not resist the application or withdraws its opposition.

- Final amended EHC plan incorporating the amendments it agrees to make.

- A copy of the EHC plan, appendices and supporting documents, where these were not submitted by the parent or the young person with the appeal.

- Any supplemental evidence and professional reports currently available to the local authority on which it intends to rely.

- Detailed grounds setting out why the parts of the application are omitted, and detailed grounds setting out why the application is resisted, and any legal points.

In relation to late evidence, while the Tribunal's automatic directions, as outlined above, set a deadline, in the case of *H.J. v London Borough of Brent*[3] the Upper Tribunal made it clear that any party may apply for permission to rely on late evidence lodged after the date. Evidence should not be excluded simply because it was lodged late – the overriding considerations are the overriding objectives of the Tribunal and procedural fairness.

Working document

According to the Tribunal's procedure, a working document should be worked on by both parties. It is therefore important that the parents or the young person who appeal provide a version of the working

---

3   [2010] UKUT 15 (AAC).

document and that the Tribunal provides a key which, in rough terms, is the parent or young person's proposed amendments – they should be in bold type, and where they strike things out in the statement, this should be in bold type struck through. The authority's amendments should be in italics, and italics underlined where both parties agree.

The process of a working document identifies the issues in dispute very effectively, and if well drafted by both sides, can reduce the time of the hearing considerably. These are complex cases, and Tribunal members read the evidence beforehand, providing an extremely efficient service to determine appeals. Remember that Judge Tudur referred to 84 per cent of appeals succeeding wholly or partially, which is a very high level of appeals succeeding.

It is important for those representing the parents, or the parents and the local authority, to ensure that all relevant witnesses are available on the day.

Most cases take a day, but as matters have become more complex (and, it is anticipated, with the new EHC plans, matters will be more complex), cases are sometimes adjourned or listed longer (meaning that the Tribunal lists a case for either a day, half a day, or more than one day later). When a hearing is adjourned, the Tribunal is able to give directions to be complied with, which include particulars of additional evidence, statements to be filed, or action to be taken by the date of the adjourned hearing.

However, unanticipated events require adjournments, which may include witnesses being ill or unavailable. Normally the Tribunal will find a day convenient to the parties, their witnesses and professional advisers. However, the Tribunal often wishes to avoid unnecessary delay. In one case, where a parent did not have a witness who was unable to come from Norway at short notice, as the evidence of the expert was central to the issue in the case, and it was plainly important, in fairness the High Court demanded an adjournment (see *Lucy v Royal Borough of Kensington and Chelsea*).[4] In *R. v Cheshire County Council, ex parte C.*,[5] the appellant had engaged a solicitor who was

---

4   [1997] EWHC 23 (QBD).
5   [1998] ELR 66 (QBD).

unable to attend, but had arranged for an expert witness to attend in his place, and represent the appellant. On the eve of the hearing, the educational psychologist went down with flu and an adjournment was refused. Sedley J. stated that fairness required the Tribunal to grant an adjournment, and where the Tribunal could be satisfied that an application to adjourn was based on the absence of the wholly unnecessary witness or representative, that it would be right to refuse the adjournment. In *B. v Hounslow London Borough Council and Vassie*,[6] the mother of a seven-year-old girl could not replace her childcare arrangements for a severely autistic child, as all three possible carers became unavailable – she could not leave the child and had to stay at home. An adjournment was refused, and the High Court set aside the decision.

Leaving aside adjournments, on arrival at the Tribunal, the Tribunal will normally set out a list of issues that it considers it should determine at the hearing. These are informed by the evidence filed, and include that contained in the parents' additional evidence. In relation to this, it is useful if they not only send in their expert evidence, but also provide an overall summary of their case as well as a working document, to describe the issues from their point of view, once they have had the opportunity to read the local authority's response. The Tribunal will therefore have had the opportunity to consider both parties' cases, the expert evidence, and the working document.

A Tribunal will normally set its own procedure under the Rules, and therefore how it deals with the list of issues will be dependent on the Tribunal itself on the day. It may ask for each issue to be addressed in turn by both sides; it may ask for both sides to address all issues on need sequentially, and then provision sequentially, before turning to the appropriate school.

Case law requires the Tribunal to be satisfied that the school in Part 4 must meet the needs in Parts 2 and 3, and therefore it is not normally appropriate to jump to Part 4 unless there is an exceptional circumstance.

---

6   [2000] Ed CR 680.

A case can be won on appeal on two issues:

- that the EHC plan does not adequately reflect the child's needs or provision. If this includes the parents seeking a different school, the issue will be that the authority's proposals cannot meet need or provide for need, then the case will be won on that basis; or

- the issue of Section 9 – if the local authority's provision either exceeds the costs of the parents' choice of school or the costs are roughly equivalent, normally as a result of Section 9, the parents will succeed.

Section 9 of the Education Act 1996 includes all public
money – i.e. all tax payer's – money that is spent

One issue that can make a major difference, therefore, is cost, and we now return to this point. In *Haining v Warrington Borough Council* the Court of Appeal considered the meaning of the words 'public expenditure' in Section 9 of the 1996 Act. The facts of the case were relevant – the local authority's case of a School Plus respite care provision was more expensive than the parents' choice of school, which included a residential provision. The Court of Appeal decided that the meaning of Section 9, in relation to public expenditure, covered all public expenditure, and was therefore wider than that considered in Schedule 27 of the 1996 Act, which is reproduced in the same form in Section 39 of the 2014 Act. The Court considered three options in the second part of the judgment, namely, should public expenditure cover all public expenditure, was it simply the education budget or was it simply the local authority's expenditure? In the leading and sole judgment, Lord Dyson M.R. made it quite clear that public expenditure meant all public expenditure. This would therefore include not only expenditure on education transport, the cost of social care, including respite care, but also, in some cases, the fact that benefits would be paid if a child remained at home. But if the child goes to a residential placement, benefits are not paid, and therefore public expenditure is reduced, which can be credited against the expenditure on the parents' choice of school. The judgment is therefore extremely important on these issues.

In deciding the case, a number of established cases confirmed this issue. It is worth mentioning the judgment of Judge Pearl in the Upper Tribunal in *K. v London Borough of Hillingdon*, which also held that the Tribunal should look at the whole picture.

This then leaves the issue within many appeals of how you work out, particularly within a school's operative situation, whether expenditure is real, has already been incurred and paid for, and is therefore a nil cost. If, for example, the local authority school has spare places, and it is a special school, there may be a nil cost because it is pre-funded. These issues were most recently considered in *E.H. v Kent County Council*, after a series of cases in the Court of Appeal. In looking at the individual costing in a particular school, the Court of Appeal first of all pointed out that the local authority's budgetary arrangements for an individual school would usually be a sensible starting point. For academies, this would currently be the Education Funding Agency. Sullivan L.J. pointed out that the basic cost of a pupil place, often called the 'age-weighted pupil unit' in the past, together with additional costs:

Specifically incurred in respect of the child in question, for example transport costs or the cost of therapy or learning support if an additional therapist or any support assistant has to be employed by the school, or if an existing therapist or learning support assistant has to be paid to work additional hours (if it is satisfied that these are additional costs) are a fair reflection to the cost to the public purpose of educating the child at the school.[7]

So if, for example, in the mainstream school, the child requires learning support assistant help, specialist teaching help and therapy input, the cost of that specific help would normally be directed to the particular child as required by the EHC plan, which would reflect the true cost of the place at school. However, as the Court of Appeal made clear in *Haining v Warrington*, in some cases, the issue of costs may be very much wider.

---

7   [2011] UKUT 71 (AAC).

CHAPTER 9

APPEALS FROM THE FIRST-TIER TRIBUNAL AND ENFORCEMENT

Introduction

When making a decision, SENDIST must produce a decision orally or in writing, according to Regulation 41 of *Tribunals and Inquiries, England and Wales, The Tribunal Procedure (First-tier Tribunal), (Health, Education and Social Care Chamber) Rules 2008.*[1] Oral decisions are rarely given, however, and in all cases, notice and a written decision must be sent. An appeal goes to the Upper Tribunal, and from there, with permission to appeal (as this is a second statutory appeal from the Upper Tribunal) to the Court of Appeal, and ultimately to the Supreme Court. It is very rare, however, that such cases ever get to the Supreme Court – as far as the authors can recall, only one such case ever reached the House of Lords (the predecessor of the Supreme Court).

If a parent or a local authority is dissatisfied with an appeal, they must appeal the decision within 28 days (Rule 46(2)). An application for permission to appeal must be made in writing, and the following must be sent to the Tribunal by no later than 28 days:

- written reasons for the decision;

- notification of amended reasons for or correction of the decision following a review; or

- notification that an application for the decision to be set aside has been unsuccessful.

---

1   See www.justice.gov.uk/downloads/tribunals/general/consolidated_TPFtT_HESC Rules2008asat010411.pdf.

The latter point refers to Rule 45, which allows a decision to be set aside in certain circumstances. It is therefore relevant to consider this rule before considering the application for appeal or review. Under Rule 45, a Tribunal may set aside a decision or part of a decision, or remake a decision or relevant part, if it is:

- in the interests of justice to do so; and

- one or more of the conditions set out below are satisfied, which are:

  » a document relating to the proceedings was not sent or was not received at an appropriate time by a party or party's representative;

  » a document relating to the proceedings was sent to the Tribunal at an appropriate time;

  » a party or a party's representative was not present at the hearing or related proceedings; or

  » there has been some other procedural irregularity in the proceedings.

A party applying for a decision or part of a decision to be set aside must make a written application to the Tribunal so that it is received no later than 28 days after the date on which the Tribunal gave notice of appeal of the decision.

According to Rule 44, the Tribunal has the jurisdiction to correct clerical mistakes or accidental slips or omissions, but an application under this rule will obviously not alter the decision in any substantial way, as it only deals with minor typographical or factual errors of no practical importance.

Rule 45 applies to the circumstances mentioned earlier in Chapter 8, where, during the hearing of an appeal, an essential witness or representative, or indeed the appellant, is unable to attend the hearing due to unexpected events (see *R. v Cheshire County Council, ex parte C.*,[2] and the other cases mentioned). It also includes cases

---

2   [1998] ELR 66 (QBD).

where documents have not been sent or fail to arrive, or where there is a procedural mistake resulting in unfairness.

Application for permission to appeal and its consideration

If the application for appeal is delivered outside of 28 days, under Rule 46(4), the Tribunal has jurisdiction to extend the time. This is only in exceptional circumstances, however, and good reasons must be given.

The application itself must: identify the decision of the Tribunal to which it relates; identify the error or errors of law in the decision; and state the result the party making the application is seeking.

The Tribunal's decision can be challenged in relation to substantive points of law, procedural unfairness, or alternatively, irrationality, which are normally called 'Wednesbury issues' by lawyers. The Courts, however, are generally reluctant to be drawn into the substantial merits of the factual dispute between the parent and the local authority. As the Court put it in *R. v Kingston upon Thames and Hunter*,[3]

> The jurisdiction of this Court, on appeal such as the present, is of course limited. It can only upset a decision of the Tribunal if the appellant shows that it was made unlawfully. In other words, the Court must ask whether the Tribunal, in making its decision, applied the correct principles of law, whether it failed to take into account any material factor, whether it took into account any immaterial factor, or whether it reached a decision which was irrational. In other words, one which no reasonable Tribunal reasonably could have reached.[4]

It would therefore be much more difficult to show that the Tribunal acted irrationally, or reached a decision which no reasonable Tribunal could have reached. Points of law, however, are more likely to be successful. Even now, the role of Section 9 of the Education Act 1966, considered earlier with reference to the case of *Haining v Warrington*,

---

3   [1997] ELR 223 (Admin.).
4   *R. v Kingston upon Thames and Hunter* [1997] ELR 223 (Admin.) 230(h)–231(b).

has still not been fully determined, particularly in relation to its effect on Section 33. Case law on challenges to the form and content of the Statement already mentioned, such as *R. v The Secretary of State for Education and Science, ex parte E.*[5] and *L. v Clarke & Somerset County Council*,[6] dealing with the issue of specific provision to illustrate points of law on the interpretation of the Act or regulations, are good examples of issues that will arise. As EHC plans are new, and as the regulations surrounding them are new, and the cases considered earlier are based on the old law, appeal issues will arise. Cases based on the old law remain good, and were intended to be preserved as a result of the requirements, for example, for specific provision (arising as a result of assurances given by Edward Timpson MP, Minister for Children's Schools and Families, to the Education Select Committee). Thus these cases have continued application.

However, with the extension of legal obligations on local authorities, the fact that the EHC plan is a more complex document, and that the definition of educational provision has been expanded in Section 21(5), this means that new points will arise. Indeed, aside from the issue of what is and is not public resources, as considered in the case of *Haining v Warrington* set out above, there are still a number of issues of law that could potentially arise. What can be said is that where the statute has kept the same test for assessment for making an EHC plan, and for the educational contents of the plan that are mandatory, the law remains remains exactly the same as prior to the 2014 Act on the essential specific issues as to criteria in law for a statutory assessment, making an EHC Plan, and as to the contents of that plan which remain mandatory. The case law which is established still applies.

The issue of costs and resources, however, are likely to occupy further appeals. Not only are there issues about the extent of public expenditure, but also regarding individual expenditure on a particular child or young person (see *E.H. v Kent County Council*).[7]

---

5   [1992] 1 FLR 377 (CA).

6   [1998] ELR 129 (QBD).

7   [2011] EWCA Civ 709 (CA).

A major subject of challenges to Tribunal decisions is the fact that the reasons are unlawful and inadequate, although failure to give reasons is not in itself an error of law. It is normally regarded to be an error of law and justifying a rehearing if it fails to cover significant issues. Case law on this is very clear; it is based on the duty of the Courts and Tribunals to give reasons (see, for example, *Flannery and Another v Halifax Estate Agencies Ltd,*[8] where the judge did not state why he preferred one expert's evidence over another). In Tribunal cases, this is obviously very important, as experts are often crucial to the decision.

There are a number of decisions on these issues (for good analysis of the duty to give reasons, see *R. (B.) v Vale of Glamorgan County Council*[9] and *H. v Kent County Council and the Special Education Needs Tribunal;*[10] the leading authority is *R. (on the application of J.F.) v Croydon LBC*).[11]

The Tribunal's own conduct could come into question as being unfair, although such circumstances are exceptional. In *Richardson v Solihull Metropolitan Borough Council,*[12] the Court of Appeal made it clear that Tribunals could not give evidence to themselves, so that the parties did not know the situation, although in this case, the Tribunal did not act improperly. However, in *Harrow Council v A.M.,*[13] Judge Mark determined that the Tribunal had acted unfairly in that it took into account evidence using its own experience, which it did not disclose to either party to the appeal, and set aside a decision on that basis.

There is no case where this has become a major point as yet in relation to the European Convention on Human Rights, as the law concerning children and young people with special needs is normally very tightly set out in order to ensure that they are protected.

---

8   [2000] 1 WLR 377 (CA).
9   [2001] ELR 529 (CA).
10   [2000] ELR 660.
11   [2006] EWHC 2368 (Admin.).
12   [1998] ELR 318 (CA).
13   [2013] UKUT 0157 (AAC).

As already indicated, it is not intended here to give a full outline of what may be the subject of an appeal, but the above are all reasonable examples.

Additional factors in applying for reviews

Rule 48(2) allows an application for a review only in SEN cases, within 28 days, with a power to extend time in exceptional circumstances, where circumstances relevant to the decision have changed since the decision was made.

Examples of this type of situation have arisen where essential information or evidence has not been disclosed to the Tribunal, and where this emerges at a later date, or the situation has changed and the child has regressed, or something to do with the provision on offer cannot be delivered (see *A. v Kirklees Metropolitan Borough Council*[14] and *Chapple v Suffolk County Council*).[15]

Additionally, it should be remembered that a duty on all parties is to disclose all relevant evidence and not to disguise it (see Sullivan J. in the *Croydon* case, reported as *R. (on the application of J.F.) v Croydon LBC*).[16]

Tribunal's decision in relation to an application for permission to appeal

On receiving an application for permission, the Tribunal can:

- review the decision;

- grant permission to appeal;

- refuse permission to appeal, in which case it must send the record of its decision, and a statement of reasons for such a refusal or notification of the Right to Appeal;

- give permission to appeal on limited grounds.

---

14   [2001] ELR 657 (CA).
15   [2011] EWCA Civ 870 (CA).
16   [2006] EWHC 2368 (Admin.).

In all circumstances, reasons for its decision must be given.

Any application for an appeal must clearly set out the outcome sought, that is, a rehearing or a variation of the decision in a significant manner. The Tribunal is now frequently reviewing decisions when previously it would have been considered a matter for appeal to the Upper Tribunal (which has now replaced the High Court). However, the Right of Appeal must be exercised on a point of law under Section 11 of the Tribunals, Courts and Enforcement Act 2007. Where an application is made for permission to appeal, in practice, it appears that the First-tier Tribunal normally deals with such applications by having one of the permanent judges (there are normally four) make a decision on the application for permission to appeal. In some cases, tribunal judges are now identifying errors of law in the First-tier Tribunal's decision and deciding to review the tribunal's decision rather than sending the matter to the Upper Tribunal. Although the regulation permits a tribunal to review its decision where there is an error of law, it is concerning that the matter is not sent to the Upper Tribunal in some cases, because it is within the jurisdiction of the Upper Tribunal to decide points of law.

However, Rule 49 applies to the review of a decision. A Tribunal may only review a decision if:

- it is satisfied that there is an error of law in the decision; or

- it is an application for a review in SEN cases.

A Tribunal may take action in relation to the decision following a review without giving each party an opportunity to make representations, and if that happens, the notice must state that each party may apply to set aside the decision and have it reviewed again on that basis.

The problem with a review is that, technically, it does not, in some cases at least, give rise to a Right of Appeal as a result of the provisions in Section 9 of the Tribunals, Courts and Enforcement Act 2007, and can therefore create difficulties. If there is no Right of Appeal following a review, the correct way to proceed is to apply for Judicial Review to the Upper Tribunal.

If permission to appeal is granted or if it is refused, there is a right to apply to appeal to the Upper Tribunal. The application, again, must be made within 28 days, and must set out in detail the errors of law, attaching the relevant decision and evidence on which the appeal is based.

If permission to appeal is initially refused, there is a right to apply for an oral hearing, and it is quite significant that a number of cases that have become leading cases were initially refused permission to appeal, but as a result of oral hearings, went ahead. These include *Chapple v Suffolk County Council,*[17] *S.K. v London Borough of Hillingdon,*[18] and *Haining v Warrington*, mentioned earlier.

The Upper Tribunal decides cases on the same principles set out previously, such as an error of law, procedural unfairness, failing to take into account material evidence, defective reasons, and irrationality.

As in the First-tier Tribunal, there is no order for costs on either side in the Upper Tribunal; the same cost rules apply, namely, that costs can only be ordered if a party or its representative has acted unreasonably in bringing, defending or conducting proceedings (Regulation 10 of the 2008 Upper Tribunal Rules).

The Upper Tribunal can often act quite slowly, so it is often important to seek expedition; it is normally understanding, however, and will deal with SEN cases urgently and give them priority, so far as its workload allows.

An appeal from the Upper Tribunal again lies with permission to appeal to the Court of Appeal from the Upper Tribunal itself, and the application should be made within 28 days. (Part 52 of the Civil Procedure Rules govern appeals to the Court of Appeal.) However, permission is granted more sparingly for appeals from specialist Tribunals than these appeals. In *Cooke v Secretary of State for Social Security,*[19] the Court of Appeal considered the criteria that should be applied in relation to applications for permission to appeal from a specialist Tribunal, in that case, the Social Security Commissioner.

---

17 [2011] EWCA Civ 870 (CA).
18 [2011] ELR 165 (AAC).
19 [2002] 3 All ER 279 (CA).

It is therefore important to show the issues that can be regarded as important points of law or practice. Such cases in which permission has been granted are, for example, *Haining v Warrington, E.H. v Kent County Council*,[20] and *Chapple v Suffolk County Council*.

Enforcement of Tribunal decisions

Regulations require that Tribunal decisions be implemented within a set period of time, which is normally five weeks in EHC plan appeals. It is not uncommon, however, for parents, having succeeded in an appeal, to discover that the local authority is unable to make the full provision, and that significant elements of the provision are missing. In these circumstances, parents should bear in mind that a child or young person often has a right to obtain legal aid, although in many cases now, parental income is taken into account. However, for young people who are on benefits (as they have a severe disability or mental health problem), legal aid is normally available. There are currently, however, only four legal aid providers (see the SEN Code of Practice for details).

As long as an EHC plan is clear and specific, and the Courts can enforce provision, there is a plain mandatory statutory duty to deliver provision. In *R. (N.) v North Tyneside*,[21] although speech therapy was quite clearly specified in the Statement, the authority failed to deliver it, arguing that it was under no duty to deliver it because it considered that it was no longer necessary. Sedley L.J, in the main judgment on behalf of the Court of Appeal, who unanimously set aside the judgment to the court below, made it clear that the duty to deliver under a Statement was non-delegable, and simply had to be delivered.

The main remedy is therefore Judicial Review. Parents could go to the Local Government Commissioner, but they will normally require the parent to complain through the local authority complaints system, which will take much longer. An alternative would be to make a direct complaint to the Secretary of State under complaint powers

---

20   [2011] EWCA Civ 709 (CA).
21   [2010] ELR 312 (CA).

in the Education Act 1996. If parents find Judicial Review either too expensive or not available because they need legal aid and cannot obtain it, a complaint to the Secretary of State is slower and less effective, but can still be much better than a complaint to the Local Government Commissioner, although they may eventually award some compensation, and, in fact, have done so in a number of cases.

CHAPTER 10

25 COMMON PROBLEMS

Problem 1: Local authority refusing a request for a statutory assessment

Aquila had real difficulties in his mainstream primary school, and was making absolutely no progress and was very unhappy. I hoped that by moving him to the independent sector that the smaller class sizes would solve the problem. Aquila's difficulties have continued, however, and the attainment gap has grown wider. Aquila's school tells me that he requires a great deal more provision than they routinely offer, and suggested I apply to the local authority for a statutory assessment in order to obtain the additional provision that Aquila requires. Unfortunately my request for a statutory assessment has been refused. The letter I have received from the local authority says that there are insufficient records of the action taken by Aquila's school, and that the records must demonstrate that relevant and purposeful action has been taken.

Answer

Section 36 of the Children and Families Act 2014 does not require any particular form of record keeping, and it does not require any particular remedial action by Aquila's school to have taken place. The test in Section 36(3) of the Act is, 'Whether it may be necessary for special educational provision to be made for the child or young person.' This will depend on the critical mass of provision that Aquila in reality requires, and the amount of provision that could be delivered in a local maintained school without an EHC plan. Provision must be genuinely and not theoretically available. It is therefore not sufficient for the local authority to simply point to the local offer.

Problem 2: Difficulties with respite provision/ Staff training may now be educational provision

My daughter Seanne has a really good understanding, but as she is non-verbal, with physical difficulties, this makes it very difficult for her to communicate her needs. We have had difficulties with her respite provision. We were provided with overnight respite by social services at a local centre. Despite having explained to staff on a number of occasions how to put her brace on, Seanne has come home with the brace upside down, resulting in pressure sores, bruising and blisters. She is plainly in severe pain, but is unable to communicate this to staff. When she is in pain and distressed, she cannot learn, and so is unfit for school for the next few days. Seanne loves going to school.

Answer

By virtue of Section 21(5) of the Children and Families Act 2014, social care provision that educates or trains a child or young person is now *educational* provision. Plainly the provision at the overnight respite setting is interfering with your daughter Seanne's education. Staff training is clearly required in order to make the provision work, and to ensure that it stops interfering with your daughter's education. The training of staff at the social services respite provision should therefore be incorporated as an educational need and educational provision in Sections B and F of the EHC plan. This means that social services should provide proper staff training, tailored to your daughter's needs, to stop the interference in your daughter's education.

Problem 3: Withholding documentary evidence

After a bitterly disputed annual review meeting, in which the headteacher of my son's school insisted that Richard, my son, had made enormous progress, and no longer needed most of the provision in his Statement, my local authority amended Richard's Statement and I have now submitted an appeal to SENDIST. During the appeal I submitted a Data Protection Act search requiring a copy of both Richard's school records as well as the local authority's records.

The local authority's records (but not the school records) contain letters from the headteacher asking for top-up funding explaining why the provision was needed, and that the school could not afford the provision set out in Richard's Statement. The headteacher appears to have made this application because the local authority told her that she had to. The application for top-up funding was subsequently refused. In terms of timing, this accounts for the subsequent bitterly contested annual review meeting. I would have preferred it if the headteacher had explained the reasons for recommending a reduction in Richard's provision.

The Data Protection Act material supplied has plainly been weeded by the school, but not the local authority. (This means that the school has, unlawfully, taken out from the material it supplied documents that it finds embarrassing. The material which the school found embarrassing was, however, included in the local authority's material.) Now what do I do?

Answer

You are quite right, it would have been preferable had Richard's headteacher been more open and honest, because you could have simply instituted proceedings for Judicial Review against the local authority that has a statutory obligation to make the provision set out in Richard's EHC plan. Nevertheless, you are now in the middle of a SENDIST appeal, so I would immediately submit this correspondence that you found on the local authority's file because it reveals that the case for the reduction in Richard's EHC Plan provision is not genuine.

You also have a number of other potential courses of action: first, a complaint to the Information Commissioner who polices the Data Protection material against Richard's school for withholding this documentation. You also have disability discrimination claims under the Equality Action 2010 against both Richard's school as well as your local authority. In relation to the disability discrimination claim against Richard's school, you may wish to submit it, and ask for it to be joined with the current EHC plan appeal (i.e., heard at the same time). This will create some interesting dynamics within the appeal. A disability discrimination claim can, however, only be made against the local authority in the County Court, and you have only six months to submit a disability discrimination claim.

Problem 4: Whose job is it anyway?

My local authority is saying it is the responsibility of the school to arrange the provision specified in Michael's Statement/ EHC Plan. At our school they are saying that they cannot provide the support set out in Michael's EHC plan (formerly Statement) due to the funding changes.

Answer

A school is not legally expected to provide funding for all of the support set out in an EHC plan (or Statement). Section 42(2) of the Children and Families Act 2014 makes funding for EHC plan provision (and currently Statements of SEN, while these remain) the local authority's legal obligation. The local SEN funding policy cannot change this statutory duty. The local authority may be required to fund this provision by means of a procedure known as Judicial Review in the Administrative Division of the High Court. Michael's school should theoretically be in a position to contribute the first £10,000 to Michael's statemented provision. If Michael's school has this money and is not spending it, then it is at risk of a disability discrimination claim made to SENDIST by you, under the Equality Act 2010. Nevertheless, this budget is 'notional', and in some schools the funding is just not available because of the number of children who have SEN – the budget just does not spread that far. If this is the case, the local authority cannot refuse to provide all of the provision in Michael's Statement, including the first £10,000.

Problem 5: Statement/EHC Plan top-up funding

Rosie attends a local special school. Her school has told me that they can't afford to provide what is in her Statement because they are being offered a set amount of top-up funding per pupil by the local authority, and *not* what is actually required in Rosie's Statement.

Answer

Section 42(2) of the Children and Families Act 2014 requires your local authority to fund the special educational provision set out in Rosie's EHC plan (and Statements of SEN, while these remain). A set amount of top-up funding for Rosie's Statement does not discharge this legal responsibility, unless this amount will, in fact, genuinely pay for what is in her EHC plan (or Statement of SEN, while these remain). The way forward is Judicial Review proceedings in the Administration Division of the High Court to compel your local authority to discharge their statutory functions properly. A disability discrimination claim under the Equality Act 2010 is also a possibility.

Problem 6: Disagreement between school and local authority about whether funding is enough

My son Edward's school and the local authority disagree on the amount of money needed to pay for the provision in his EHC plan. His school says they haven't enough money, and the local authority says they have. I feel trapped in the middle of a dispute. As a result, Edward is not receiving the provision in his EHC plan (or Statements of SEN, while they remain).

Answer

The simple answer is again, that the local authority has a statutory duty to make this provision under Section 42(2) of the Children and Families Act 2014 where there is an EHC plan (or Statement of SEN, while these remain). Proceedings in the Administration Division of the High Court, to make the local authority discharge its statutory function properly, is the obvious solution. There may, however, be an underlying problem, dependent on the wording of the EHC plan. If it is insufficiently specific, there may be a legitimate disagreement between the school and the local authority on the amount of money required. It may be that Edward's school is costing on the basis of a different level of provision to the local authority, because they have different views about what the wording in Edward's Statement requires and Edward's needs. It may be necessary, first, to have the issue of what provision is, in reality, required, and the issue of specificity resolved.

Problem 7: Refusal to undertake a Statutory Assessment

My local authority is saying that Theo's needs are within the £10,000 that his primary school has available for him, and is refusing a statutory assessment.

Answer

The legal test for a statutory assessment has nothing to do with any set figure such as £10,000. The legal test is whether a statutory assessment is necessary (Section 36(3) of the Children and Families Act 2014). In looking at necessity, the critical issue is the amount of provision that is, in reality, required by Theo, and can be made by the school. Provision must be genuinely and not theoretically available, and must be appropriate in the sense that it has to be reasonably effective to meet Theo's needs.[1]

The costing of provision by a local authority is often inadequate. It is not unknown for local authority officers to cost learning support assistant or speech and language therapy provision on the basis of the most junior and inexperienced teaching assistant or therapist, despite the complexity of the child's requirements, or, for that matter, on the basis of outdated historic salary scales. A Freedom of Information Act search can be used to check the local authority and school's costings, but you need to establish in detail exactly what Theo requires.

---

1   *R. v Surrey County Council Education Committee, ex parte H.* [1985] 83 LGR 219 (QBD).

Problem 8: Refusal to undertake a Statutory Assessment

My school SENCO is saying that the local authority are telling her that any child who does not need 12.5 hours of support is not entitled to an EHC plan (or Statement). If this is right, this means that Kamilla is not entitled to an EHC Plan.

Answer

Support for 12.5 hours is likely to represent £10,000 of the time of the most junior and inexperienced learning support assistant/ teaching assistant. What your SENCO has accepted undoubtedly in good faith is that the legal position as explained to her by the local authority is right. This is not the case. The legal test is based on the issue of necessity, that is, the critical mass of provision, which in reality is required, including provision other than just a learning support assistant (for example, specialist dyslexia teaching, input from an ASD advisory teacher, speech and language therapy, paediatric occupational therapy and physiotherapy). The legal test is whether a statutory assessment is necessary. Section 36(3) of the Children and Families Act 2014 does not create any artificial 12.5-hour threshold.

Problem 9: Refusal to undertake a Statutory Assessment

Following a statutory assessment of my daughter Gudrun's needs, the local authority are saying that they are within £10,000 and they are refusing an EHC plan (Statement). I have discussed this with my daughter's school, and they don't see how they can possibly make further provision for her; that was why they applied for statutory assessment in the first place.

Answer

The issue, again, is the critical mass of provision required, and whether the school without an EHC plan can in reality deliver the provision Gudrun requires. Provision must be genuinely and not just theoretically available, regardless of any funding arrangements with the school.[2] You have a right of appeal to SENDIST that must be exercised within two months of the local authority's decision. Use this and obtain some good independent expert evidence to support your appeal. Note that although school staff will say things privately to a parent, they are often not prepared to say the same thing publicly, which may offend the local authority.

Problem 10: Personal budgets

I am thinking of accepting a personal budget for the provision that my son Andrew requires. The level of funding offered is sufficient only for a low-level skill mix. What I need is a specialist speech and language therapist in ASD (which costs more than the amount of money I am being offered), and I also need a paediatric occupational therapist with postgraduate training in sensory integration dysfunction. The local authority funding is not sufficient for this either. Further, the teaching assistant support is sufficient only for a low-level skill mix.

Answer

If your proposed EHC plan is very specific as to the skill mix required, and it is clear that the local authority is not going to fund your direct payments to a sufficient level to buy what is in reality required, then I strongly suggest you reject the direct payments option.

The local authority has an enforceable legal obligation to provide exactly what is in the EHC plan if it is educational provision. Unfortunately there is no Tribunal appeal against a local authority failing to provide sufficient funding, and once you accept the personal budget, the local authority's duty is treated as having been discharged. It is possible, of course, that the local authority is not offering you enough money, because your EHC plan is insufficiently specific, in which case, you need to ensure that the EHC plan is more specific, and appeal to SENDIST to achieve this if this is resisted by the local authority.

---

2   *R. v Oxfordshire County Council, ex parte Pittick* [1996] ELR 153 (QBD).

Problem 11: Refusal to undertake a Statutory Assessment: discrepancy in progress

My daughter Lenka's school won't refer her for a statutory assessment because they say she is doing fine and making progress, and that I shouldn't be so negative. Lenka doesn't seem to be making any progress at all to me, and she certainly can't reproduce at home what the school claims. What can I do?

Answer

You have a legal right to ask the local authority to undertake a statutory assessment yourself. You are not dependent on Lenka's school making this request for you. You will, however, need evidence to demonstrate that a statutory assessment is necessary, particularly if you are in disagreement with Lenka's school over the issue of progress. First of all I suggest that you make a Data Protection Act request for all school records, and second, that you instruct your own independent experts including a good independent educational psychologist. It is also possible to have flawed National Curriculum levels checked using independent experts.

Problem 12: Transport: fit for learning

My daughter Katarina is only five, and attends a local special school. In this area of London the traffic is very heavy in the mornings and her taxi picks other children up en route. Katarina is the first child to be picked up at 7am, and with the other children that need to be picked up, and the amount of traffic, it is taking two hours for her to get to school, and she isn't then really fit to learn on arrival.

Answer

The Courts have already looked at this issue and decided in a case called *R. v Hereford and Worcester County Council, ex parte P.*[3] that a child was entitled to 'non-stressful' transport. This particular case involved a

---

3   [1992] 2 FLR 207 (QBD).

child with Down's syndrome. The minibus took a circuitous route and the journey was about an hour each way. We suggest you point this out to your local authority, and in the event that alternative arrangements are refused, we suggest Judicial Review in the Administrative Division of the High Court.

Problem 13: Funding for college

My son Colum is 19. Social services said they would provide two years at college, not three. We have asked for an EHC plan as Colum has a Section 139A Learning Difficulties Assessment (LDA). Are we bound by the social services decision that they would only provide two years at college, and not three?

Answer

Setting aside the issue of the legality of social services telling you that they would only provide two years and not three, when you have a Section 139A LDA (this wasn't lawful at all, and could have been challenged, even under the old system), the answer is no, you are not bound by that social services decision.

EHC plans are subject to an annual review, in the same way as Colum's previous Statement was subject to an annual review every year at school. What happened next when Colum was still at school depended on the annual review, and social services could not have brought the Statement to an end.

The situation will be exactly the same once Colum has an EHC plan; continued provision will be dependent on Colum's annual review, and if the provision involves education or training, you will have a right of appeal to SENDIST, who are not bound by any views that social services have historically expressed about what they will and will not fund. What happens is not going to be for social services to decide.

Problem 14: Parent-funded provision

I am currently putting in place two hours and 20 minutes of tuition per week (paid for by myself), and my son Liam's school is putting in one hour per week to address his handwriting, which is delivered by one of Liam's teachers. With this input, Liam is just about keeping pace.

The SENCO at the school has told me that Liam's social emotional development is not the school's concern. I have also been told that whatever the NHS says, Liam will not get an EHC plan, and one reason for this is that Liam's grades are good.

Answer

There is some merit in the point that Liam's grades are good. Success in these cases (i.e., EHC plan with additional provision) is generally based on the child's failure. Your interventions have prevented a failure in terms of headline attainment scores. However, case law *C. v Lambeth London Borough Council and Another*[4] means that all the provision put in place, including that made by you as well as by the school, must be taken into account. Further, paragraph 6.23 of the SEND Code of Practice states that:

> [It] should not be assumed that attainment in line with chronological age means that there is no learning difficulty or disability. Some learning difficulties and disabilities occur across the range of cognitive ability and, left unaddressed, may lead to frustration which may manifest itself as disaffection, emotional or behavioural difficulties.

Much will depend on the critical mass of provision that Liam in reality requires. A parent has the right to make a request for a statutory assessment. The test remains one of necessity, under Section 36(3) of the Children and Families Act 2014. What does Liam require, in fact, and can it be delivered without an EHC plan? As you plainly do not have the support of Liam's school, independent expert evidence will be essential.

---

4   [1999] ELR 350 (QBD).

Problem 15: Inadequate specification in EHC Plan

I have received a proposed EHC plan for my son Preston. It says that the speech and language therapist will make three contacts (termly) of 60 minutes each to provide Preston with suitable input that may take the form of direct work, group therapy, liaison and training. The type and frequency of therapy intervention will be reviewed annually as a minimum, but may be amended in accordance with therapists' advice. In addition, there is no paediatric occupational therapy from a therapist with postgraduate training in sensory integration difficulties. The LA officer told me that they cannot put in an EHC Plan what is not available locally.

Answer

On this wording, Preston could receive three hours of individual direct speech and language therapy per year; alternatively, it could be three hours of group therapy (and the concern here is that therapeutic input in a group, unless the group is very carefully matched, may not meet the needs of each individual child and only meet the needs of the group). Equally on this wording, Preston may never see the speech and language therapist at all.

You simply don't know what you are going to receive. The EHC plan is therefore inadequately specified. There is also the skill mix issue – is the therapist the one who is appropriate to Preston's particular needs? What sort of skill is actually required to deliver Preston's speech and language therapy? In relation to his paediatric occupational therapy, the same issues arise. The educational provision set out in any EHC plan (Section 37(2) of the Children and Families Act 2014) must be specified. Further, the Courts have considered this issue and have taken the view that provision should be 'so specific and clear as to leave no room for doubt as to what has been decided is necessary.'[5] In relation to paediatric occupational therapy, it allows the level of support to be changed without any need for an amendment of the EHC plan that would trigger a Right of Appeal.

---

5   *L. v Clarke & Somerset County Council* [1998] ELR 129 (QBD).

In *E. v Rotherham Metropolitan Borough Council*,[6] the Court took the view that such wording was a fundamental infringement of the policy of the Right of Appeal. This wording was therefore held to be unlawful. If the evidence is that paediatric occupational therapy from a paediatric occupational therapist with postgraduate training in sensory integration difficulties is required as educational provision, the local authority cannot refuse to include it in the education sections of the EHC Plan, simply because it is not available in the area. The local authority must include this provision in the educational sections of the EHC Plan and, if necessary (assuming local NHS Trust does not have a paediatric occupational therapist with postgraduate training in sensory integration dysfunction available) buy it in from the independent sector (i.e. private practice).[7]

Problem 16: Disability discrimination: access arrangements

Jonathan is dyslexic and has had learning support since he was nine years old. He is very bright, and took his controlled assessment in Year 10 and in the first term of Year 11 in the same way as everyone else, without any extra time to do them. I recently asked whether extra time (they call it 'access arrangements') had been put in place for Jonathan's GCSE examinations, and it hadn't.

Answer

The Courts have decided that the school is responsible for examination arrangements.[8] As time is an important factor here, you could instruct an independent educational psychologist, and depending on their findings, ask them to complete an application for access arrangements form for you.[9] However, such an application now, with the examinations

---

6   [2002] ELR 266 (Admin.).
7   *R v. Harrow LBC ex parte M* [1997] ELR 62 (QBD).
8   *ML v Kent County Council* (2013) ELR 364.
9   See www.edexcel.com/iwantto/Pages/access-arrangements.aspx for a copy of the form.

fast approaching, is a bit late in the day. Concessions should have been put in place for Jonathan's controlled assessments. The Joint Council for Qualifications (JCQ) documents entitled *Controlled Assessments: Outlining Staff Responsibilities* (for use by exam office staff) and *Access Arrangements, Reasonable Adjustments and Special Consideration* set out the procedures and responsibilities for making an application for access arrangements at the appropriate time, stating that the SENCO should 'ensure access arrangements have been applied for', and once applied for and the application is accepted, access arrangements are valid for 26 months.

Any application for access arrangements should normally be made towards the end of Year 9, so that appropriate adjustments can be made in controlled assessments and tests in Years 10 and 11. A concise summary of the application procedure for access arrangements can be found at www.pearlstraining.co.uk. This outlines the procedure clearly and it states that an application should be made before the beginning of the course, in Years 7 to 9 for GCSEs, and any assessment is valid for 26 months from the date of the assessment.

Failure to apply for examination concessions for a child with a well-established learning difficulty is undoubtedly disability discrimination, whether in the maintained or independent educational sectors. However, in the independent sector (where the parent is paying the school fees), this would also amount to a breach of contract because of Section 13 of the Supply of Goods and Services Act 1982 that creates an implied contractual term about care and skill where the supplier is carrying out a service.

Contractual damages may well include the reimbursement of two years' school fees if the examination results (as a consequence of a breach of contract) result in examination achievements that are very different to Jonathan's very good academic potential, and that suggest that his specific learning difficulties were sabotaged due to the failure to apply for concessions at the start of his course.

Problem 17: Voluntary Care, Section 20, Children Act 1989e

My daughter Addie's SEN include ASD, severe learning difficulties and a range of severely challenging behaviours. She is non-verbal. Addie is now bigger than I am and is physically enormously powerful. When Addie lashes out and bites, she does not link her actions to consequence. She is also very unpredictable, with no obvious triggers for her behaviour. I have said on a number of occasions that I cannot continue to have Addie at home. It is simply not safe. I had to lock me and her little sister in the bathroom on one occasion recently, and use my mobile to summon help. Addie is also a danger to herself – she runs off at any opportunity and we have locks on the windows and doors. We cannot be vigilant all of the time, and there is a serious and obvious risk, both to Addie and to members of the public.

Despite saying to our social worker that we cannot continue to accommodate Addie, all we have received are short periods of respite, and our social worker says that this cannot exceed 75 days in a total period of any 12 months. I have also been told that we should be having LAC (looked-after child) reviews, but our social worker says that these are not necessary.

Answer

You have made a request for voluntary care under Section 20(1)(c) of the Children Act 1989. If it was not in writing, make a request in writing now. Your local authority is obliged to provide accommodation for Addie. This is an absolute duty.

It appears that your local social services may be trying to evade the implications of Section 20 by claiming that Addie's accommodation is provided pursuant to Section 17 of the Children Act 1989 or the Housing Act 2004 when, in fact, you have triggered the Section 20(1) duty.

The reason that this appears to be the case is that accommodation provided pursuant to Section 17 of the Children Act 1989 is excluded from the definition of being 'looked after', and your social worker is saying that an LAC review is not necessary.

Added to this, your social worker is telling you that the short breaks that Addie receives cannot exceed 75 days in total in any period of 12 months. This clearly derives from Regulation 48 of the Care Planning, Placement and Case Review (England) Regulations 2010. Regulation 48(2)(a) specifically excludes children not in the care of the responsible authority. Local authorities cannot lawfully evade the implications of Section 20 by claiming that accommodation is provided pursuant to Section 17 of the Children Act 1989 or Housing Acts.[10]

Unfortunately it is necessary on occasion to institute Judicial Review proceedings if an extensive placement is needed. The law on this issue is clear, but delay can represent a cost saving to cash-strapped social services' departments.

Problem 18: Omissions from the EHC Plan

I have received my son Tim's proposed EHC plan. Section F, which sets out Tim's SEN provision, leaves out much of the provision he needs. I rang the local authority officer, and she told me that she couldn't include the provision in the independent expert reports I obtained because Tim's school couldn't deliver what the experts say is needed.

Answer

The officer you discussed your EHC plan with is taking the wrong approach. It is not a question of fitting Tim's SEN provision in Section F to the educational placement in Section I, but of considering whether Tim's current school is fit to meet the provision in Section F.[11] The legal position is that if provision is educationally necessary, it must be included in the EHC Plan. If the provision is not available at Tim's school, then the local authority is responsible for putting the

---

10   *R. (M.) v Hammersmith and Fulham LBC* [2008] UKHL 14 (HL) 24 (Baroness Hale).
11   *R. v Kingston upon Thames and Hunter* [1997] ELR 223 (Admin.).

provision in place and if necessary they must go to the independent sector (private practice) and buy the provision in, so that it is delivered at Tim's school.[12]

Problem 19: Funding a specialist placement yourself

I have submitted an appeal to SENDIST against the content of Raais's EHC plan. This includes the school named in Section I. I would prefer Raais to start the new academic year at the specialist placement I would like named in Section I of his EHC plan. I am thinking of taking out a loan to cover the first term's school fees, and asking SENDIST to reimburse the school fees incurred while waiting for the outcome of the appeal.

Answer

SENDIST does not have the legal power to order backdated school fees incurred while waiting for the outcome of a SENDIST appeal (*R. v Secretary of State for Education and Science, ex parte Davis*[13] and approved by the Court of Appeal in *Slough Borough Council v Special Educational Needs and Disability Tribunal and Others*).[14] You also need to bear in mind that even the strongest case on paper can lose on the day. If your appeal is unsuccessful, do you have the resources to maintain the placement, or will Raais have to leave? If so, how will a second move affect him?

Problem 20: Does an appeal delay the implementation of the EHC Plan?

The provision in Charlotte's EHC plan is insufficient, and she really needs help as quickly as possible. If I appeal, will this delay Charlotte receiving the provision she needs?

---

12   *R v. Harrow LBC ex parte M* [1997] ELR 62 (QBD).
13   [1989] 2 FLR 190.
14   [2010] EWCA Civ 668 (CA).

Answer

No. In *R. v Secretary of State for Education and Science, ex parte Davis*, which concerned legislation preceding the Education Act 1996, it was held that the local authority was responsible for putting in place the provision in a Statement as soon as it was finalised, notwithstanding any outstanding appeal. The Court of Appeal affirmed this principal in *R. v Barnet London Borough Council, ex parte G.*[15] under the 1996 Act. The same principal should therefore continue to be applied in the case of EHC plans under the Children and Families Act 2014. Charlotte should therefore receive the provision set out in her EHC plan while you appeal for more.

Problem 21: Missing provision

I have my proposed EHC plan. Some of the provision Geoffrey currently receives is missing, so I asked my local authority officer about this. She says they don't have to include anything that the school is going to provide. Is this right?

Answer

No. The EHC plan must be made in respect of the whole child. All of the provision to meet the child's needs, including provision that would be made by the school without the need for extra support, must be included.[16]

Problem 22: EHC Plans for dyslexia

I was told that you can't get a Statement for dyslexia. Does the same apply to an EHC plan?

---

15   [1998] ELR 281 (CA).
16   *R. v The Secretary of State for Education and Science, ex parte E.* [1992] 1 FLR 377 (CA).

Answer

I am afraid you were misinformed. Neither the Education Act 1996 nor the Children and Families Act 2014 specifically exclude dyslexia or any other learning difficulty. There is no specific legal ban. You could get Statements of SEN for dyslexia and you can also obtain an EHC plan for dyslexia. The test in Section 36(3) of the Children and Families Act 2014 is whether it is necessary. In other words, the issue is the critical mass of provision required by the individual child. If, for example, your child's dyslexic difficulties are severe and persistent, and daily sessions of specialist dyslexia teaching from a teacher additionally qualified and experienced in teaching dyslexic children is required, together with a substantial amount of input from a teaching assistant, you may well have a case for an EHC plan.

Problem 23: The local offer

I have looked at the local offer and seen some dyslexia-friendly schools listed. Is my son Alex entitled to a place at one of these schools?

Answer

No, he is not. The local offer is not an individual entitlement; it is a comprehensive list of what is available locally. You can only ask. The advantage of an EHC plan (and Statement of SEN, while these continue to exist) is that if your request is refused, you can put together your evidence and appeal to SENDIST. If the Tribunal decides in your favour, both your local authority and the school must comply with the Tribunal's decision.

Problem 24: Costings: expensive mainstream placements

My daughter Suzuko currently attends a local mainstream school. In reality she needs far more provision than the school can offer. I have obtained some independent expert reports and costed the additional provision needed in her current school. It would be far less expensive for the local authority to place Suzuko in a specialist setting in the independent sector, and with highly specialist input I feel her rate of progress would accelerate. I have explained this to the local authority officers, but they say they don't place children in the independent sector.

Answer

Bespoke provision in a mainstream school, if properly costed, can be more expensive than a specialist setting. In this situation I suggest an appeal to SENDIST. The Tribunal is not bound by local authority policies or what individual officers say. You have Section 9 of the Education Act 1996 on your side, and the decision of the Court of Appeal in *Haining v Warrington Borough Council*. If the Tribunal agrees with your costing, and orders your local authority to place Suzuko at the school you have identified, then the local authority will have no choice and must comply with the order.

Problem 25: Increase of school fees at school named in Statement/ EHC Plan

I went to Tribunal a couple of years ago and obtained a specialist placement for Hassan. The school fees have increased and my local authority won't pay. I don't want Hassan to lose his place; this hasn't been suggested, but I worry and feel embarrassed about the whole situation. Will I be asked to pay the outstanding balance?

Answer

This does happen from time to time, and you shouldn't be asked to pay the balance. The local authority is legally required to maintain the EHC plan (and Statements, while they exist), so Hassan's placement is not at risk. Personally I would go and have a quiet word with the school bursar, point out that this is a contractual issue between the school and the local authority, and suggest that the bursar approaches the school's solicitors to recover the outstanding school fees as a sundry debt. This is the most inexpensive and quickest way to resolve this, and to put your mind at rest.

APPENDIX 1

REASONS FOR APPEAL: TWO EXAMPLES

Below are two examples of reasons for appeal. One is for a severely dyslexic child, and the other is for a young person who lacks capacity with severe autism and other complex difficulties. If using the examples below as a template, amend the details accordingly to reflect the particular needs of your own child or young person.

EXAMPLE 1: IN THE SPECIAL EDUCATIONAL NEEDS DISABILITY TRIBUNAL

Appeal No.

BETWEEN

Kevin Bloggs
(by his parents Fred Bloggs and Frederica
Bloggs as the alternative person)

Appellants

and
Mountainshire County Council

Respondent

REASONS FOR APPEAL
KEVIN BLOGGS
D.O.B 11.04.1995

1. Background

1.1   This is an appeal under Section 51 of the Children and Families Act 2014 and Regulation 64(2) of the Special Educational Needs and Disability (SEND) Regulations 2014 due to capacity issues that arise in this case.

1.2   This appeal is against the child and young person's special educational needs (SEN) (Section B). The special educational provision required by the child and young person (Section F), the educational placement (Section I) of an Education, Health and Care (EHC) plan issued by Mountainshire County Council on 11 October 2014.

1.3   A mediation certificate has been obtained and is enclosed.

1.4   Kevin is now 19. Where a young person lacks capacity, references to 'young person' in Section 51 of the **Children and Families Act 2014** are to be read as references to both the young person and the alternative person who, by virtue of **Regulation 64(2) of the SEND Regulations 2014**, are Fred and Frederica Bloggs, Kevin's parents.

1.5   Although Fred and Frederica Bloggs very much love and cherish Kevin, after much thought and an honest appraisal of his increasing needs and their ability to meet them, they came to the conclusion that it was simply not possible to accommodate Kevin in their family home or to meet his needs. Sadly, as responsible parents, Fred and Frederica Bloggs had no alternative but to recognise their own limitations and that the severity of Kevin's needs created a serious and obvious risk to the safety of both them, his siblings and also to Kevin. He was originally accommodated under **Section 20** of the **Children Act 1989**, and is now accommodated under **Section 21** of the **National Assistance Act 1948** locally, in local authority accommodation provided by adult social care, and will continue to attend a local authority-maintained special school, King Richard III School in Mountainshire, until the end of the current academic year.

2. Child or Young Person's Special Educational Needs (Section B)

2.1 Part 2 of Kevin's Statement should specify each and every one of Kevin's needs in accordance with **Section 37(2) of the Children's and Families Act 2014** and *R. v The Secretary of State for Education and Science, ex parte E.*[1] which held that if a child's needs are not correctly identified, the provision cannot be appropriate.

2.2 On this basis, we suggest the following amendments are required to appropriately specify the section of Kevin's EHC plan dealing with his special educational needs (Section B):

i) Section B should make it clear at the outset, that Kevin is severely autistic, basically non-verbal, and displays considerable Pica behaviours.

ii) Section B should also record that he is now bigger and stronger than many adults, including his father and mother.

iii) This section should additionally record that there has been a significant deterioration in Kevin's behaviour, both at school and at home. Section B currently considerably understates the position.

iv) Section B currently records: 'Kevin can become frustrated and display inappropriate behaviours if he is unable to get his own way or if he cannot communicate his needs. His behaviour can be challenging at times.'

It is not considered that this passage accurately reflects the situation. The most recent risk assessment states:

---

1   [1992] 1 FLR 377 (CA).

Kevin has been getting increasingly aggressive recently without any triggers and he uses his weight and size to try and get what he wants. Kevin will target the person stopping him. Due to Kevin's behaviour in the car, the taxi driver taking him to school crashed into the crash barrier taking the side of the taxi off. It is no longer safe to travel with Kevin in a car or without a two-to-one escort.

And also:

Kevin does at times slap, pinch, scratch or kick carers, this can be for no apparent reason and he is very fast at doing this. He might also barge people out of the way and abscond, and he needs two-to-one support in the community to ensure his safety and that of others. Kevin has also started to display negative behaviour towards other children and adults. This behaviour is not done aggressively, as he can be happy and smiling and still slap people. As Kevin is getting bigger and stronger he can physically hurt people without this being the intention.

And in addition: 'He is obsessed by seeking out liquid (he has caused extensive water damage to his parents' house) and items he can put in his mouth including stones, leaves and grass.'

In relation to school, Dr Jean Davies, consultant and adolescent psychiatrist, and Hillary Hands, learning disability nurse, both visited King Richard III School, and state in their letter of 13 July 2013: 'There is also a long list of behaviours displayed at school, divided into the physical – where he bites, kicks, runs off and self-harms, and the sensory where he spits, urinates, trying to get access to water and playing with fluids. They now use an adult treadmill or rowing machine to help him calm down. Kevin needs constant supervision and has two-to-one staffing. If he is not getting attention, he will slap staff, he does enjoy upsetting staff.'

They also comment in the same letter that: 'Kevin does not understand personal space and he can get very close to people and stare at them. This can be intimidating for people who do not know Kevin. Kevin is not aware of the dangers of eating plants, bulbs, household items and objects/liquids etc.' and will place anything and everything in his mouth. Teaching and care staff must be alert at all times to prevent the serious and obvious risk created by his behaviour.

Section B should also state that Kevin has a significant sensory processing disorder. The Learning Disability Nurse, in her letter of 5 September 2014, refers to the issue of adult-sized gym equipment (a treadmill or rowing machine) to help calm him down. This should be referred to as Kevin's sensory processing disorder in Section B of his EHC plan. The explanation is to be found in the report by Katie Cloud, NHS Trust paediatric occupational therapist. She notes: 'The use of adult gym equipment to manage Kevin's need for sensory input and calm him down will also contribute to his fitness and strength.'

2.3   In summary, therefore, Section B does not adequately record the following issues:

- self-harm

- aggressive and challenging behaviours

- personal space

- Pica behaviours

- sensory issues

- awareness of risk and danger

- transport.

3. Special Educational Provision (Section F)

3.1   This section of Kevin's EHC plan does not specify sufficient special educational provision and training to address his learning difficulties as required by **Section 37(2) of the Children and Families Act 2014** and case law on the issue of specificity commencing with *L. v Clarke & Somerset County Council*[2] which held 'that provision should be specific and clear to leave no room for doubt as to what has been decided is necessary', and Para. **9.69** of the **SEND Code of Practice**.

3.2 We would therefore suggest that this section of Kevin's EHC plan should be amended to include:

a) Curriculum: we would like Kevin's curriculum to be replaced with the following: 'A developmental "Waking Day" curriculum providing for the development of Kevin's life, independence and social skills.'

b) Educational setting

   i) An educational setting capable of providing a 'Waking Day' curriculum, for 52 weeks of the year, which is structured, intensive and autistic-specific and differentiated by staff with relevant qualifications, training and experience to take account of Kevin's particular needs.

   ii) Kevin's educational setting will provide on staff speech and language therapy, paediatric occupational therapy delivered by a paediatric occupational therapist with postgraduate training and experience in sensory integration dysfunction, and clinical psychology involved in the development of Kevin's behavioural management plans. The HPC-registered speech and language therapist, occupational therapist and clinical psychologist will work collaboratively with specialist teaching and care staff.

   iii) Kevin's educational setting will integrate both therapy and the advice of clinical psychology into Kevin's day-to-day learning activities across the curriculum

---

2   [1998] ELR 129 (QBD).

and into his 'Waking Day'. The therapists and clinical psychologists will be available to trouble shoot at all hours of the 'Waking Day', including before school, evenings and weekends. There should also be provision of consistent programmes for trained staff available to deliver them throughout Kevin's 'Waking Day'.

iv) Kevin's educational setting will provide a peer group of children with autistic spectrum disorders, associated difficulties, and similar cognitive, language and communication and sensory and motor skill profiles.

v) Kevin's educational setting will provide a structured 'Waking Day' with predictable routines so that Kevin understands and can predict what is expected of him.

vi) Kevin's educational setting will minimise transitions, and changes to his routine will be introduced one step at a time. Kevin's educational setting will liaise closely with his family regarding any change.

vii) Kevin's educational setting will pre-plan changes in his routine or activities (including any anticipated change in the class teacher or group of pupils with whom he works) with guidance and frequent reassurance to help him manage and adapt to any new or unfamiliar situation.

c) Life skills, self-help and independence skills: Kevin needs to develop his life, self-help and independence skills. Provision to address this issue including details of the qualification/ experience of the professionals devising, implementing and monitoring this provision will be required. This programme should be consistent with Kevin's 52-week 'Waking Day' curriculum.

d) Behavioural programme: in view of the deterioration of Kevin's behaviour, a behavioural management plan is required. While behavioural management is currently included in Kevin's EHC plan, this relates only to the development of 'Kevin's behaviours at home and in the community.' The EHC plan provides that the programme is devised and monitored by the SENCO in conjunction with the class teacher and supported by a teaching assistant. Given the deterioration in the situation both at school and in the community, we take the view that this provision is inadequate, and that a behaviour management programme, with input from a clinical psychologist, should be in place consistently through Kevin's 52-week 'Waking Day' curriculum.

e) Speech and language provision: over the years Kevin's communication skills have made very little progress. We therefore seek greater input from an HPC-registered speech and language therapist experienced in working with young people with ASD with severe learning difficulties. This input should be delivered consistently as part of Kevin's 52-week 'Waking Day' curriculum and take place within his residential educational setting.

f) Occupational therapy: we seek quantified input of occupational therapy from an HPC-registered paediatric occupational therapist, with postgraduate training and sensory integration dysfunction, and experienced in working with young people with ASD with severe learning difficulties. This input should be delivered as part of Kevin's 52-week 'Waking Day' curriculum and take place within his residential educational setting.

g) Training: a continuous and professional development training programme is required for all staff working directly with Kevin at his school, whether teaching, supporting or providing care. This will provide:

i) Advice, information and support to meet Kevin's SEN, enabling appropriate awareness and understanding management skills, together with the knowledge of the current best practices in dealing with Kevin's learning difficulties.

ii) Training and demonstrations of activities delivered by an HPC-registered speech and language therapist and HPC-registered occupational therapist, and clinical psychologist.

4. Placement (Section I)

4.1 Mountainshire County Council considers that King Richard III Special School is an appropriate educational setting to meet Kevin's needs and has named it in Section I of his EHC plan.

4.2 Kevin has been at King Richard III Special School since 2003. It is the parental case that this school is not appropriate to meet Kevin's learning difficulties. Kevin is now 19, and his physical size is now larger than many adults. The use of adult-sized gym equipment also means he is extremely fit. The exacerbation of Kevin's behavioural difficulties, both at school and in the community, have led to a situation in which he now presents a considerable danger both to himself and others. Fred and Frederica Bloggs believe that Kevin requires a specialist ASD-specific residential school setting which can provide a 52-week 'Waking Day' curriculum for pupils with ASD and challenging behaviours, as outlined in Section 3 of this appeal, in order to address Kevin's limited progress and regression in many areas.

4.3 Kevin requires the specialisation and consistency of this type of setting. Without it, it is likely his difficulties will continue to exacerbate. Kevin is a danger to himself and others and, without a 52-week 'Waking Day' curriculum, there are likely to be increasing adverse consequences. Kevin requires specialist input, not containment.

4.4 King Richard III's assertion that they are managing is noted. That is not the correct test. **Paragraph 6.17** of the SEND Code of

Practice provides that the key test of the need for action is evidence that current rates of progress are less than expected.

4.5 **Paragraph 6.17** observes that less than expected progress can be characterised in a number of ways, including progress that:

- is significantly slower than peers starting from the same baseline;

- fails to match or better the child's previous rate of progress;

- fails to close the attainment gap between the child and their peers;

- widens the attainment gap.

4.6 **Paragraph 6.18** recognises instances where a pupil needs to make additional progress with wider developmental or social needs, which plainly applies to Kevin.

4.7 Having regard to the test set out in **paragraphs 6.17 and 6.18**, the attainment gap between Kevin and his peers has demonstrably widened. He is not matching or bettering his previous rate of progress; in fact, he has regressed in many areas. He is not demonstrating an improvement in self-help, social or personal skills; again, he has regressed. Kevin is not demonstrating improvements in his behaviour; again, there is regression. It is difficult to see on any of the above tests, set out at **paragraphs 6.17 and 6.18** of the **SEND Code of Practice**, how it can be logically maintained that Kevin is making expected progress, particularly in the situation in which he now needs two-to-one support in all settings, and as a consequence, has been placed initially in Section 20 accommodation and is now accommodation provided under Section 21 of the National Assistance Act 1948.

4.8 A placement has been offered at Fine View School, Steep Street, Waterfall City, Mountainshire, and Kevin's family request that Fine View School should be named in Section 1 of Kevin's EHC plan, which can make provision for him until the age of 25.

EXAMPLE 2: IN THE SPECIAL EDUCATIONAL NEEDS AND DISABILITY TRIBUNAL

Appeal No.

BETWEEN

Hermione Granger

Appellant

and

Mountainshire County Council

Respondent

REASONS FOR APPEAL

DANIEL GRANGER

D.O.B 01.01.01

---

1. Background

1.1 This is an appeal under Section 51 of the Children and Families Act 2014 against Section B the child and young person's special educational needs (SEN) (Section B), the special educational provision required by the child and young person (Section F) and the educational placement (Section I) of an Education, Health and Care (EHC) plan issued by Mountainshire County Council on 19 September 2014.

2. Child or Young Person's Special Educational Needs

2.1 Daniel's EHC plan is deficient in failing to identify all of his special educational needs (SEN) contrary to Section 37(2) of the Children's and Families Act 2014 and the decision of the Court of Appeal in *R. v The Secretary of State for Education and Science, ex parte E.*[3] which held that if the needs are not correctly identified, the provision can be appropriate. It is in

---

3   [1992] FLR 1 377 (CA).

particular not lawful or appropriate to describe Daniel's SEN as being 'described in detail in the attached Appendices'. The EHC plan must set out in detail the child's needs, which are, in particular:

i) Daniel is of average verbal ability and high visual ability;

ii) Daniel has severe specific learning difficulties;

iii) Daniel has severe difficulties with spelling skills – he is currently some three-and-a-half years behind his chronological age;

iv) Daniel has difficulties in auditory and visual short-term memory skills (not recognised in the EHC plan);

v) Daniel has difficulties with fine motor control skills (not recognised in the EHC plan);

vi) Daniel has difficulties with reading skills, particularly reading accuracy, comprehension and speed – in reading accuracy he is functioning nearly five years behind his chronological age;

vii) Daniel has difficulties with number skills – oral calculation skills in particular are weak;

viii) Daniel has a need for help in the development of skills in learning;

ix) Daniel has a need for in-class support to enable him to access the Curriculum.

3. Special Educational Provision Required by the Child or Young Person (Section F)

a) In failing to specify all of the special educational provision that Daniel requires for his SEN, the local education authority (LEA) has failed in its duty to comply with Section 37(2) of the Children and Families Act 2014, and failed to comply with the guidelines laid down in the SEND

Code of Practice and the law as contained in the decision of the Court of Appeal in *R. v The Secretary of State for Education and Science, ex parte E.*,[4] which held that all of the provision required to meet the child's needs should be set out, including provision that would be made by the school without the need for extra support.

b)   Daniel's EHC plan does not set out all of the needs to be met by the school and the LEA, as it is required to do so by law.

c)   Overall, the provision section in the EHC plan is vague and non-specific, and contains little of substance.

d)   Daniel requires a very detailed and specialist provision as follows:

   i)   Learning skills: to help with the development of motor and memory skills, Daniel needs to follow a course such as the 'Instrumental Enrichment Programme' by Professor Reuven Feuerstein or the 'Somerset Thinking Skills Development Course' by Blague and Ballinger – 2 hours per week arranged in short frequent daily sessions spread evenly over the week. Daniel should follow a structured multi-sensory language programme such as 'The Dyslexia Institute Skills Development Programme – Literacy', 'Alpha to Omega' by Hornsby and Shear or 'Dyslexia: A Training Course for Learners and Teachers' by Kathleen Hickey – 5 hours per week targeted skill-based teaching required with the lessons being arranged in short frequent daily sessions spread evenly over the week.

   ii) Number skills: to help Daniel with his difficulties in oral calculation skills and to help him develop additional competencies in number skills, he requires one hour per week structured multi-sensory teaching. The provision required for Daniel should be delivered

---

4   [1992] FLR 1 377 (CA).

by a teacher who has the appropriate specialist qualifications in teaching children with specific learning difficulties such as the RSA or BDA Diploma, and should be delivered on a one-to-one basis or in a small group (no more than 5 or 6 pupils). If Daniel is to be placed in a mainstream school, he will require a further 15 hours' in-class support to enable him to access the Curriculum and to catch up on the lessons he has missed.

4. Educational Placement (Section I)

4.1 In all, the provision required for Daniel is in excess of 8 hours per week of specialist teaching and 5 hours' in-class support. It is very detailed and specialised, and requires a considerable input over the week. The LEA would find it very difficult for this type of provision to be delivered effectively in a mainstream school. In addition, Daniel would find it very difficult to cope with the National Curriculum.

4.2 In view of the impracticability, both for Daniel and the LEA, in coping with such a programme in a mainstream school, a more appropriate placement and a more efficient use of resources would be for the LEA to place Daniel in a residential school for children with specific learning difficulties providing small teaching groups, individual specialist teaching and a modified specialist curriculum such as Hogwarts, where his educational, emotional and social needs can continue to be met throughout the day in a carefully structured and caring environment.

4.3 Finally, it is to be noted that in the educational placement section (Section I) of the EHC plan, the local authority has not actually named a school.

EXPERT REPORTS: TWO EXAMPLES

Independent experts need a forensic approach in relation to the specification and quantification of special educational provision, including health and training provision, which is educational in nature.

It is always advisable to seek good independent expert advice and professional advice. There are many good educational and medical professionals working with children who have SEN. However, not all are familiar with SENDIST's very specific requirements, set out in their practice direction, or case law relating to the specificity and quantification of provision, listing of documents and a Statement of Truth which is applicable in the field of SEN.

Good independent experts will provide quantified advice on the basis of a child's needs, as opposed to what the NHS or local authority is willing or able to provide. It is preferable to have a thorough job done by independent experts.

Expert witness work is a specialisation in its own right, a point not always appreciated. Specialist treatment is very different to report writing for these specific judicial purposes, and the ability to give evidence well before SENDIST is a quite separate and distinct additional skill as well.

Parents often ask, what does a good independent expert report look like, and how does it differ from an LA or NHS report? These example reports are fictional, but are adapted from real reports from experts who work regularly in the Special Educational Needs & Disability Tribunal, whose work has been successful and is considered competent. The facts in the reports are examples for the purposes of this book. The reports have been adapted for the purposes of giving examples, as previously Dr Harry Chasty did, when he provided sample reports for the first book issued by Jessica Kingsley Publishers, *Young Adults with Special Needs* by John Friel and Dr Harry Chasty, in this field. The format of the reports are therefore intended to provide guidance to parents, advisors and professionals.

EXAMPLE 1: OCCUPATIONAL THERAPY REPORT

Name:	XXXXX
Address:	XXXXX
Date of Birth:	XXXXX
Chronological Age:	XXXXX
Date of Assessment:	XXXXX
Date of Final Report	XXXXX
Appeal Number:	XXXXX

The contents of this report are confidential and may not be communicated or copied without permission of the author or the client's parents.

Table of Contents

22. Statement of Compliance and Truth   page 42

1. Curriculum Vitae

1.1   This section originally contained information regarding the expert's background history and qualifications.

2. Instructions and Issues

2. a)   I have been instructed by XXXXX, XXXXX's mother, to conduct a full occupational therapy assessment for her. This is firstly to establish her occupational therapy needs, and secondly to contribute to the information presented in her Statement of SEN regarding therapy provision and selection of an appropriate education placement.

2. b)   XXXXX is placed in the reception class of XXXXX, a special needs unit based within XXXXX Primary School. Her mother is particularly concerned that she does not receive adequate occupational therapy or speech and language therapy, and that this is limiting her ability to make progress within her education setting. The areas of need that present particular concern to XXXXX are related to XXXXX's communication, sensory, motor, and daily living skills.

3. Approach Used in Conducting the Assessment for this Report

3. a)   'Occupational therapy is a client-centred health profession concerned with promoting health and well-being through occupation. The primary goal is to enable people to participate successfully in the activities of everyday life. Occupational therapists (OTs) achieve this outcome by enabling people to do things that will enhance their ability to live meaningful lives or by modifying the environment to better support participation

(World Federation of Occupational Therapists 2011, What is Occupational Therapy?, About Occupational Therapy).[1]

3. b)   I will consider the child within her total environment: home, family and school, and also the functional impact of developmental, health and social history.

3. c)   Although formal assessment scores are a useful measure, there are times when observation of the child's performance of the assessment task, particularly noting qualitative features, is a more useful indication of a child's functional ability. How a child approaches a task can be as important as the overall result, particularly in relation to assessing executive difficulties.

3. d)   My assessment focuses on obtaining details of base line motor, sensory and daily life skills. I visited XXXXX in her school environment and then spent time with her and her mother at her home.

4. Background Information

Medical history

This section originally contained confidential information regarding the child.

Family history

This section originally contained confidential information regarding the child's family.

Educational history

XXXXX attends the XXXXX unit at XXXXX Primary School and is in Reception Class.

---

1   World Federation of Occupational Therapists, Copyright 2011, What is Occupational Therapy? About Occupational Therapy Page, (online). Available: http://www.wfot. org/AboutUs/AboutOccupationalTherapy/WhatisOccupationalTherapy.aspx (13.03.2012).

5. Current Assessment

Assessment context

5. a) XXXXX was observed within her class group and then on the same day with her mother at her home. Assessment focused on sensory, gross and fine motor skills, and play. XXXXX's poor attention and language limits the formal assessments available, particularly in relation to assessing motor skills.

5. b) XXXXX's existing history indicates poor attention, difficulty in engaging in activity, need for adult assistance in undertaking more demanding visual perceptual tasks, fine motor delay, self-stimulatory behaviour limiting her ability to engage in play, and delayed self-help skills.

Occupational therapy input

5. c) **Report XXXXX:** This report summarises two sessions held with Behaviour Support Team member XXXXX. It refers to sensory assessments undertaken on previous occasions but does not reassess any skills formally. It reports that XXXXX has 'developed' her awareness of her surroundings.

XXXXX's sensory needs are described as a 'mixed picture', and particularly in relation to proprioception. 'Sensory processing and modulation difficulties' are mentioned but not clearly described. Advice provided includes use of chew toys, use of gym balls for deep pressure and use of weighted equipment.

Although not described as such, this amounts to a sensory diet, but the oversight and careful management is not provided, and so does not meet either the necessary rigour described in the sensory integration literature or training and professional standards in terms of responsibility for other staff implementing the programme.

There is no attempt to assess or remediate the impact of sensory processing difficulties on XXXXX's gross or fine motor skills.

These appear significant and particularly relate to feeding and fine motor skills.

5. d)   **Occupational Therapy Advice for an Assessment of Special Educational Needs**: this report notes:

XXXXX has significant sensory processing and modulation difficulties.

Fine motor skills: issues are noted from initial assessment. On XXXXX an improved pencil grip is described and activities suggested.

Self-help and independence: total dependence in dressing and undressing is identified but no reason for this described.

Attention and learning: XXXXX is described as inconsistent in attending and as visually distracted.

Ongoing therapy by a sensory integration-trained occupational therapist is recommended in the form of a termly review of XXXXX's sensory processing and modulation.

5. e)   **Sensory Profile Report, XXXXX, Behaviour Support Assistant, 05.07.2013**: this is a descriptive report not based on any standardised measures.

Assessments undertaken

5. f)   *Peabody Developmental Motor Scales Second Edition (PDMS-2) (M. Rhonda Folio and Rebecca R. Fewell)*: researchers have gathered evidence that appears to verify the theoretical position that motor skills are improved through intervention. Folio (1975), DuBose and Folio (1977), Harris (1981), Jenkins, Fewell and Harris (1983), Campbell and Stewart (1986), Boucher and Doescher (1992), and Block and Davis (1996), have demonstrated that children receiving targeted motor

intervention programmes that promote the identified sequential skills make significant gains in motor development.

The Page 2 Examiners Manual PDMS-2 PDMS-2 is composed of six subtests that measure interrelated motor abilities that develop in early life. It was designed to measure motor skills in children from birth to five years of age.[2]

5. g) *Greenspan Social-Emotional Growth Chart:* (Stanley I. Greenspan) this is a screening questionnaire for infants and young children, and although XXXXX is a little older than its intended assessment group, it is useful for highlighting the level of her emotional social development. It identifies functional emotional milestones focusing on larger emotional patterns that define healthy emotional functioning and provide purpose to many mental purposes. These milestones include the capacity to: engage with a range of emotions, including joyful intimacy and assertiveness; experience, express, and comprehend a variety of emotional signals; and elaborate a range of feelings with words and symbols (pretend play). Appropriate emotional experiences during each of these phases help develop critical cognitive, social, emotional, language, and motor skills.

5. h) The *Sensory Processing Measure™ (SPM™):* (Parham and Ecker) SPM™ gives a complete picture of children's sensory functioning at home, at school, and in the community. Recognising that sensory processing problems often manifest differently in different environments, this set of three integrated rating scales assesses sensory processing, praxis, and social participation in primary school children. The assessment's unique multi-environment approach can evidence why a child who functions well in a highly structured classroom may have problems in a more relaxed setting.

Grounded in sensory integration theory, the SPM™ provides norm-referenced standard scores for two higher-level integrative functions – praxis and social participation – and five

---

2   FOLIO, M.R., FEWELL, R.R, (2000). Examiner's Manual. PDMS-2. Second Edition. PRO.ED, Texas

sensory systems (visual, auditory, tactile, proprioceptive, and vestibular functioning). Within each system, it offers descriptive clinical information on processing vulnerabilities, including under- and over-responsiveness, sensory-seeking behaviour, and perceptual problems.

5. i) *Adaptive Behaviour Assessment System® – Second Edition (ABAS® – II):* this norm-referenced assessment of adaptive behaviour measures skills that are important to everyday life. Adaptive skills as measured by the ABAS® – II are defined as those practical, everyday skills required to function and meet environmental demands, including effectively and independently taking care of oneself and interacting with other people. It uses three adaptive domains – conceptual, practical and social – and ten skill areas. The assessment contributes to a comprehensive, diagnostic assessment of individuals who may be experiencing difficulties with the daily adaptive skills that are necessary to function effectively within a normal environment, given the typical demands on individuals of the same age. It identifies strengths and weaknesses and specific adaptive skills.

5. j) Informal clinical observations: these are a series of non-standardised activities carried out by the child and observed by the experienced therapist. They provide information about the maturity of the nervous system and sensory processing faculties. The therapist can then make clinical judgments regarding the quality and level of performance of the child.

5. k) Parental questionnaire: this is a detailed description of the child from the parental perspective. It provides valuable information on the child's history and current difficulties. It considers motor, sensory, perceptual and functional skills.

6. School Visit

This section originally contained information regarding the assessment at school.

Home Visit

This section originally contained information regarding the assessment at home.

Discussion of assessment results and clinical observations

7. Motor Skills

7. a)   PDMS-2: because of her language difficulties and difficulties with conforming to specific instruction, it is not possible to use this assessment formally, and my comments below can only be used as an informal guide to XXXXX's motor developmental level.

The six subtests

7. b)   Gross motor skills

Reflexes: measures the child's ability to automatically react to environmental events; 31–32 months.

Stationary: measures the child's ability to sustain control of his or her body within its centre of gravity and maintain equilibrium; less than 31 months.

Locomotion: measures the child's ability to transport his or her body from one base of support to another; less than 22 months.

Object manipulation: measures the child's ability to throw, catch and kick balls; about 24 months.

7. c)   Fine motor skills

Grasping: measures the child's ability to use his or her hands and fingers; about 16 months; about 25 months.

Visual-motor integration: measures the child's ability to integrate and use his or her visual perceptual skills to perform complex eye–hand coordination tasks; skills are scattered in this field, but in the region of 20 months.

7. d) Informal use of this assessment of motor ability tells us that XXXXX does have significant underlying motor difficulties. Her performance of motor skills reflects her poor motor planning difficulties, and remediation of this will require skilled occupational therapy input and access to appropriate equipment and space.

Motor skills: clinical observations

7. e) XXXXX has ligamentous laxity and associated sensory-seeking behaviour relating to her need for added sensory input.

7. f) XXXXX's righting and equilibrium reactions are in place but slow to elicit.

The righting reactions are important in establishing a vertical or upright posture against gravity and a continuous head-torso axis. The equilibrium responses are patterns that maintain balance of the whole body in the dynamic relationship between the shifting of one's centre of gravity through space and one's base of support.

Equilibrium reactions are those highly integrated complex automatic responses to changes in posture and movement aimed towards restoring balance.

7. g) When lying prone over a large therapy ball, XXXXX was able to support her weight on outstretched arms for a short period, but only if she had help to position herself. She had difficulty in adapting her posture and particularly in use of rotational movement of her trunk. She is anxious about moving out of her centre of gravity unless well supported.

7. h) XXXXX's seated and standing posture was good; however, she nevertheless requires correct seating and table heights to prevent compromising her fine motor skills.

7. i) XXXXX has hypermobility and tires if she has to walk far, and uses a pushchair for longer distances.

7. j) XXXXX enjoys climbing but cannot judge when it is safe for her. Her poor motor planning limited her ability to climb into the swing seat. She cannot ride a bike, and in order to begin developing these skills, she needs access to equipment and a programme to develop her scooting skills. In both fine and gross motor activity XXXXX has poor bilateral integration (the simultaneous coordination of both sides of the body).

7. k) XXXXX has very immature fine motor skills, and development of these skills is limited by her poor attention and issues with motor planning.

8. Oro-Motor Skills

8. a) XXXXX was slow to make the transition to solid food; she frequently gagged and disliked lumpy textures. She is avoidant of new or different tastes and textures, and took time to move to a spouted beaker. Her limited diet is also increasing her bowel problems.

8. b) Her mother describes her as a messy eater, and she does not chew with a mature rotational chew but will rather squash her food against the side of her mouth.

8. c) Currently her 'safe' foods include toast, battered chicken nuggets, battered fish, potato waffles, chips/fries, cream crackers, bread sticks, cracker bread, yoghurts (particularly from a tube), chocolate mousse and pureed fruit pots. These foods fall into two distinct groups: dry and crisp/crunchy, and smooth semi-liquid. This is a pattern typical of a child with sensory processing issues who does not adequately register sensory information in the mouth and lips and so gains additional stimulation from hard, crunchy food. The pureed-type textures she can swallow as a liquid and these do not require as much

manipulation in the mouth. She finds mixed textures particularly difficult.

8. d) XXXXX frequently seeks oral sensory input by putting her fingers in her mouth, suggesting that she has poor registration of sensory input.

8. e) XXXXX urgently requires her occupational therapist and speech and language therapist together to develop and deliver a programme based on the MORE programme (or similar) to remediate these issues. MORE (Motor, Oral, Respiration, Eyes) is an acroynm for a treatment model designed to help therapists look at the qualities of interventions that enhance mouth, sensory and postural functions.[3] Central to the MORE approach is the process of coordinating sucking, swallowing, and breathing, the SSB synchrony. Problems with the synchrony are felt to influence many elements of sensori-motor development, including speech and language, regulation, postural control, feeding and hand–eye coordination.

9. Sensory Processing

Approximately 5–10% of the non-disabled population and 30% of children with disabilities experience atypical responses to sensory stimuli that interfere with their ability to fully participate in home, school and community activities.[4]

The *Diagnostic and Statistical Manual of Mental Disorders, Fifth Edition* of the American Psychiatric Association (DSM-5)[5] clinicians' manual includes the addition of sensory issues to the new diagnostic criteria for autism.

The sensory system is made up of eight senses: vision, smell, taste, touch, hearing, balance, movement, and referred emotion. These senses keep us informed about input coming from outside

---

3   OETTER P., RICHTER E. W., FRICK S. M., 1995. M.O.R.E. Integrating the Mouth with Sensory and Postural Functions. 2nd Edn. Minnesota: PDP Press Inc.
4   Baranek, 1998; *Ahn et al.*,2004.
5   http://www.dsm5.org/Pages/Default.aspx

and inside our bodies. Together these senses give us constant information and feedback about our environment. When our system is inadequately regulated, it creates responses in the central nervous system that prevents adequate or appropriate interface with the environment and those in it.

Those with autism typically have a combination of over- or under-aroused senses. Each child has his or her own unique sensory profile. Only when their individual sensory profile is established can work begin with the child to regulate their senses appropriately.

The Sensory Processing Measure (Parham and Ecker) Results and Discussion

9. a) Assessment results: Home form

T score mean 50 Standard deviation 10	T score range 40–59 Typical range	T score range 60–69 Some problems	T score range 70–80 Definite dysfunction
	Home	Home	Home
Social participation			
Vision			
Hearing			
Touch			
Taste and smell			
Body awareness			
Balance and motion			
Planning and ideas			
Total sensory systems			

9. b) Assessment results: Classroom form

T score mean 50 Standard deviation 10	T score range 40–59 Typical range	T score range 60–69 Some problems	T score range 70–80 Definite dysfunction
	School	School	School
Social participation			
Vision			
Hearing			
Touch			
Taste and smell			
Body awareness			
Balance and motion			
Planning and ideas			
Total sensory systems			

Some problems

Mild to moderate difficulties

Definite dysfunction

Significant sensory processing problem that may have a noticeable effect on the child's daily functioning.

9. c)   There are stark differences between the home and school results, particularly in relation to XXXXX's motor skills. There appears to be both misunderstanding of the questions, and discrepancies with her mother's and my observations by the school staff member who filled in the form. For example, in relation to 'Vision' she is described as only occasionally being distracted by nearby visual stimulus; my observation was that XXXXX was continually visually distracted and she is scored as 'Never' staring intensely as people or objects, yet there is a qualifying handwritten comment saying XXXXX occasionally stares at objects.

9. d)   There are in particular great discrepancies in relation to XXXXX's 'Body awareness' and 'Balance and motion'. Staff observations are markedly different from mine. For example, XXXXX is described as occasionally having difficulty in moving her body to a rhythm, while I observed XXXXX as unable to do this at all when asked. It is perhaps because XXXXX is generally passive that her sensory modulation issues are less evident in the classroom; however, my observation is that she has significant issues that are limiting her ability to focus and function in the classroom setting. The regular presence of a sensory integration-trained occupational therapist in the classroom to coach staff in understanding how sensory processing issues are limiting XXXXX's performance, and how these can be remediated, is urgently required.

9. e)   In the home form 6 out of 7 scale areas fall in the 'Definite dysfunction' range, and at school 3 out of 7; the remaining three are in 'Some problems'.

9. f)   The 'Social participation' scale measures the child's participation in social activities in the home and community. XXXXX's score in 'Definite dysfunction' demonstrates her pervasive social problems across multiple settings with both other children and adults.

9. g)   The 'Vision' scale represents a range of visual processing vulnerabilities including over- and under-responsiveness to stimulation, excessive seeking of visual input and problems with perception and ocular motor function. XXXXX's 'Definite dysfunction' score at home and 'Some problems' at school indicates that she will find visually rich environments distracting, and may try to avoid environments that are visually overwhelming.

9. h)   The 'Hearing' scale represents auditory processing vulnerabilities of over- and under-responsiveness, seeking behaviour and perceptual difficulties. XXXXX's score in the 'Some problems'

range at home and 'Definite dysfunction' indicated that she is struggling to cope with processing auditory sensory input.

9. i) The 'Touch' scale represents tactile defensiveness (over-responsiveness) to tactile information under-responsiveness and sensory-seeking behaviours. XXXXX has a mixed response in this field and some difficulties at home and school. I believe these are related to her poor fine motor performance.

9. j) The 'Body awareness' scale refers to the proprioceptive sensory system with receptors in muscles and joints, and provides the child's ability to sense where the various parts of their body are in relation to each other and objects in the environment. Functional proprioception, along with balance and muscle control, is essential to coordinated movement and tool use. This scale assesses increased sensory-seeking behaviour and disordered perception of these sensory stimuli leading to inability to judge and control the force, direction or speed of her movement. XXXXX scores 'Definite difficulties' in this field at home, but no issues are noted at school.

9. k) The 'Balance and motion' scale refers to the vestibular sensory system, the child's ability to sustain balance and remain upright against gravity, and relates directly to the execution and control gross motor activity. XXXXX scores in the 'Definite dysfunction' range at home, but no issues are noted at school, except her need to swing.

9. l) The 'Planning and ideas' scale refers to 'praxis', the ability to conceptualise, plan and organise movements in order to complete unfamiliar motor tasks. This is a higher-level cognitive function that depends on the integration of multiple sensory systems. This scale considers two elements of praxis: (1) 'ideation', the ability to create a mental image of a novel task; and (2) 'motor planning', the ability to plan and organise novel motor actions. At home and school XXXXX scores a very high score in the 'Definite dysfunction' range, indicating profound difficulties in her ability to initiate, problem-solve or

execute novel motor tasks and severe problems in overall daily functioning.

9. m) The 'Total sensory systems' scale is a composite score of the five sensory systems (vision, hearing, touch, body awareness, and balance) plus items representing taste and smell, and represents general dysfunction in sensory processing. XXXXX scores in the 'Definite dysfunction' range at home and 'Some problems' at school.

9. n) In my opinion, these scores indicate the presence of sensory processing issues that will limit XXXXX's ability to learn, and her need for an educational environment where her particular sensory needs are managed and appropriate sensory strategies provided.

9. o) The parental questionnaire indicates that XXXXX:

- seeks touch

- prefers loose-fitting clothing

- is fussy about certain fabrics against her skin (denim jeans)

- likes cuddles

- has difficulty standing in a queue

- is wary of touching certain textures – particularly unfamiliar foods

- is generally okay with having dirty hands, but it can become too much for her to tolerate and she will want her hands cleaned

- dislikes nail cutting and tooth brushing (although she has recently become more tolerant of this)

- mouths objects often (except for new or unfamiliar foods)

- prefers being barefoot

- likes playgrounds, slides and roundabouts; although she likes swinging at school, this is in a moulded seat that surrounds her rather than a flat exposed seat that she does not like to try

- is 'wriggly'
- sometimes bangs into things
- likes rough and tumble play, likes to be chased and tickled
- sometimes presses hard when using a drawing tool
- is fearful of heights
- dislikes bright sunlight
- is sensitive to sound and distracted by noise
- sometimes appears to switch off, sometimes by rocking or head banging on the sofa
- has periods during the night when she sleeps poorly and will rock her head from side to side.

9. p)   During his/her assessment I noted that XXXXX:

- seeks sensory input through touch and movement
- chooses to opt out of situations where she is likely to become over-stimulated by seeking an activity, such as looking at a catalogue.

The new nosology proposed for the diagnostic categories uses 'sensory processing disorder' as a global umbrella term that includes all forms of this disorder, including three primary diagnostic groups (sensory modulation disorder, sensory discrimination disorder, and sensory-based motor disorder), and the subtypes found within each.[6]

---

6   Position Statement on Terminology Related to Sensory Integration Dysfunction, *SI Focus* magazine, Summer 2004. Lucy Jane Miller, Ph.D., OTR, Executive Director of the KID Foundation and Associate Professor at the University of Colorado Health Sciences Center; Sharon Cermak, Ed.D., OTR/L, Professor at Boston University; Shelly Lane, Ph.D., OTR/L, Professor at Virginia Commonwealth University; Marie Anzalone, Sc.D., OTR, Assistant Professor at Columbia University; and Jane Koomar, Ph.D., OTR/L, Director of OTA-Watertown and President of the Spiral Foundation.

9. q) XXXXX has a processing disorder, pattern 1: sensory modulation disorder (SMD), which has some features of sensory over-responsivity and significant features of sensory under-responsivity. She may not be registering incoming sensory input, particularly in relation to tactile and vestibular-proprioceptive input. XXXXX does display some sensory-seeking behaviours; these may be related to XXXXX's attempts to increase her arousal level. Additionally XXXXX has pattern 3: sensory-based motor disorder, subtype 2: dyspraxia.

Pattern 1: Sensory modulation disorder

Sensory modulation occurs as the central nervous system regulates the neural messages relating to sensory stimuli. SMD results when a person has difficulty responding to sensory input with behaviour that is graded relative to the degree, nature or intensity of the sensory information. Responses are inconsistent with the demands of the situation, and inflexibility adapting to sensory challenges encountered in daily life is observed. Difficulty achieving and maintaining a developmentally appropriate range of emotion and attention often occurs.

SMD SUBTYPE 1: SENSORY OVER-RESPONSIVITY

People with sensory over-responsivity (SOR) respond to sensation faster, with more intensity or for a longer duration than those with typical sensory responsiveness. Over-responsivity may occur in only one sensory system (e.g., tactile defensiveness) or in multiple sensory systems (e.g., sensory defensiveness). SOR prevents people from making effective functional responses. Difficulties are particularly evident in new situations and during transitions. More intense responses generally occur if the stimulation is unexpected rather than self-generated. In addition, sensory input often has a cumulative effect; thus, a sudden exaggerated response may occur to a seeming trivial event because of the accumulated events of the day. Sympathetic nervous system activation is a marker of SOR (Miller et al., 1999), which may result in exaggerated fight, flight, fright, or freeze responses (Ayres, 1972a).

SMD SUBTYPE 2: SENSORY UNDER-RESPONSIVITY

People with sensory under-responsivity (SUR) disregard, or do not respond to, sensory stimuli within their environment. They appear not to detect incoming sensory information. This lack of initial awareness may lead to apathy, lethargy, and a seeming lack of inner drive to initiate socialisation and exploration. Failure to respond to pain (e.g., bumps, falls, cuts) or extreme temperatures (hot or cold) are typical. Compensatory strategies may lead to procrastination and people with SUR are often labelled 'lazy' or 'unmotivated'. Commonly SUR is not detected in younger children. However, because people with SUR need high-intensity salient input to become involved in a task or interaction, when such children are older, the necessary arousal level to participate across contexts may not be available. SUR occurring in tactile and proprioceptive systems usually leads to poor tactile discrimination and a poor body scheme with clumsiness. Thus, people with SUR often have concomitant sensory discrimination disorder (SDD), dyspraxia, or both.

SMD SUBTYPE 3: SENSORY SEEKING/CRAVING

People with sensory seeking (SS) crave an unusual amount or type of sensory input, and seem to have an insatiable desire for sensation. When unable to meet sensory needs, children may become explosive and aggressive. Extreme SS can disrupt attention so profoundly that learning is compromised or activities of daily living are difficult to complete. SS may also occur to obtain enhanced input when reduced perception of sensation occurs. SS often occurs as the person tries to increase his or her arousal level. Specific, directed types of sensory input, however, can have an organising or self-regulatory effect. Some children with SOR will engage in SS behaviours as an attempt at self-regulation (e.g., stereotypical in a child with autism).

Pattern 3: sensory-based motor disorder

People with sensory-based motor disorder (SBMD) have poor postural or volitional movement as a result of sensory problems.

SBMD SUBTYPE 2: DYSPRAXIA

Dyspraxia is an impaired ability to conceive of, plan, sequence, or execute novel actions. People appear awkward and poorly coordinated in gross, fine or oral–motor areas. Visual–motor deficits are also common in this disorder. People with dyspraxia seem unsure of where their body is in space, and have trouble judging distance. They usually have poor skills in ball activities and sports. Because people with dyspraxia are unable to generate new ideas of what to do, they may resort to rigid or inflexible strategies, perseverating and preferring the familiar to the novel. Daily activities, such as using utensils and dressing, are often slow to develop or are imprecise.

9. r) There are a number of sensory approaches that are necessary to ensure XXXXX is able to develop her motor skills and improve her attention. A sensory diet, regularly monitored by an experienced occupational therapist, will help manage her sensory-seeking behaviour and help her maintain a more aroused and alert state. Also a sensory integration treatment programme designed to provide opportunities for her to develop her motor planning in relation to gross, fine and oro-motor skills.

The 'sensory diet', a term developed by occupational therapist Patricia Wilbarger, is an individualised activity programme providing the sensory input a person's nervous system needs to stay focused and organised throughout the day. A person whose nervous system is 'high' will need more calming input, while someone who is more 'low' will need more arousing input to remain on task.

9. s) Educational psychologist Colin Newton 12.12.2012 notes that XXXXX has a range of sensory sensitivities relating to tactile, auditory, olfactory and visual stimuli. Additionally he describes a range of movement difficulties that are particularly characterised by poor praxis.

9. t) Occupational therapy and physiotherapy reports from August 2011 identify the presence of sensory processing and motor planning issues.

Tactile input is the sense of touch and includes texture, temperature and pressure. It includes not only the skin covering your body, but also inner skin linings such as inside the mouth.

Vestibular sensation is detected in our inner ear in a structure called the semi-circular canals or the labyrinth. In combination with detecting movement, we also sense the downward pull of gravity with our vestibular receptors. The vestibular system is often referred to as our sense of balance, and is also intimately connected to receptors of auditory (hearing) and visual senses.

Proprioception is the unconscious awareness of sensations coming from one's joints, muscles, tendons and ligaments, the 'position sense'. This sense underlies one's ability to place body parts in a position in space and to grade movements (i.e., the ability to judge direction of force and pressure).

10. Planning and Organisation Skills (Executive Skills)

Executive skills are basic to learning, and progress in executive functioning is developmental and varies from child to child. These skills are closely linked, and the same behaviour may reflect weaknesses in more than one skill.

10. a) XXXXX's issues with praxis and attention indicate that she will have poor executive skills and will require a variety of structures to help her begin learning independently. These will include a visual timetable and use of technology (apps such as ChorePad to provide structure, motivation and stimulus to facilitate independence in learning and life skills).

11. Attention and Concentration

11. a) XXXXX's attention was very limited except when she was focused on looking at a catalogue. She frequently looked away from an activity that requires visual monitoring, and spent extended periods gazing out of the window.

12. Daily Living Skills

12. a) When prompted, XXXXX will attempt to pull down her trousers. She is not able 'to pull bottoms up/down' or to 'use a knife and fork', as described by Ginevra Holmes in her 21.02.2013 report. She can take her socks off and positions herself for clothes over her head or arms through sleeves. Otherwise XXXXX is entirely dependent on adult support to complete her personal care activities.

12. b) XXXXX has recently begun to tolerate having her teeth brushed and will put the brush towards her mouth unassisted, but then bites down on the brush.

Adaptive Behaviour Assessment System: Second Edition (ABAS – II): Results and discussion

This assessment evaluates whether the individual demonstrates the functional skills necessary for daily living without the assistance of others, and identifies areas of strength and weakness.

12. c) Results: Parent form

Skill areas	Composite	Scaled score
Communication		
Community use		
Functional pre-academics		
Home living		
Health and safety		
Leisure		
Self-care		
Self-direction		

Social		
Motor		

12. d)

Composite	Composite score, mean of 100	Percentile rank
GAC*		
Conceptual		
Social		
Practical		

Note: *GAC = general adaptive composite.

12. e)   Results: Classroom form

Skill areas	Composite	Scaled score
Communication		
Functional pre-academics		
School living		
Health and safety		
Leisure		
Self-care		
Self-direction		
Social		
Motor		

12. f)   Motor skills area: there were 14 answers guessed and 3 unanswered out of a total of 27, which renders this section un-scorable, and means a GC score cannot be calculated. It suggests that the member of staff concerned is unfamiliar with XXXXX's motor skills, and reinforces my contention that, assuming it is completed by the same member of staff, the scores in the school sensory processing measure results relating to motor skills are not reliable.

12. g)

Composite	Composite score, mean of 100	Percentile rank
GAC*		
Conceptual		
Social		
Practical		

Note: *GAC = general adaptive composite.

- Conceptual skills include: receptive and expressive language, reading and writing, money concepts and self-direction.

- Social skills include: interpersonal relationships, responsibility, self-esteem, gullibility, naiveté, following rules, obeying laws, and avoiding victimisation.

- Practical skills include: basic maintenance activities of daily living (eating, mobility, toileting and dressing), instrumental activities of daily living (meal preparation, house keeping, transportation, taking medication, money management and telephone usage) together with occupational skills and maintenance of safe environments.

12. h)   XXXXX gains low scores in all skill areas and in all composite scores. I have no reason to believe that her motor skills performance at school was sufficient to give XXXXX a GAC score higher than that gained at home. This indicates her need for a structured integrated programme of activity to build her practical independent living and learning skills. This will need to take particular account of her language, motor and executive difficulties.

13. Communication, Play and Social-Emotional Development

13. a)   I did not observe XXXXX participate in any symbolic play; she responds to individual interaction particularly when her sensory

arousal level is managed and increased affect used to sustain her attention.

Greenspan Social Emotional Growth Chart

13. b)   XXXXX does not obtain a complete score at any level, and stops scoring after level 5b (25–30 months).

13. c)   Her score summary indicates **possible challenges** in 'social emotional growth' and **emerging mastery** of 'sensory processing'. XXXXX requires work at all levels including basic early self-regulation (level 1) in order to continue the developmental sequence. The emotional stages described are:

> 1. Exhibits growing self regulation and interest in the world (0–3 months)
>
> 2. Engages in relationships (4–5 months)
>
> 3. Uses emotions in an interactive purposeful manner (6–9 months)
>
> 4a. Uses a series of interactive emotional signals or gestures to communicate (10–14 months)
>
> 4b. Uses a series of interactive emotional signals or gestures to solve problems (15–18 months)
>
> 5a. Uses symbols or ideas to convey intentions or feelings (19–24 months)
>
> 5b. Uses symbols or ideas to express more than basic needs (25–30 months)
>
> 6. Creates logical bridges between emotions and ideas (31–42 months)

13. d)   XXXXX responds well to use of heightened affect, and this, combined with good sensory management, will enable her to participate in longer interactive play sessions.

13. e) XXXXX will require individual sessions from either a speech therapist or occupational therapist using intensive interactive techniques in order to develop her symbolic play and interaction skills.

13. f) There is an established relationship between sensory processing, attention and language development, suggesting that joint working between speech and language therapy and occupational therapy will be necessary to further XXXXX's progress.

> The relationship between language development and sensory integration was explored through single case experimental studies of one female and three male aphasic children ranging in age from 4 years, 0 months to 5 years, and 3 months. Other agencies had assessed all the children in the area of language development at least 6 months before the start of occupational therapy. Three of the four children had received either speech therapy, special education specific to aphasia, or both, before starting occupational therapy. Additional baseline data on language expression and comprehension, as well as on sensory integrative functioning, were gathered before beginning a year of occupational therapy that involved sensory integration procedures. Inspection of rate of language growth before and after starting occupational therapy showed a consistent increase in rate of growth in language comprehension concomitant with occupational therapy compared to previous growth rate.[7]

14. Summary

Summary of occupational therapy needs

14. a) My current assessment identifies XXXXX's main areas of difficulty within the context of occupational therapy as:

---

7   Am J Occup Ther. 1981 Jun;35(6):383-90. Ayres AJ, Mailloux Z PMID: 6166198 (PubMed - indexed for MEDL)

- a sensory processing disorder characterised by poor modulation of her arousal level (predominantly low arousal), and motor planning issues (praxis); XXXXX has significant difficulty sustaining the middle ground (being neither over- nor under-aroused), and being able to sustain this well-regulated middle ground is vital to learning

- immature gross and fine motor skills

- very limited independent life skills (not yet using the toilet independently)

- limited play and interaction

- poor attention, particularly when visually distracted.

15. Recommendations

General recommended actions

15. a)   XXXXX requires:

- an environment where the staff are trained to understand the needs of children with autism, sensory issues and motor learning difficulties;

- a programme of specified, targeted activities to develop motor and interaction skills at break time;

- structured programmes delivered daily and described in detail, where targets are identified and achievable within a prescribed period; in relation to motor skills and life skills, these need to be written jointly by teaching staff, the occupational therapist and parents;

- motivating activities need to use rewards and motivators to maintain XXXXX's involvement;

- a programme for developing XXXXX's independent living skills and in particular a toileting programme consistently implemented across home and school.

16. Occupational Therapy Recommendations

16. a) XXXXX will require weekly occupational therapy sessions of 60 minutes, 35 minutes for treatment, and 25 minutes to update a programme delivered on a daily basis by support staff and to liaise with parents and the speech and language therapist.

16. b) The person delivering this daily programme must be experienced in working with children with ASD and trained in the needs of children with sensory motor difficulties. Sensory integration-trained occupational therapists must be an integrated part of the school staff and on hand to provide support and advice within the classroom setting. The daily programme of occupational therapy activities will include work on oro-motor, fine and gross motor skills, and functional independence skills, and this will be combined with establishing a sensory diet that is monitored and adapted by the occupational therapist.

16. c) At this stage XXXXX is physically small enough to be provided with an appropriate sensory integration programme using mobile equipment, but as she grows she will require fixed suspended equipment. She will require access to a space large enough to accommodate her sensory integration programme. This is not to be confused with a 'sensory room' that is not related to sensory integration treatment, and does not provide XXXXX with experiences that are meaningful to her sensory motor development at this stage.

16. d) In addition, training regarding XXXXX's sensory motor development will need to be provided for all staff working with her, and in particular for the member of staff delivering her programme. This member of staff will need to attend all her weekly sessions. There must be access to a space where appropriate climbing and suspended equipment can be used. And the occupational therapist must spend time every week in the classroom to demonstrate, coach and model to all staff how effective sensory management works for children with ASD.

16. e) XXXXX requires an occupational therapist to provide:

- individual sensory integration-based treatment to develop her motor planning skills;

- monitoring of seat and desk;

- a daily programme of motivating activity to develop motor skills delivered by the support worker, including activities to develop pre-writing skills and oro-motor skills;

- a sensory diet and environmental sensory management modulation;

- support in a programme of functional life skills, at this stage focusing on toileting and dressing;

- training for school staff through weekly presence in class and an ongoing programme of termly formal sessions;

- liaison with parents, the speech and language therapist and education staff.

16. f) The therapist must be trained and experienced in using sensory integration techniques. The therapist needs experience of working with children with autism.

16. g) A 'sensory diet' must be monitored frequently by a therapist trained in sensory integration (which is considered extended scope practice by the College of Occupational Therapy). Dr G. Kelly, Reader in Occupational Therapy at Ulster University, and Course Director for the MSc in Sensory Integration, proposes that to deliver sensory integration-based treatment, a therapist requires two years' postgraduate training in sensory integration. Input from an occupational therapist without this training can only use sensory integration theory as a 'common-sense' approach.

16. h) Therapy needs to be seen as an educational need and must therefore be in Part III of XXXXX's Statement of SEN.

16. i) Therapy must be integrated into school so that strategies taught in therapy can be used across the curriculum.

16. j) The occupational therapist should be involved in the writing of XXXXX's Individual Education Plan (IEP), and work closely with staff to achieve these targets. The therapist should also reassess and report to her annual review. This is in addition to her specified treatment time.

Appendices

17. Documentation Referred to for this Report

18. Additional Information Sensory Processing

Sensory integration evidence for intervention

- Evidence-Based Practices and Treatments for Children with Autism

Reichow, B. Doehring, P. Cicchetti, D. V. Volkmar, F. R. (Eds.). (2011) Evidence-Based Practices and Treatments for Children with Autism, p. 269. New York: Springer

> Overall, the data supporting the sensory integrative approach is promising, whereas the data related to isolated sensory strategies is problematic.

> However, from findings of the majority of studies that investigated the sensory integrative approach, it is felt that there is emerging evidence to support the use of the sensory-integrative approach for individuals with ASD… (p.9)

- Sensory Abnormalities in Autism. A brief report.

Klintwall L., Holm A., Eriksson M., Carlsson L.H., Olsson M.B., Hedvall A., Gillberg C., Fernell E. Research in Developmental Disabilities. 2011 Mar- Apr;32(2):795-800. Epub 2010 Dec 15.

The findings provide support for the notion that sensory abnormality is very common in young children with autism. This symptom has been proposed for inclusion among the diagnostic criteria for ASD in the upcoming DSM-V.

- Abnormal Response to Sensory Stimuli

Abnormal response to sensory stimuli are among the most consistently impairing problems from childhood to adulthood and affect almost all individuals diagnosed with 'classic autism' (Billstedt, Gilberg, & Gilberg, 2007; Leekham, Nieto, Libby, Wing, & Gould, 2007 Research in Developmental Disabilities Volume 32, Issue 2, March–April 2011, Pages 768–773).

- Effectiveness of Sensory Integration Intervention in Children With Autism Spectrum Disorders

Effectiveness of Sensory Integration Intervention in Children With Autism Spectrum Disorders: A Pilot Study. Pfeiffer, Koenig, Kinnealey, Sheppard and Henderson (2011).

Pre-tests and post-tests measured social responsiveness, sensory processing, functional motor skills, and social-emotional factors. Results identified significant positive changes in Goal Attainment Scaling scores for both groups; more significant changes occurred in the sensory integration group, and a significant decrease in autistic mannerisms occurred in the sensory integration group.

19. Suspended Equipment

19. a) It would be impossible to provide XXXXX with an appropriate sensory integration treatment programme without vestibular stimulation; with younger children this can be achieved with mobile equipment, but XXXXX will require fixed suspended equipment as she grows. Clinical observations indicate that she has significant motor processing difficulties related to vestibular-proprioceptive processing.

19. b) Sensory integration treatment is defined as 'a program of intervention involving meaningful therapeutic activities characterised by enhanced sensation, especially tactile,

vestibular, and proprioceptive, and adaptive interaction.' Bundy, Lane, & Murray, 2002, p. 479. Sensory Integration Theory and Practice (2nd ed.) Philadelphia: F.A. Davis

19. c)   *Fidelity measures*

Development of a Fidelity Measure for Research on the Effectiveness of the **Ayres Sensory Integration Intervention**.

Parham, L. D., Roley, S. S., May-Benson, T. A., Koomar, J., Brett-Green, B., Burke, J. P., et al. (2011). Development of a fidelity measure for research on the effectiveness of the Ayres Sensory integration_ intervention. American Journal of Occupational Therapy, 65, 133–142. doi: 10.5014/ajot.2011.000745 ASI intervention.

The purpose of the Ayres Sensory Integration Fidelity Measure, developed by the Sensory Integration Research Collaborative (SIRC), is to provide a tool that will enable documentation of whether intervention is carried out in accordance with the essential procedural aspects of Ayres Sensory Integration intervention.

Occupational therapists working in sensory integration treatment are encouraged to adhere to the fidelity measures used in researching sensory integration treatment.

Part 3: Physical environment

- Adequate space for flow of vigorous physical activity 4.79 (0.42).

- Flexible arrangement of equipment and materials for rapid change of the intervention environment 4.84 (0.38).

- No less than three hooks for hanging suspended equipment, minimal distance between hooks 2.5–3ft (i.e., enough room to allow for full orbit on suspended equipment) 4.21 (1.08).

- One or more rotational devices attached to ceiling support to allow 360° of rotation 4.79 (0.42).

- Quiet space (e.g., tent, adjacent room, or partially enclosed area) 4.68 (0.48).

- One or more sets of bungee cords for suspended equipment 4.42 (0.84).

- Mats, cushions, pillows (available to be used to pad floor underneath all suspended equipment during intervention) 4.95 (0.23).

- Equipment adjustable to child's size 4.69 (0.48).

- Therapist monitors accessible equipment for safe use 4.95 (0.23).

- Unused equipment stored or placed so children cannot fall or trip 4.74 (0.45).

- Documentation of routine monitoring of equipment safety (e.g., ropes and bungee cords not frayed) 4.78 (0.43).

- Variety of equipment available (e.g., bouncing equipment such as trampoline; rubber strips or ropes for pulling; therapy balls; swings (platform swing, square platform, glider swing, frog swing, flexion disc, bolster swing, tire swing, net swing); scooter and ramp; weighted objects such as balls or bean bags in a variety of sizes; inner tubes; spandex fabric; crash pillow; ball pit; vibrating toys, massagers, tactile material; visual targets; ramps; climbing equipment; barrel for rolling; props to support engagement in play, e.g., dress-up clothes, stuffed animals, and dolls; materials for practising daily living skills, e.g., school supplies, clothing, and shoes with laces).

Developmental dyspraxia

When practitioners use the term 'developmental dyspraxia' in sensory integration theory they refer specifically to a disruption in sensory processing and motor planning. Dyspraxia is distinct from developmental coordination disorders (DCD), which DSM-IV characterises as a marked impairment in the development of motor coordination that is not the result of another medial condition that greatly interferes with activities in daily living or academic performance (APA, 1994). Dyspraxia is a more specific term than DCD and is likely to be a subtype of DCD. Dyspraxia relates to the organisation of movement and motor planning and, in the occupational therapy literature, generally includes deficits in sensory processing. Taken from 'Towards a Consensus in Terminology in Sensory Integration Theory and Practice; Part 2; Sensory Integration Patterns of Function and Dysfunction'. Published by the American Occupational Therapy Association, Inc. June 2000. Shelly J. Lane, Lucy Jane Miller, Barbra E. Hanft.

The College of Occupational Therapy's Publication 'Occupational Therapy Evidence Developmental Coordination Disorder (DCD) Fact Sheet' states:

Occupational therapists play a significant role in the diagnosis of DCD as part of a multi-disciplinary pathway (Missiuna et al., 2008). There is evidence that intervention by occupational therapists can enable children and young people with DCD to develop strategies to manage and/or overcome the difficulties they experience with everyday activities that are important to them (Dunford 2011).

Occupational therapy intervention will include:

- helping those around the child and the child themselves to understand the nature of their difficulties;

- offering individualised task-orientated approaches focused on the direct teaching of functional skills; this includes a cognitive approach based on the learning of specific tasks;

- addressing difficulties observed during assessment such as fine motor skills, visual perceptual skill and planning and organisational skills;

- encouragement of an active lifestyle to help prevent secondary impairments.

'Evidence supports occupational therapy intervention within schools, in teaching skills including handwriting, scissor skills, and increasing participation in PE and playground activities.'

'Cost savings are not necessarily immediate but the evidence shows that in the long term, if not addressed, DCD has negative impact on education, health, social participation and employment.' http://www.cot.co.uk/sites/default/files/commissioning_ot/public/Developmental-Co-ordination-Disorder.pdf

20. Standards of Practice

College of Occupational Therapists Code of Ethics and Professional Conduct Revised Edition 2010

Section 5. Professional Competence and Standards

DELEGATION

5.2 If you delegate interventions or other procedures you shall be satisfied that the person to whom you delegate is competent to carry them out. In these circumstances, you, as the delegating occupational therapist, retain responsibility for the occupational therapy care provided to the user (HPC 2008, standard 8).

5.3 You should provide appropriate supervision for the individual to whom you have delegated responsibility.

The HCPC Standards of conduct, performance and ethics say:

Whenever you give tasks to another person to carry out on your behalf, you must be sure that they have the knowledge, skills and experience to carry out the tasks safely and effectively. HCPC (2008) Standards available at: www.hpc-uk.org/publications/standards.

Sensory integration training

Postgraduate Sensory Integration Modular Pathway[8]

SENSORY INTEGRATION MODULE 2/3: FROM ASSESSMENT TO PRACTICE

- The Sensory Integration Module 2 and old Sensory Integration Module 3 courses have been merged into a new updated Sensory Integration Module 2/3 course, as part of the revised accreditation of the modular pathway in conjunction with our partner, the University of Ulster.

- Recent advances in neuroscience support the application of the theory of sensory integration as a treatment approach with children, adolescents, adults and older adults.

- This course aims to develop participants' skills in evaluation and clinical reasoning based on a sensory integration framework. It builds on the theory of sensory integration from the 'Sensory Integration I Theory and Intervention' course to enable participants to use this knowledge in the evaluation and clinical reasoning process in the context of their specific client group. A comprehensive evaluation requires a broad spectrum of information obtained through clinical observation, questionnaires, interviews and standardised assessment. Interpretation of this information is promoted through analysis and clinical reasoning.

- You must have passed the Sensory Integration Module I assessment within the last five years in order to register for the Sensory Integration Module 2/3 with accreditation.

International Coalition for Education in Sensory Integration (ICE-SI)

- It is recommended by ICE-SI that in order to undertake this training route and to be accredited, a therapist must have had undergraduate training to practise as an occupational

---

8   www.sensoryintegration.org.uk/si-modular-pathway

therapist, physiotherapist or speech and language therapist. This undergraduate education including anatomy and physiology and the process of assessment, therapeutic intervention and evaluation specific to a profession, enables the participant/student to apply the theory and principles of sensory integration within their everyday practice of occupational therapy, physiotherapy or speech and language therapy.

- It is recommended by the ICE-SI and the Network that sensory integration as a therapeutic frame of reference and treatment approach is undertaken by occupational therapists, physiotherapists and speech and language therapists.

- Good practice recommends that all sensory integration therapy must be supervised by a therapist with postgraduate education in sensory integration (minimum Module 2/3 or equivalent), who will monitor and adapt the assessment and treatment programme as required.

21. Statement of Compliance and Truth

Statement of Compliance

In accordance with Section 35.10(2) of the Civil Procedure Rules 1998, I understand my duty as an Expert Witness is to the Court. I understand that my overriding duty is to assist the tribunal in matters within my expertise, and that this duty overrides any obligation to those instructing me or their clients. I confirm that I have complied with that duty and will continue to do so. I have given details in this report of any matters which might affect the validity of this report.

Statement of Truth

In accordance with Section 35.10 (2) of the Civil Procedure Rules (1998), I confirm that I have made clear which facts and matters referred to in this report are within my own knowledge and which are not. Those that are within my own knowledge I confirm to be true. The opinions I have expressed represent my true and complete professional opinions on the matters to which they refer.

EXAMPLE 2.

Educational psychologist

Chartered psychologist

Educational psychology report for

xxxxxxxxx

D.O.B.:		Age:	9 years
			5 months
School:		Date of assessment:	
School year:	4	Report issued:	

Solicitor: Mrs Melinda Nettleton

Table of Contents

1. Qualifications and Experience

This section contains the details of the expert's qualifications and experience, key publications and training packages, chapters in books and commissioned work.

2. Referral and Background Information

2.1. General

2.1.1   XXXX was referred for assessment by parents.

2.1.2   I was provided with the following paperwork: this section contains annual review reports, local authority SALT (speech and language therapy), OT (occupational therapy) and EP (educational psychologist) reports, specialist teacher reports, Individual Education Plans (IEPs), school reports, private reports commissioned by parents and correspondence that was considered relevant.

2.2. Information from home

2.2.1   XXXX is the younger of two children who lives with both parents in a stable family situation. Mother and father have experienced some difficulties in relation to reading, spelling, maths, speaking and coordination.

2.2.2   Mother informed me that the pregnancy and birth of XXXX were normal.

2.2.3   XXXX spoke a few words at the age of 13 months but did not progress until he received speech and language therapy.

2.2.4   XXXX has a history of developmental difficulties in relation to motor skills. He experienced problems with throwing and catching a ball, dressing, cycling, eating, drawing and colouring and coordination. Parents report that he is now developing well, with practice. However, they note that he has clumsy fingers and hands. When he goes to the toilet, he still finds it hard to wipe himself; he then emerges with his trousers crooked. When parents try to help him, he now pushes them away as he says that this annoys him and makes him embarrassed.

2.2.5   When XXXX was three years of age, he had encephalitis. No ongoing problems are reported as a result of this.

2.2.6   XXXX does not experience difficulties with sleeping or behaviour; however, he has problems in relation to concentration.

2.2.7   No problems are reported in relation to sight or hearing. He does not take medication.

2.2.8   XXXX attended XXXX Nursery School and then XXXX Primary School, where he has been since XXXX.

2.2.9   XXXX is described by his parents as being sociable, but they are aware that due to his very poor speech, other children find it hard to relate to him.

2.2.10   XXXX was affected by the death of his grandmother in XXXX. In XXXX, his best friend left school suddenly without warning or explanation (due to his parents moving house); XXXX was worried that he may have died.

2.2.11   XXXX *enjoys*: football, swimming, riding, Lego, jigsaw, books, cinema, theatre, family outings and research for school pictures. He *does not enjoy*: working 'hard' at school.

2.2.12   Parents report that their son is starting to be aware that others do not understand his speech, and as a result he withdraws into himself at times. It is hard for him to join in games and to establish close friendships. He tries to compensate by not talking or avoiding situations.

2.2.13   He wanted to stand for the school council but did not as he felt that people would not listen to him or take him seriously. He was also very worried about asking questions on a recent school outing to XXXX Castle; he was worried that the guides would not understand him. Parents wanted him to join the Scouts; he did not because he was worried that the boys would make fun of his speech. He has experienced some negative responses to his speech – in the form of physical pushing and teasing.

2.2.14   XXXX tries to be independent. He changes for swimming, buys his own sweets and magazines – but is not confident about counting his change. He is also not secure in telling the time.

2.2.15   Parents are aware that XXXX is not reaching his potential and are very worried about secondary school in particular. They are also worried that he might find himself in a situation out of his control and have to try and explain himself to a stranger who would not understand him. XXXX is now asking to be home educated.

2.3. Information from school

2.3.1   Information was kindly received from Mr XXXX, class teacher. He informed me that XXXX is performing at *below-average* levels for all of: reading, writing, spelling, comprehension, speaking/listening, maths, science, history and geography.

2.3.2   Mr XXXX described XXXX as a boy who enjoys hands-on and visual learning styles. He noted that he is slow, distractible and lacks interest in his work. Socially, he is accepted by his peer group, although he is better with younger children.

2.3.3   XXXX has been assessed by a range of professionals for his 'complex learning difficulties' – an educational psychologist, speech therapist, occupational therapist and specialist teachers.

2.3.4   XXXX receives termly visits from a speech and language therapist and a specialist teacher. He further receives a fortnightly visit from a private speech and language therapist. He attends a privately funded school. He is in receipt of 15 hours' weekly support from a learning support assistant and 30 minutes per week SENCO support.

2.3.5   Testing was carried out in school. Results are as follows:

- *Personal and social development*: interaction and working with others – P7 without support, P7 with support.

- *Independent and organisational skills*: P7 without support, P9 with support.

- *Attention*: P7 without support, P9 with support.

- *Standardised scores at chronological age 9.4 years*:

- Salford *Reading* (June 2007), reading age – 4.5

- Nelson *Spelling* (June 2007), 5.10 (stated to be below level of test)

- *Current attainment*: (I understand from the parents that there is some disagreement about these figures relating to what they were told and what has been written)

- *English*: speaking/listening 1C, reading 1B, writing 1C

- *Maths*: using and applying P8; number P8; shape, space and measurement P8

- *Science*: scientific enquiry 2b; life processes and living things 2b; materials and properties 2c, physical processes 1a

2.3.6   Mr XXXX's main concerns relate to:

- slow progress

- poor levels of concentration

- difficulty making himself understood.

3. Child's Views

3.1.1   XXXX told me that he gets tired in school. He has one best friend in school and no one out of school.

3.1.2   XXXX told me that his teachers often talk too quickly for him and he then loses understanding.

3.1.3   XXXX uses an orange-coloured overlay to help him read, but he doesn't use it much as he is not too sure that it changes very much.

3.1.4   XXXX told me that he enjoys football and playtime at school. He pointed out that he does not like being bullied.

4. Appearance and Behavioural Observations

4.1.1   XXXX arrived with both his parents. He had not been in the room long when he asked them whether they would send him to a school where he would not be bullied.

4.1.2   The rapport between us was good. However, I suspect due to his severe speech and language difficulties, he tended to speak when spoken to, rather than initiate conversation.

4.1.3   Once the assessment began, he seemed to enjoy the challenge of the cognitive tests. However, he showed frustration when faced with literacy tasks.

4.1.4   He was in constant motion throughout our time together. He showed signs of impulsivity rather than calm and measured thinking.

4.1.5   There were many instances when I had to repeat questions/instructions to him. When reading, he tended to omit or repeat the line. He reverses letters and numbers when writing on occasion.

4.1.6   Watching him on stairs, he showed signs of unsteadiness.

5. Test Results

Cognitive testing

I tested XXXX using the Weschler Intelligence Scale for Children – Fourth Edition (WISC-IV). This is an updated psychometric assessment which is individually administered and used for the assessment of the cognitive ability of children aged 6 years 0 months to 16 years 11 months. The WISC-IV provides subtest scores that represent intellectual functioning in specific cognitive domains (verbal comprehension, perceptual reasoning, working memory and processing speed) as well as a full-scale general intellectual ability. [See Appendices for further information.]

Great care must be taken when linking IQ scores with predicted academic success, as the connection is not exact. Other factors such as quality and quantity of appropriate teaching, attitude, motivation, persistence etc. will have an effect.

- On the day of testing the following results were established. It should be noted that, as with any test, results may fluctuate slightly from day to day, and are therefore not set in stone. However, they are likely to be close to current levels of functioning.

- Percentile scores show where a person is in relation to others of their age. They range from 1 at the lowest to 99 at the highest.

- Raw scores are the total number of points gained. The scaled scores are the scores related to children of this age. 10 is the mean of the Scaled Scores and 7–13 is average.

- Very few tests are absolutely precise. Scores on a retest may vary slightly, as no one functions in exactly the same way on different occasions. As such, results are given with a 95% level of confidence.

5.1.1   XXXX's unique set of thinking and reasoning abilities make his overall intellectual functioning difficult to summarise by a single score on the Wechsler Intelligence Scale for Children – Fourth Edition (WISC-IV). His verbal reasoning abilities are much better developed than his non-verbal reasoning abilities.

5.1.2   Making sense of complex verbal information and using verbal abilities to solve novel problems are a relative strength for

XXXX. Processing complex visual information by forming spatial images of part-whole relationships and/or by manipulating the parts to solve novel problems without using words is a less well-developed ability.

5.1.3   XXXX's verbal reasoning abilities as measured by the **Verbal Comprehension Index** (VCI) are in the **Low Average** range and above those of only 19% of his peers (VCI = 87; 95% confidence interval = 81–95). The VCI is designed to measure verbal reasoning and concept formation. XXXX's performance on the verbal subtests contributing to the VCI is somewhat variable, although it is not especially unusual. Examination of XXXX's performance on individual subtests provides additional information regarding his specific verbal abilities.

5.1.4   XXXX's non-verbal reasoning abilities as measured by the **Perceptual Reasoning Index** (PRI) are in the **Extremely Low** range and *above those of only 2% of his peers* (PRI = 69; 95% confidence interval = 64–79). The PRI is designed to measure fluid reasoning in the perceptual domain with tasks that primarily assess non-verbal fluid reasoning and perceptual organisation abilities. XXXX performed comparably on the perceptual reasoning subtests contributing to the PRI, suggesting that his visual-spatial reasoning and perceptual-organisational skills are similarly developed.

5.1.5   XXXX's ability to sustain attention, concentrate and exert mental control is in the **Borderline** range. He performed *better than approximately 3% of his peers* in this area (**Working Memory Index** = 71; 95% confidence interval 66–81). XXXX's abilities to sustain attention, concentrate and exert mental control are a weakness relative to his verbal reasoning abilities. *Such a weakness in mental control will make the processing of complex information more time-consuming for XXXX, draining his mental energies more quickly as compared to other children his age, and result in more frequent errors on a variety of learning tasks.*

5.1.6 XXXX's ability in processing simple or routine visual material without making errors is in the **Borderline** range when compared to his peers. He performed *better than approximately 5% of his peers* on the processing speed tasks (**Processing Speed Index** = 75; 95% confidence interval 69–87).

5.1.7 Tables of cognitive scores

VERBAL COMPREHENSION SUBTEST SCORE SUMMARY

Subtests	Scaled score	Percentile rank
Similarities	8	25
Vocabulary	9	37
Comprehension	6	9

PERCEPTUAL REASONING SUBTEST SCORE SUMMARY

Subtests	Scaled score	Percentile rank
Block design	4	2
Picture concepts	7	16
Matrix reasoning	4	2

WORKING MEMORY SUBTEST SCORE SUMMARY

Subtests	Scaled score	Percentile rank
Digit span	6	9
Letter-number sequencing	4	2
(Arithmetic)	3	1

PROCESSING SPEED SUBTEST SCORES SUMMARY

Subtests	Scaled score	Percentile rank
Coding (CD)	4	2
Symbol search (SS)	7	16

Attainment testing

The Wechsler Individual Achievement Test – Second Edition (WIAT-II) provides an assessment of reading, language and numerical attainment in one test. It is a reliable source of information about an individual's achievement skills and it allows the assessment of problem-solving abilities by evaluating the process as well as the scores. It is directly linked to the WISC-IV, and as such, additionally provides comparisons of achievement and ability. It is designed to be used by young people between the ages of 4 to 16 years 11 months in the UK.

Summary of WIAT-II subtest scores

5.2.1   *Reading:* XXXX presents a diverse set of skills on different aspects of reading. His performance on the reading comprehension and single word reading tests is very poor indeed. He was unable to carry out the pseudo word reading test. Reading has not taken off as yet. Errors in the single word reading test included:

- confusion of the names and sounds of letters

- difficulty rhyming sounds in words: 'sit' for 'sea'; 'what' for 'how': 'be' for 'people'; he had no idea as to how to attempt words such as 'you', 'school', 'then', 'fly'.

- In the **Reading Comprehension Test,** he struggled with single word phrases and single sentences designed for children aged 6. He was unable to read any of the passages shown him.

5.2.2   *Mathematics:* XXXX's skills in mathematics are diverse and may not be adequately summarised by a single number. He performed slightly higher on tasks that evaluated his ability to add and subtract one- to three-digit numbers and to multiply and divide two-digit numbers (numerical operations standard score = 61) than on tasks that required him to understand numbers, consumer mathematics concepts, geometric measurement, basic graphs and to solve one-step word problems (mathematical reasoning standard score = 43).

- XXXX's skills in **Mathematical Reasoning** are within the **Extremely Low** range and *better than those of only approximately <0.1% of children his age.*

- His **Numerical Operations** subtest score is *above that of approximately 0.5% of his peers,* still within the **Extremely Low** range.

5.2.3   *Listening comprehension:* XXXX performed in the **Low Average** range on tasks that required him to identify the picture that best represents an orally presented descriptor or to generate a word that matches the picture, as indicated by his listening comprehension standard score (89). His skills in this area *exceed that of approximately 23% of students his age.* Scores were as follows:

- Receptive language: 12 of a possible 16

- Sentence comprehension: 8 of a possible 10

- Expressive language: 3 of a possible 15.

- He found it particularly difficult to retrieve words he wanted to say, although he clearly understands a great deal more than he can say.

5.2.4   *Written language*

Spelling:

On tasks that required him to correctly spell verbally presented words XXXX performed in the **Extremely Low** range. He achieved a spelling standard score of 43. His skills in this area *exceed those of only approximately <0.1% of students his age.* He was unable to write words such as 'look', 'hand', 'candy', 'two'.

5.2.5   *Written languages, free writing:* XXXX was unable to write. He refused the use of a computer and didn't want to use a pen. He was fully aware that he was unable to perform the task. In response to the request that he try to complete the sentence starting with: 'On a rainy day, I like...' he wrote the word 'nothing', which he wrote as 'ongfojwi'. He was unable to control the pen, and the letters were formed in a shaky manner.

5.2.6 SUMMARY OF WIAT-II ATTAINMENT SUBTEST SCORES

Subtests	Standard score	95% Confidence Interval	Percentile	Age equivalent
Word reading	40	36–44	<0.1	4:00
Reading comprehension	53	47–59	0.1	
Pseudo word decoding			Unable to do this test	
Numerical operations	61	51–71	0.5	6:00
Mathematical reasoning	43	35–51	<0.1	5:04
Spelling	43	36–50	<0.1	4:08
Listening comprehension	89	76–102	23	8:04
Writing			Unable to do this test	

5.3   Ability-achievement discrepancy analysis predicted method

The WISC-IV has the advantage of being linked with the WIAT-II (Second Edition) to provide information on both cognitive ability and academic achievement in children. Predicted levels of achievement are statistically calculated to children of this intellectual ability.

5.4.1   XXXX's scores on the WIAT-II were compared to the levels of achievement predicted for a student with his general cognitive ability, as indicated by his verbal comprehension score of 87 on the WISC-IV. Significant differences between actual and predicted achievement scores are reported in this section.

5.4.2   Reading: XXXX displays difficulty with achievement in reading. The difference between his actual and predicted scores is significant and highly unusual. Thus, this is an area in which XXXX needs specialist dyslexia assistance in helping him further develop his skills. **Word Reading** (actual standard score = 40), reading comprehension (actual standard score = 53) and **Pseudoword reading** (no score) are all **areas of difficulty** for XXXX.

- The difference between XXXX's actual and predicted scores on the **word reading** subtest (52 points) is both **significant and highly unusual**, and indicates a specific weakness in tasks that required him to correctly read a series of printed words.

- For the **Reading Comprehension** subtest, the discrepancy between his actual and predicted scores (38 points) is also **significant**, suggesting a specific weakness in tasks that required XXXX to read sentences and paragraphs and to answer questions about what was read. He was unable to correctly apply phonetic decoding rules when reading a series of nonsense words.

5.4.3 Mathematics: XXXX displays difficulty with achievement in mathematics. He scored much lower on the mathematics composite (actual score = 44) than expected for a child with his general cognitive ability (predicted score = 92).

- The difference between his actual and predicted scores is **significant and highly unusual**. Thus, this is an area in which XXXX needs specialist dyslexia assistance in helping him further develop his skills. Both **Mathematical Reasoning** (actual standard score = 43) and **Numerical Operations** (actual standard score = 61) are areas of difficulty for XXXX.

- The difference between XXXX's actual and predicted scores on the **Mathematical Reasoning subtest** (49 points) is both **significant and highly unusual**, and indicates a specific weakness in tasks that required him to understand numbers, consumer mathematics concepts, geometric measurement, basic graphs and to solve one-step word problems.

- For the **Numerical Operations** subtests, the discrepancy between his actual and predicted scores (32 points) is also **significant**, suggesting a specific weakness in tasks that required XXXX to add and subtract one- to three-digit numbers and to multiply and divide two-digit numbers.

5.4.4   Spelling: this is a particular area of difficulty for XXXX. Specifically, there is a noteworthy difference between his spelling subtest score (43) and the level of achievement anticipated for a student with his cognitive ability (predicted score = 94). This **significant and highly unusual** difference indicates a specific weakness on tasks that required him to correctly spell verbally presented words.

5.4.5 PREDICTED-DIFFERENCE METHOD

	Predicted score	Actual score	Expected difference	Significant difference Yes/No
WIAT-II subtest				
Word reading	92	40	52	Y
Reading comprehension	91	53	38	Y
Pseudo word decoding	94	**No score**		Y
Numerical operations	93	61	32	Y
Mathematical reasoning	92	43	49	Y
Spelling	94	43	51	Y
Listening comprehension	92	89	3	N

Statistical significance is expressed by the word 'significant'. 'Highly unusual' is used when the difference is even greater.

6. Test of Visual Motor Integration

6.1.1   Due to XXXX's significant difficulties in learning, I administered the Beery-Buktenica developmental test of **Visual-Motor Integration** (VMI) together with its supplementary tests. The

VMI is designed to assess the extent to which individuals can integrate their visual and motor abilities. XXXX attempted to move his whole body to draw the shapes. He used his right hand to draw and held his head close to the paper. His control of the writing implement is very poor.

Standard score	66
Scaled score	3
Percentile	1
Descriptor	Very low

6.1.2   Visual Perception (Supplementary test)

This is a considerably more demanding test in terms of both visual acuity and visual perception. However, all the test shapes are considerably larger and fewer than the printed letters that children encounter in their books.

Standard score	100
Scaled score	10
Percentile	50
Descriptor	Average

6.1.3   Motor Coordination (Supplementary test)

The first three tasks are related to early gross and fine motor control. The remaining tests assess the child's ability to control hand and finger movements – to see if the child can draw within a targeted area.

Standard score	Below the bottom score
Scaled score	Less than the 1st
Percentile	0.02
Descriptor	Very low

7. Emotional Assessment

Further testing on self-esteem was carried out using the Beck Youth Inventory. This is a test in the form of a questionnaire on which the child is asked to monitor his own feelings and responses. He scored at an 'average' level, but only at the lower end of the score, and within two marks of 'lower than average'. From his general behaviour and his comment about wanting to go to a school where he is not bullied, it is my view that his self-esteem is deteriorating and will continue to do so as he gets older and realises the difficulties and restrictions he has compared to his peers. It is vital therefore that he is placed in an appropriate, supportive and nurturing environment.

8. Summary and Conclusions

8.1.1   XXXX is a 9-year 5-month old child who has a severe speech and language impairment, dyspraxia, dyslexia and dyscalculia. His language needs are so poor that it was not possible to carry out a full phonological test investigating phonological awareness, phonological memory and rapid naming. He finds it particularly difficult to retrieve the word he wants to say, although he appears to understand a great deal more than he can say. It is my view from scores on the listening comprehension test as well as general interaction, that he is a child who is very much brighter than his scores would suggest. It is as though there is 'a child inside' trying to get out.

8.1.2   At this assessment, he completed the WISC-IV, WIAT-II, Beery-Buktenica and Beck Youth Inventory – Self-esteem. His overall cognitive ability, as evaluated by the WISC-IV, cannot easily be summarised because his verbal reasoning abilities are much better developed than his non-verbal reasoning abilities. XXXX's reasoning abilities on verbal tasks are generally in the low average range (VCI = 87), while his non-verbal reasoning abilities are significantly lower and in the extremely low range (PRI = 69). XXXX's general working memory abilities are in the borderline range (WMI = 71), and general processing speed abilities in the borderline range (PSI = 75). XXXX's abilities to sustain attention, concentrate and exert mental control are a weakness relative to his verbal reasoning abilities.

8.1.3 COMPOSITE SCORES SUMMARY

Scale	Composite score	Percentile rank	95% Confidence Interval	Qualitative description
Verbal comprehension (VCI)	87	19	81–95	Low average
Perceptual reasoning (PRI)	69	2	64–79	Extremely low
Working memory (WMI)	71	3	66–81	Borderline
Processing speed (PSI)	75	5	69–87	Borderline

XXXX demonstrated relatively weak skills in mathematical reasoning, numerical operations, pseudo word decoding, reading comprehension, spelling, writing and word reading.

8.1.4 SUMMARY OF WIAT-II ATTAINMENT SUBTEST SCORES

Subtests	Standard score	95% Confidence Interval	Percentile	Age equivalent
Word reading	40	36–44	<0.1	4:00
Reading comprehension	53	47–59	0.1	
Pseudo word decoding			No score	
Numerical operations	61	51–71	0.5	6:00
Mathematical reasoning	43	35–51	<0.1	5:04
Spelling	43	36–50	<0.1	4:08
Listening comprehension	89	76–102	23	8:04
Writing			No score	

8.1.5 RELATIVE STRENGTHS AND WEAKNESSES TABLE

Relative strengths	Relative weaknesses
Listening comprehension	Speech and communication
Visual perception	Fine and gross motor skills
Congenial	Working Memory
Desire to achieve	Self-esteem
	All aspects of reading
	All aspects of writing
	All aspects of mathematics
	Social skills

8.1.6   Table of progress: it is not possible to produce a progress table showing literacy, numeracy and listening comprehension scores over time as assessed by educational psychologists, as such tests have hitherto not been used.

9. Further Support and Assessment

9.1.1   XXXX should attend a school for children with severe speech and language difficulties and one where dyslexia methodologies are used for the teaching of literacy and numeracy.

9.1.2   The provision of speech, language and communication therapy with a qualified and experienced specialist speech and language therapist should be provided in a whole-school specialist setting. This provision should be quantified as set out by such a therapist.

9.1.3   The provision of occupational therapy with a qualified and experienced specialist occupational therapist should be provided in a whole-school specialist setting. This provision should be quantified as set out by an occupational therapist.

9.1.4   The environment needs to be sympathetic and supportive, with small classes of up to 6–8, a high staff-to-pupil ratio, and reduced auditory distractions.

9.1.5   The curriculum needs to be fully differentiated and taught using multi-sensory techniques at all times.

9.1.6   XXXX must receive tutoring in the 'pre-requisites for learning' in order that he can begin to both acquire literacy and numeracy skills and access the National Curriculum. This will entail intensive work on: speech, language and communication, memory skills, processing speed, phonological awareness, phonemic awareness, visual spatial skills, auditory skills and motor skills development and awareness.

9.1.7   XXXX needs to receive all literacy and numeracy teaching in one-to-one or small group situations (up to 3 pupils) using nationally published, structured, sequential multi-sensory courses with a proven track record of success for *numeracy and literacy* on a *daily basis* for a minimum of *45 minutes each*. Dyslexia-trained teachers should deliver this; they should hold additional postgraduate qualifications recognised by OCR, RSA, BDA, Hornsby or equivalent.

9.1.8   All XXXX's teachers should have specialist knowledge of teaching children with severe speech, language and communication disorders with on-site therapeutic input delivered by an in-house specialist speech and language therapist.

9.1.9   A paediatric occupational therapist with postgraduate training in sensory integration dysfunction should be working with XXXX so that therapy is integral to the delivery of the curriculum, so that therapy informs teaching and teaching informs therapy.

9.1.10 It is important to note that XXXX *should not* be placed in a Language Unit in a mainstream school. In my view, his language, motor skills, literacy and numeracy needs are so severe that he must be placed in an appropriate full-time specialist language setting where his needs can be met and his skills developed throughout the day, every day. A placement with therapists on site will ensure that therapy informs teaching and teaching informs therapy.

9.1.11   Moreover, XXXX is a vulnerable child who finds it extremely difficult to make himself understood. He is a prime target for bullying – as unfortunately he already knows. Mainstream education is highly inappropriate for him.

9.1.12   XXXX will require 'in-class support' for all lessons that require reading and/or writing skills at this time. His teaching assistant will need to have completed courses on working with children with speech and language difficulties and/or dyslexia – ideally both.

9.1.13   XXXX's educational setting should provide a quiet environment with minimal distractions and good acoustic listening conditions in which background noise, reverberation and noise by other children can be minimised.

9.1.14   XXXX should be in receipt of a learning and memory skills development course which should be scheduled, either as a specific lesson or alternatively 'chunked' into classroom lessons throughout the curriculum, so that the skills learned can be generalised across all subjects. This should be taught twice a week and reinforced across the curriculum.

9.1.15   XXXX will require tuition in word processing once he has developed basic knowledge of sounds and words. He will also need word processing facilities and software available on a daily basis. The frequency and duration of this tuition should be delivered by a specialist who understands the needs of children with his complex needs; a laptop should be provided.

9.1.16   Regular and close liaison with XXXX's parents should take place so that any difficulties can be rapidly and professionally dealt with, and schoolwork and specific teaching approaches, including guidance to help with generalisation and reinforcement of activities and learning through XXXX's working day, can be supported at home.

9.1.17   XXXX should make good progress with such a provision. If he does not receive it, he is highly likely to experience deteriorating self-esteem and ultimately low motivation. In my experience, this often leads to behavioural difficulties. His school and home should monitor his development in relation to this.

9.1.18   There is a strong body of evidence that academic self-concept is derived primarily from reading achievements and other school achievements, over and above other factors, including home background factors. In the Dunedin Multidisciplinary Child Development Study (Chapman, Lambourne and Silver (1990) it was found that academic self-concept at age 11 appeared to be influenced primarily by reading achievement and academic self-concept at age 9. Academic self-confidence at age 9 was influenced by reading achievement at age 7. The same study found that:

> For less skilled readers, slower progress in reading has more generalised effects on processes that underlie a broader range of tasks and skills than just reading. Further study showed that children with reading difficulties probably display an eroding motivation in achievement situations that increases the likelihood of failure in the future.

and

> The effect of low academic self-concept and frequently associated feelings of learned helplessness may result in children giving up easily in the face of difficulty and never persisting long enough to discover that success may be possible (Butkowsky and Willows (1998).

9.1.19   It is a similar story for children who have expressive speech disorders. Caroll and Snowling (2004) note that 'The results of the present study confirm the view that children with expressive speech impairments…are at high risk of reading difficulties and are on a continuum with children at family risk of dyslexia.' Furthermore, Bishop and Adams (1990) found that children with spoken language difficulties that had not resolved by the age of 5.5 years had widespread reading difficulties and spelling delay at the age of 8.5 years. It confirms how important it is that XXXX is provided with appropriate support and provision.

9.1.20   A continuing training programme for all of the staff who work with XXXX in school, either teaching or supporting, should be organised. This will provide advice, information and support to meet his specific needs. This will also develop appropriate awareness, understanding and management skills, together with knowledge of current best practice in dealing with children with this range of special needs.

9.1.21   XXXX's school should make arrangements in order to ensure that staff will be able to attend training sessions and convey a clear expectation of attendance at training sessions to staff.

9.1.22   The setting, monitoring and re-setting of short-term educational targets should be devised through XXXX's IEP. Targets will be based on the overall objectives given above.

9.1.23   Teaching staff, speech and language therapists and paediatric occupational therapists should set targets for XXXX in his IEP, particularly making reference to his skill needs. There should be regular termly liaison between teaching, therapy staff, XXXX and his parents for this purpose.

10. Useful Guidelines

10.1.1   XXXX's family should help him identify and cope with his feelings by encouraging him to verbally label and openly discuss emotions or by demonstrating that we all experience emotions.

10.1.2   Family and teachers are encouraged to give XXXX appropriate chores or responsibilities to be performed regularly to build his sense of self-worth and value as a member of the home and classroom. Chores appropriate to XXXX's age and ability will reduce the likelihood of failure.

10.1.3 As XXXX may be discouraged about his academic progress, family and teachers are encouraged to provide praise for sincere efforts that end in failure and minor accomplishments.

10.1.4 Family or teachers could ask XXXX what his peers do for fun, and develop a programme requiring him to do one thing for fun each day.

10.1.5 XXXX's teachers may help him cope with failures by openly discussing difficulties, emphasising successes, or marking work positively (that is, marking all of the correct, rather than the incorrect, answers).

10.1.6 XXXX's family may help him cope with failures by openly discussing difficulties and emphasising successes. Sharing examples of others' failures will help demonstrate open discussion.

10.1.7 XXXX may need help from family and teachers to recognise his successes or verbalise his accomplishments.

10.1.8 Emphasise XXXX's successes by having him keep a daily record of his accomplishments and discussing the results with him each day. The daily record may also be used to create graphs for reinforcement of XXXX's progress.

10.1.9 Instruct XXXX in the use of positive coping statements when he encounters difficult situations or experiences failure (e.g., 'Oh, I made a mistake. Next time I'll be more careful and maybe I'll get it right').

10.1.10 XXXX's teachers could regularly display samples of his as well as other pupils' work. These samples might include classroom assignments, tests or computer work on which XXXX did well.

10.1.11 XXXX's family may help him complete his homework assignments by providing a location where he can be monitored. A pre-arranged, unobtrusive, non-punitive signal, such as a tap on the shoulder, may be used as a means of bringing XXXX back on task. It is recommended that he not do his homework in an unsupervised room, as this affords too many opportunities for distraction.

10.1.12 XXXX's teachers are encouraged to interrupt his daydreaming or off-task remarks, and refocus his attention to the task.

10.1.13 XXXX's tasks should be short, well within his attention span, varied and gradually increased in length. For example, XXXX could be instructed to write an alphabetic letter ten times on paper, make the same letter by rolling ropes of clay and draw the letter ten times on an individual blackboard.

10.1.14 Whenever possible, distractions should be minimised in XXXX's study area. For example, XXXX's desk could be placed near the teacher or in an area with minimal classroom traffic.

10.1.15 XXXX should benefit from a mixture of high- and low-interest tasks. For example, teachers could follow a lecture with a hands-on activity. He is more likely to maintain attention when presented with a variety of tasks rather than a series of either high-interest or low-interest activities.

10.1.16 Longer tasks may be divided into smaller parts that can be completed at different times. For example, a page of 12 numerical operations could be cut into three sections so XXXX completes only four problems at a time.

10.1.17 In order to ensure XXXX's understanding of a task, it may be helpful if instructions are presented one at a time and he is asked to repeat the instruction prior to proceeding with the task.

10.1.18 Teachers could assist XXXX in maintaining attention by altering the volume, tone and rate of verbal presentations.

10.1.19 XXXX's teachers may need to use an approach that is activity-based so that XXXX is actively engaged in a series of short activities with frequent feedback.

10.1.20 Teachers and therapists can repeat and simplify instructions, using cues, prompts or models to elicit correct responses.

10.1.21 Teachers are encouraged to limit instruction primarily to one-to-one or small group settings, reserving large group settings for maintenance activities of learned skills, games, songs and stories.

10.1.22 XXXX may need to be encouraged to increase self-monitoring by asking himself, 'Did I understand everything this person said?' and double-checking with the speaker.

10.1.23 XXXX's teachers and parents are encouraged to use concise verbal directions by explaining tasks with as few words as possible. Verbal directions may also be clarified with visual cues and demonstrations.

10.1.24 Teachers are encouraged to establish a series of successive increases in reward requirements for XXXX's communication attempts. For example, during the first week, teachers reward non-verbal gestures; during the second week, teachers reward one-word, structured responses.

10.1.25 Teachers and family can assist XXXX's verbal communication by reinforcing his ability to correctly label concrete objects, feelings and abstract concepts.

10.1.26 XXXX's teachers could break large assignments down into a series of smaller units.

10.1.27 XXXX's language development may be enhanced through rhyming activities. For example, XXXX could create new songs or rhymes by substituting rhyming words for existing words.

10.1.28 XXXX's short-term memory and vocabulary abilities can be improved with games at home, such as 'Simon Says' or 'I went to market'.

10.1.29 XXXX's teacher and family can assist with XXXX's language development by participating in story-time activities. For example, a story is read several times, with each reading including a change to the characters, action or sequence. XXXX's task is to identify and describe the part of the story that has changed. XXXX could also be asked to complete an incomplete story or to participate in dramatisation of a story.

10.1.30   Teachers and therapists are encouraged to use concrete language and materials geared to XXXX's level of language processing.

10.1.31   As XXXX has difficulty in processing language formed as questions, teachers could limit direct questioning as a teaching technique.

10.1.32   In order to develop problem-solving skills, XXXX's family/teachers may ask him to identify as many solutions to a problem as possible. They can then assist him in identifying the pros and cons of an alternative solution, choosing a course of action and evaluating the results.

10.1.33   XXXX is encouraged to generate as many solutions as possible for potentially stressful situations. Family and teachers may assist XXXX in generating and evaluating possible solutions.

10.1.34   XXXX should be encouraged to ask frequent questions to ensure his understanding of task requirements or academic material.

10.1.35   XXXX may benefit from being asked to verbalise the steps he will use to complete a daily routine (e.g., dressing) or an assigned task. He can then use self-talk during the task to reinforce the sequencing of the steps required for successful completion.

10.1.36   XXXX may need to be taught the steps required to solve a problem or complete a task and be given the opportunity to rehearse the steps. Whenever possible, XXXX can be offered a logical structure or procedure in solving problems.

10.1.37   XXXX's family may assist his development of effective organisational skills. For example, family members could work with XXXX to identify and describe the necessary steps to successfully complete a task.

10.1.38 Organising new information into visual categories that are meaningful may help XXXX remember the information more easily and accurately.

10.1.39 Teachers may elect to use visual cues to teach procedures or skills involving sequencing or serialisation to help XXXX retain the facts and skills being taught.

10.1.40 XXXX may benefit from sequence-learning activities that address auditory, visual and general readiness skills to prepare him for reading and mathematics.

10.1.41 Teachers and family are encouraged to assist XXXX by participating in activities designed to teach sequential reasoning skills. For example, a story could be developed in which XXXX is the central character. XXXX can then be asked to select pictures that illustrate the sequence of events. He can then 'read' the story back to his parents/teacher.

10.1.42 Teachers and family can encourage XXXX to identify what happened before and after an event in a story.

10.1.43 XXXX would likely benefit from structured or peer activities that allow him to excel. For example, XXXX could be paired with a younger child who he could help with a simple task or be appointed leader in a favourite learning activity.

10.1.44 XXXX may need encouragement to learn ways of handling social situations appropriately and successfully without conflict. Role-playing is an engaging method for practising these skills.

10.1.45 XXXX's family is encouraged to engage in activities that promote communication and enrich XXXX's verbal environment. For example, family members could take turns recounting the day's events, telling short stories, or sharing jokes or riddles.

10.1.46 Teachers, other adults and family are encouraged to engage XXXX in social interaction. If direct communication is inappropriate for the situation, frequent eye contact with XXXX is recommended.

10.1.47 XXXX could benefit from increased opportunities at home to improve his visual-motor abilities, such as activities involving cutting, pasting, tracing and colouring. Holidays provide an excellent opportunity for family activities involving these skills in an enjoyable and positive environment.

10.1.48 When XXXX watches television, he could benefit from watching educational television programmes that promote reading and vocabulary development in specific academic content areas.

10.1.49 XXXX may benefit from practising new skills in several different ways. For example, to reinforce his learning of new vocabulary words, he could finger-paint or mould letters with clay into words, practise with flash cards and create sentences with the words.

10.1.50 Family and teachers can assist XXXX in learning beginning consonant sounds by asking XXXX to identify objects that begin with the same sound.

10.1.51 Family and teachers can develop a set of playing cards that contain pictures of household items or common objects. They can then ask XXXX to select a card, name the object and describe what the object is used for.

10.1.52 XXXX's family and teachers could participate in activities to improve XXXX's language development and verbal categorisation ability. For example, naming games can be developed in which XXXX is asked to list as many objects as he can based on a specific characteristic (e.g., red, round, soft, furry).

10.1.53 XXXX's family and teacher could assist him by participating in activities that teach positional words (e.g., on/in/on top/left/right). For example, XXXX could be asked to physically demonstrate a positional word by performing some action (e.g., sitting on the chair; getting into the car).

10.1.54 XXXX's family and teacher could assist him by participating in activities that teach attributes of objects. For example, the game 'I spy' could be played in which XXXX attempts to name a visible object based on characteristics described by another.

10.1.55 Family and teachers can encourage activities that address part/ whole relationships. For example, XXXX could be asked to identify a partially hidden object (e.g., a toy, kitchen utensil, etc.).

10.1.56 Computer programs that focus on the development of letter identification, phonemic awareness, spelling and grammar may be sources of help for XXXX.

10.1.57 Teachers may need to limit verbal instructions to one or two actions per sentence and ensure understanding.

10.1.58 Teachers may need to paraphrase or rephrase instructions.

10.1.59 XXXXX should be seated close to the source of auditory information or instructions (e.g., the teacher, television, speaker).

10.1.60 Family and teachers should encourage him to ask the meaning of any unfamiliar words.

10.1.61 Due to XXXX's auditory limitations, teachers are encouraged to demonstrate directions and instructions during oral presentations.

10.1.62 To teach relational skills specific to mass, XXXX's parents and teachers may wish to fill plastic bags with materials (e.g., polystyrene, sand, beans) to demonstrate varying weights. XXXX should then be asked to identify which of two bags is heavier or lighter.

10.1.63 To develop money skills, XXXX's parents/teachers may wish to attach coins of different denominations to index cards. Pictures could then be drawn around each coin to illustrate (e.g., picture of a girl named 'Penny'). Review the coins and provide prompts if XXXX has difficulty with recall.

10.1.64 Due to XXXX's difficulties with mathematics, he is encouraged to generalise any new skills to 'real world' applications (e.g., shopping, counting change, cooking).

10.1.65   XXXX is encouraged to learn how to use a calculator to check his work on mathematics assignments.

10.1.66   Teachers are encouraged to incorporate the use of manipulables, drawing or other engaging activities when teaching XXXX mathematical concepts or skills.

10.1.67   XXXX's family is encouraged to reinforce his school learning in the home. For example, XXXX could count the potatoes that need to be peeled or help make the grocery list by counting 'how many we have' and finding 'how many we need.'

10.1.67   XXXX's teachers should encourage pleasure reading at a level consistent with his abilities and interests.

10.1 68   XXXX is encouraged to learn a new vocabulary word each day and to record this word in a log.

10.1.69   Family and teachers can assist in building XXXX's vocabulary by encouraging him to ask for definitions of unfamiliar words during reading activities.

10.1.70   XXXX's teachers and parents can encourage XXXX to engage in pleasure reading by setting aside a few minutes each day for this activity.

10.1.71   Due to XXXX's reading difficulties, teachers should match assignments to XXXX's reading level.

10.1.72   Lessons should incorporate visual presentation rather than class discussion, especially during reading-group time.

10.1.73   In due course, XXXX may need encouragement to take an active approach to reading for learning. This approach may include discussing the subject matter prior to reading, pre-reading end-of-chapter questions and bold-faced headings, and pausing at the end of each sentence (or paragraph) to summarise or paraphrase the information.

10.1.74   Teachers and therapists are encouraged to assess homework assignments in terms of the reading demands and degree of learning enhancement.

10.1.75 XXXX is encouraged to choose reading materials with which he is most comfortable or interested to increase positive reading experiences. Most children will seek more difficult material as they gain confidence.

10.1.76 Given XXXX's difficulty with reading comprehension, he may need to be taught specific comprehension strategies such as reading for the main idea, using context clues to determine word meaning and identifying cause and effect.

10.1.77 XXXX will need assistance in choosing interesting reading materials that are at the appropriate reading level.

10.1.78 Teachers and family could assist XXXX with remembering important information by showing him how to embed important points and activities within a story that is meaningful to him.

10.1.79 Due to XXXX's reading difficulties, tape-recorded textbooks are recommended. These can be either commercially produced or produced by family, teachers or student volunteers.

10.1.80 XXXX's family are encouraged to support his efforts in completing homework while avoiding an over-emphasis on high grades. His family may wish to focus on the quality of work and timely completion of assignments.

10.1.81 It is recommended that XXXX's family set realistic expectations, goals or responsibilities on XXXX that build on his strengths and skills.

10.1.82 XXXX will benefit from a caring, positive and supportive environment. For example, XXXX's teacher might make a point of daily saying something positive, such as 'I like being your teacher and being with you' or 'I like the way you are completing that assignment'.

10.1.83 XXXX is encouraged to seek extra help from teachers or pupils when he does not understand an assignment. The teacher can suggest names of specific pupils with whom he may work best to enable him to feel more comfortable pursuing this help.

10.1.84   Teachers are encouraged to provide consistent reinforcement to XXXX for persistence, effort and independent work.

10.1.85   Teachers are encouraged to present only the essential tasks directly related to the concept being taught and present those tasks in sequence.

10.1.86   Teachers and therapists are encouraged to provide frequent, immediate feedback on XXXX's task performance. Feedback is most likely to be effective when phrased in a clear manner that provides direction in improving performance.

10.1.87   Teachers are encouraged to focus on small meaningful units of instruction, using short, simple directions and repeating them when necessary.

10.1.88   Teachers are encouraged to repeat new concepts in a variety of ways to provide XXXX with ample opportunity to generalise and internalise the new material.

10.1.89   Teachers are encouraged to ensure that XXXX has the prerequisite skills for new material.

11. Examination Provisions

In all his school and external examinations, XXXX should be allowed the provision of:

- 25% extra time
- a reader
- a scribe.

Due to his very poor speech, it should be organised so that XXXX works with a professional who knows him well, understands his speech and is therefore in the position of committing correctly to paper that which he has said.

Signed

Dr XXXX CBE
Educational Psychologist
Chartered Psychologist

Appendix 1: Evaluation Procedures

- Wechsler Intelligence Scale for Children – 4th Edition (WISC-IV UK)
- WIAT-II
  - ◦ *Reading* (single word, pseudo word, comprehension)
  - ◦ *Mathematics* (numerical operations, mathematical reasoning)
  - ◦ *Written language* (spelling)
  - ◦ *Listening comprehension*
- Free writing
- Parental questionnaire and interview
- School questionnaire
- Beck Youth Inventory – Self-esteem Questionnaire
- Beery-Buktenica developmental test of Visual Motor Integration (with supplementary tests)

Appendix 2: Description of WISC-IV subtests

Subtest	Description
Block design	While viewing a constructed model or a picture in the Stimulus Book, the child uses red and white blocks to recreate the design within a specified time limit.
Similarities	The child is presented with two words that represent common objects or concepts, and describes how they are similar.
Digit span	For Digit Span Forwards, the child repeats numbers in the same order as presented aloud by the examiner. For Digit Span Backwards, the child repeats numbers in the reverse order of that presented aloud by the examiner.
Picture concepts	The child is presented with two or three rows of pictures and chooses one picture from each row to form a group with a common characteristic.
Coding	The child copies symbols that are paired with simple geometric shapes or numbers. Using a key, the child draws each symbol in its corresponding shape or box within a specified time limit.
Vocabulary	For Picture Items, the child names pictures that are displayed in the Stimulus Book. For Verbal Items, the child gives definitions for words that the examiner reads aloud.
Letter-number sequencing	The child is read a sequence of numbers and letters and recalls the numbers in ascending order and the letters in alphabetical order.
Matrix reasoning	The child looks at an incomplete matrix and selects the missing portion from five response options.
Comprehension	The child answers questions based on his or her understanding of general principles and social situations.
Symbol search	The child scans a search group and indicates whether the target group symbol(s) matches any of the symbols in the search group within a specified time limit.
Arithmetic	The child mentally solves a series of orally presented mental arithmetic problems within a specific time limit.

Appendix 3: Description of scores on WISC-IV

Percentage of cases	2.2	6.7	16.1	50.00	16.1	6.7	2.2
Qualitative description	Extremely Low	Borderline	Low average	Average	High average	Superior	Very superior
Score	<70	70–79	80–89	90–109	110–119	120–129	130+

Appendix 4: Description of WIAT-II composites and subtests

Composite	Subtest	Description
Reading	Word reading	Assess pre-reading (phonological awareness) and decoding skills:
		Name letters of the alphabet
		Identify and generate rhyming words
		Identify beginning and ending sounds of words
		Match sounds with letters and letter blends
		Read aloud from a graded wording list
	Reading comprehension	Reflect reading instruction in the classroom:
		Match a written word with its representative picture
		Read passages and answer content questions
		Read short sentences aloud and respond to comprehension questions

	Pseudo word decoding	Assess the ability to apply phonetic decoding skills: Read aloud a list of nonsense words designed to mimic the phonetic structure of words in the English language
Mathematics	Numerical operations	Evaluate the ability to identify and write numbers: Count using one-to-one correspondence Solve written calculation problems Solve simple equations involving all basic operations (addition, subtraction, multiplication and division)
	Mathematical reasoning	Assess the ability to reason mathematically: Count Identify geometric shapes Solve single and multi-word problems Interpret graphs Identify mathematical patterns Solve problems related to statistics and probability
Written language	Spelling	Evaluate the ability to spell: Write dictated letters, letter blends and words
Oral language	Listening comprehension	Measure the ability to listen for details: Select the picture that matches a word or sentence Generate a word that matches a picture or oral description

THE SPECIAL EDUCATIONAL NEEDS AND DISABILITY REGULATIONS 2014

STATUTORY INSTRUMENTS

2014 No. 1530

EDUCATION

The Special Educational Needs and Disability Regulations 2014

Made - - - -	*4th June 2014*	
Laid before Parliament	*11th June 2014*	
Coming into force - -	*1st September 2014*	

The Secretary of State makes the following Regulations, in exercise of the powers conferred by sections 30(8) and(9), 34(6), 36(11), 37(4), 41(5), 44(7), 45(5), 46(2), 47(1) and (2), 51(4), 56(1), 67(3), 69(3)(a), and 80(1) of the Children and Families Act 2014(**a**):

PART 1

Introduction

Citation and commencement

1. These Regulations may be cited as the Special Educational Needs and Disability Regulations 2014 and come into force on 1st September 2014.

Interpretation

2.—(1) In these Regulations(**b**)—

"the Act" means the Children and Families Act 2014;

"the appropriate authority" means—

(a) in relation to a community, foundation or voluntary school(**c**) or a maintained nursery school(**d**), the governing body of the school; and

(b) in relation to an Academy school(**e**), the proprietor;

"educational institution" means a school or post-16 institution;

"health care professional" means an individual who is a member of a profession regulated by a body mentioned in section 25(3) of the National Health Service Reform and Health Care Professions Act 2002(**f**);

(**a**) 2014 c.6
(**b**) The definitions in the Act are applied throughout these Regulations.
(**c**) Community, foundation and voluntary school have the same meaning as in section 20 of the School Standards and Framework Act 1998 (c.31) ("the 1998 Act")
(**d**) Maintained nursery school has the meaning given by section 22(9) of the 1998 Act
(**e**) Academy school has the meaning given in section 1A of the Academies Act 2010 (c.32). Section 1A was inserted by section 53(7) of the Education Act 2011 (c.21) ("the 2011 Act")
(**f**) 2002 c.17

"infant school" means a primary school for the purpose of providing education for children who are of compulsory school age but have not attained the age of eight, even though it may also provide education for children below compulsory school age;

"junior school" means a primary school for the purpose of providing education for children who are of compulsory school age who have attained the age of eight;

"relevant school" means a mainstream school or a maintained nursery school;

"responsible commissioning body" has the meaning given in section 42(4) of the Act;

"the SENCO", in relation to a relevant school, means the person who has been designated to be the special educational needs co-ordinator for the school by the appropriate authority in accordance with section 67 of the Act;

"transfer between phases of education" means a transfer from—

(a) relevant early years education to school;

(b) infant school to junior school;

(c) primary school to middle school;

(d) primary school to secondary school;

(e) middle school to secondary school; or

(f) secondary school(**a**) to a post-16 institution;

"year 9" means the year of compulsory schooling in which the majority of pupils in the class attain the age of 14.

(2) Preparation for adulthood and independent living includes preparation relating to—

(a) finding employment;

(b) obtaining accommodation;

(c) participation in society.

PART 2

Children and young people with special educational needs

Assessments

Consideration of request

3. A local authority must consult the child's parent or the young person as soon as practicable after—

(a) receiving a request for an EHC needs assessment under section 36(1) of the Act, or

(b) becoming responsible for the child or young person in accordance with section 24 of the Act,

before determining whether it may be necessary for special educational provision to be made in accordance with an EHC plan for the child or young person.

Determination whether or not special educational provision may be necessary

4.—(1) Where a local authority determines that it is not necessary for special educational provision to be made in accordance with an EHC plan it must notify the child's parent or the young person in accordance with section 36(5) of the Act as soon as practicable, but in any event within 6 weeks of—

(**a**)   Primary school, middle school and secondary school have the meaning in section 5 of the Education Act 1996 (c.56) ("the 1996 Act").

(a) receiving a request for an EHC needs assessment under section 36(1) of the Act, or

(b) becoming responsible for the child or young person in accordance with section 24 of the Act.

(2) Where the local authority is considering securing an EHC needs assessment it must also notify—

(a) the responsible commissioning body;

(b) the officers of the local authority who exercise the local authority's social services functions for children or young people with special educational needs;

(c) in relation to a child—

(i) if the child is a registered pupil(**a**) at a school, the head teacher of that school (or the person holding the equivalent position), or

(ii) if the child receives education from a provider of relevant early years education, the person identified as having responsibility for special educational needs (if any) in relation to that provider; and

(d) in relation to a young person—

(i) if the young person is a registered pupil at a school, the head teacher of that school (or the person holding the equivalent position), or

(ii) if the young person is a student at a post-16 institution, to the principal of that institution (or the person holding the equivalent position).

Decision whether or not to conduct an EHC needs assessment

5.—(1) The local authority must notify the child's parent or the young person as soon as practicable and in any event within 6 weeks of—

(a) receiving a request for an assessment under section 36(1) of the Act, or

(b) becoming responsible for the child or young person in accordance with section 24 of the Act

of its decision whether or not it is necessary to secure an EHC needs assessment for the child or young person.

(2) The local authority must also notify the persons who were notified in accordance with regulation 4(2) of its decision.

(3) When notifying the child's parent or the young person of its decision that it is not necessary to secure an EHC needs assessment for the child or young person, it must also notify them of—

(a) their right to appeal that decision;

(b) the time limits for doing so;

(c) the information concerning mediation, set out in regulation 32; and

(d) the availability of—

(i) disagreement resolution services; and

(ii) information and advice about matters relating to the special educational needs of children and young people.

(4) The local authority need not comply with the time limit referred to in paragraph (1) if it is impractical to do so because—

(a) the local authority has requested advice from the head teacher or principal of a school or post-16 institution during a period beginning one week before any date on which that school or institution was closed for a continuous period of not less than 4 weeks from that date and ending one week before the date on which it re-opens;

(**a**) Pupil has the meaning in section 3 of the 1996 Act

3

(b) the authority has requested advice from the person identified as having responsibility for special educational needs (if any), in relation to, or other person responsible for, a child's education at a provider of relevant early years education during a period beginning one week before any date on which that provider was closed for a continuous period of not less than 4 weeks from that date and ending one week before the date on which it re-opens;

(c) exceptional personal circumstances affect the child, the child's parent, or the young person during the time period referred to in paragraph (1); or

(d) the child, the child's parent, or the young person, are absent from the area of the authority for a continuous period of not less than 4 weeks during the time period referred to in paragraph (1).

Information and advice to be obtained of EHC Needs Assessments

6.—(1) Where the local authority secures an EHC needs assessment for a child or young person, it must seek the following advice and information, on the needs of the child or young person, and what provision may be required to meet such needs and the outcomes that are intended to be achieved by the child or young person receiving that provision—

(a) advice and information from the child's parent or the young person;

(b) educational advice and information—

    (i) from the head teacher or principal of the school or post-16 or other institution that the child or young person is attending, or

    (ii) where this is not available, from a person who the local authority is satisfied has experience of teaching children or young people with special educational needs, or knowledge of the differing provision which may be called for in different cases to meet those needs, or

    (iii) if the child or young person is not currently attending a school or post-16 or other institution and advice cannot be obtained under sub-paragraph (ii), from a person responsible for educational provision for the child or young person, and

    (iv) if any parent of the child or young person is a serving member of Her Majesty's armed forces, also from the Secretary of State for Defence;

(c) medical advice and information from a health care professional identified by the responsible commissioning body;

(d) psychological advice and information from an educational psychologist;

(e) advice and information in relation to social care;

(f) advice and information from any other person the local authority thinks is appropriate;

(g) where the child or young person is in or beyond year 9, advice and information in relation to provision to assist the child or young person in preparation for adulthood and independent living; and

(h) advice and information from any person the child's parent or young person reasonably requests that the local authority seek advice from.

(2) Where it appears to the authority, in consequence of medical advice or otherwise, that the child or young person in question is either or both—

(a) hearing impaired;

(b) visually impaired,

and any person from whom advice and information is sought as provided in paragraph (1)(b) is not qualified to teach children or young people who are so impaired, then the advice sought shall be advice given after consultation with a person who is so qualified.

(3) When seeking advice in accordance with paragraph (1)(b) to (h), the local authority must provide the person from whom advice is being sought with copies of—

(a) any representations made by the child's parent or the young person, and

4

(b) any evidence submitted by or at the request of the child's parent or the young person.

(4) The local authority must not seek any of the advice referred to in paragraphs (1)(b) to (h) if such advice has previously been provided for any purpose and the person providing that advice, the local authority and the child's parent or the young person are satisfied that it is sufficient for the purposes of an EHC needs assessment.

Matters to be taken into account in securing an EHC needs assessment

7. When securing an EHC needs assessment a local authority must—

(a) consult the child and the child's parent, or the young person and take into account their views, wishes and feelings;

(b) consider any information provided to the local authority by or at the request of the child, the child's parent or the young person;

(c) consider the information and advice obtained in accordance with regulation 6(1);

(d) engage the child and the child's parent, or the young person and ensure they are able to participate in decisions; and

(e) minimise disruption for the child, the child's parent, the young person and their family.

Duty to co-operate in EHC needs assessments

8.—(1) Where a local authority requests the co-operation of a body in securing an EHC needs assessment in accordance with section 31 of the Act, that body must comply with such a request within 6 weeks of the date on which they receive it.

(2) A body need not comply with the time limit referred to in paragraph (1) if it is impractical to do so because—

(a) exceptional circumstances affect the child, the child's parent or the young person during that 6 week period;

(b) the child, the child's parent or the young person are absent from the area of the authority for a continuous period of not less than 4 weeks during that 6 week period; or

(c) the child or young person fails to keep an appointment for an examination or a test made by the body during that 6 week period.

Provision of advice, information and support to parents and young people

9. When securing an EHC needs assessment the local authority must consider whether the child's parent or the young person requires any information, advice and support in order to enable them to take part effectively in the EHC needs assessment, and if it considers that such information, advice or support is necessary, it must provide it.

Decision not to secure an EHC plan

10.—(1) Where, following an EHC needs assessment, a local authority decides that it is not necessary for special educational provision to be made for a child or young person in accordance with an EHC plan, the notification given in accordance with section 36(9) must be given as soon as practicable, and in any event within 16 weeks of the local authority receiving a request for an EHC needs assessment in accordance with section 36(1) of the Act, or of the local authority becoming responsible for the child or young person in accordance with section 24 of the Act.

(2) It must also notify the responsible commissioning body and the person notified in accordance with regulation 4(2)(c) or (d).

(3) When notifying a child's parent or young person in accordance with paragraph (1) the local authority must also notify them of—

(a) their right to appeal that decision;

(b) the time limits for doing so;

5

(c) the information concerning mediation, set out in regulation 32; and

(d) the availability of—

    (i) disagreement resolution services; and

    (ii) information and advice about matters relating to the special educational needs of children and young people.

(4) The local authority need not comply with the time limit referred to in paragraph (1) if it is impractical to do so because—

(a) the authority has requested advice from the head teacher or principal of a school or post-16 institution during a period beginning one week before any date on which that school or institution was closed for a continuous period of not less than 4 weeks from that date and ending one week before the date on which it re-opens;

(b) the authority has requested advice from the person identified as having responsibility for special educational needs (if any) in relation to, or other person responsible for, a child's education at a provider of relevant early years education during a period beginning one week before any date on which that provider was closed for a continuous period of not less than 4 weeks from that date and ending one week before the date on which it re-opens;

(c) exceptional personal circumstances affect the child or the child's parent, or the young person during that time period ; or

(d) the child or the child's parent, or the young person, are absent from the area of the authority for a continuous period of not less than 4 weeks during that time period.

EHC Plans

Preparation of EHC plans

11. When preparing a child or young person's EHC Plan a local authority must—

(a) take into account the evidence received when securing the EHC needs assessment; and

(b) consider how best to achieve the outcomes to be sought for the child or young person.

Form of EHC plan

12.—(1) When preparing an EHC plan a local authority must set out—

(a) the views, interests and aspirations of the child and his parents or the young person (section A);

(b) the child or young person's special educational needs (section B);

(c) the child or young person's health care needs which relate to their special educational needs (section C);

(d) the child or young person's social care needs which relate to their special educational needs or to a disability (section D);

(e) the outcomes sought for him or her (section E);

(f) the special educational provision required by the child or young person (section F);

(g) any health care provision reasonably required by the learning difficulties or disabilities which result in the child or young person having special educational needs (section G);

(h) (i) any social care provision which must be made for the child or young person as a result of section 2 of the Chronically Sick and Disabled Persons Act 1970(**a**) (section H1);

(**a**) 1970 c.44

(ii) any other social care provision reasonably required by the learning difficulties or disabilities which result in the child or young person having special educational needs (section H2);

(i) the name of the school, maintained nursery school, post-16 institution or other institution to be attended by the child or young person and the type of that institution or, where the name of a school or other institution is not specified in the EHC plan, the type of school or other institution to be attended by the child or young person (section I); and

(j) where any special educational provision is to be secured by a direct payment, the special educational needs and outcomes to be met by the direct payment (section J),

and each section must be separately identified.

(2) The health care provision specified in the EHC Plan in accordance with paragraph (1)(g) must be agreed by the responsible commissioning body.

(3) Where the child or young person is in or beyond year 9, the EHC plan must include within the special educational provision, health care provision and social care provision specified, provision to assist the child or young person in preparation for adulthood and independent living.

(4) The advice and information obtained in accordance with regulation 6(1) must be set out in appendices to the EHC plan (section K).

Timescales for EHC plans

13.—(1) When a local authority sends a draft plan to a child's parent or young person it must—

(a) give them at least 15 days, beginning with the day on which the draft plan was served, in which to—

(i) make representations about the content of the draft plan, and to request that a particular school or other institution be named in the plan; and

(ii) require the local authority to arrange a meeting between them and an officer of the local authority at which the draft plan can be discussed; and

(b) advise them where they can find information about the schools and colleges that are available for the child or young person to attend.

(2) A local authority must send the finalised EHC plan to—

(a) the child's parent or to the young person;

(b) the governing body, proprietor or principal of any school, other institution or provider of relevant early years education named in the EHC plan; and

(c) to the responsible commissioning body,

as soon as practicable, and in any event within 20 weeks of the local authority receiving a request for an EHC needs assessment in accordance with section 36(1) of the Act, or of the local authority becoming responsible for the child in accordance with section 24 of the Act.

(3) The local authority need not comply with the time limit referred to in paragraph (2) if it is impractical for any of the reasons set out in regulation 10(4)(a) to (d)

Sending the finalised EHC plan

14.—(1) The finalised EHC plan must be in the form of the draft plan sent in accordance with regulation 13(1), or in a form modified in the light of the representations made in accordance with that regulation.

(2) When sending a copy of the finalised EHC plan to the child's parent or the young person in accordance with section 39(8)(a) or 40(5)(a) of the Act, the local authority must notify them of—

(a) their right to appeal matters within the EHC plan in accordance with section 51(2)(c) of the Act;

(b) the time limits for doing so;

7

(c) the information concerning mediation, set out in regulation 32; and

(d) the availability of—

    (i) disagreement resolution services; and

    (ii) advice and information about matters relating to the special educational needs of children and young people.

Transfer of EHC plans

15.—(1) This regulation applies where a child or young person in respect of whom an EHC plan is maintained moves from the area of the local authority which maintains the EHC plan ("the old authority") into the area of another local authority ("the new authority").

(2) The old authority shall transfer the EHC plan to the new authority ("the transfer") on the day of the move or, where it has not become aware of the move at least 15 working days prior to that move, within 15 working days beginning with the day on which it did become aware.

(3) From the date of the transfer—

(a) the EHC plan is to be treated as if it had been made by the new authority on the date on which it was made by the old authority and must be maintained by the new authority; and

(b) where the new authority makes an EHC needs assessment and the old authority has supplied the new authority with advice obtained in pursuance of the previous assessment the new authority must not seek further advice where the person providing that advice, the old authority and the child's parent or the young person are satisfied that the advice obtained in pursuance of the previous assessment is sufficient for the purpose of the new authority arriving at a satisfactory assessment.

(4) The new authority must, within 6 weeks of the date of the transfer, inform the child's parent or the young person of the following—

(a) that the EHC plan has been transferred;

(b) whether it proposes to make an EHC needs assessment; and

(c) when it proposes to review the EHC plan in accordance with paragraph (5).

(5) The new authority must review the EHC plan in accordance with section 44 of the Act before the expiry of the later of—

(a) the period of 12 months beginning with the date of making of the EHC plan, or as the case may be, with the previous review, or

(b) the period of 3 months beginning with the date of the transfer.

(6) Where, by virtue of the transfer, the new authority comes under a duty to arrange the child or young person's attendance at a school or other institution specified in the EHC plan but in the light of the child or young person's move that attendance is no longer practicable, the new authority must arrange for the child or young person's attendance at another school or other institution appropriate for him or her until such time as it is possible to amend the EHC plan.

(7) Where, by virtue of the child or young person's move, another commissioning body becomes the responsible commissioning body for that child or young person, the original responsible commissioning body must notify the new responsible commissioning body of the move on the day of the move or where it has not become aware of the move at least 15 working days prior to that move, within 15 working days beginning on the day on which it did become aware.

(8) Where it is not practicable for that new commissioning body to arrange the health care provision specified in the EHC plan, it must, within 15 working days beginning with the date on which it became aware of the move, request that the new local authority makes an EHC needs assessment or reviews the EHC Plan, and where the new local authority receives such a request it must comply with that request.

8

Change of responsible commissioning body

16.—(1) This regulation applies where, in relation to a child or young person in respect of whom an EHC plan is maintained, another commissioning body becomes the responsible commissioning body for that child or young person, and the local authority which maintains the EHC plan remains the same.

(2) The original responsible commissioning body must notify the new responsible commissioning body of the change in responsible commissioning body within 15 working days beginning on the day on which it became aware of the change.

(3) Where it is not practicable for the new commissioning body to arrange the health care provision specified in the EHC plan, it must, within 15 working days beginning with the date on which it became aware that it is the new responsible commissioning body, request the local authority makes an EHC needs assessment or reviews the EHC Plan, and where the local authority receives such a request it must comply with that request.

Restriction on disclosure of EHC plans

17.—(1) Subject to the provisions of the Act and of these Regulations, an EHC plan in respect of a child or young person shall not be disclosed without the child or young person's consent except—

(a) to persons to whom, in the opinion of the local authority concerned, it is necessary to disclose the whole or any part of the EHC plan in the interests of the child or young person;

(b) for the purposes of any appeal under the Act;

(c) for the purposes of educational research which, in the opinion of the local authority, may advance the education or training of children or young persons with special educational needs, if, but only if, the person engaged in that research undertakes not to publish anything contained in, or derived from, an EHC plan otherwise than in a form which does not identify any individual including, in particular, the child concerned and the child's parent or the young person;

(d) on the order of any court or for the purposes of any criminal proceedings;

(e) for the purposes of any investigation under Part 3 of the Local Government Act 1974(**a**) (investigation of maladministration);

(f) to the Secretary of State when he requests such disclosure for the purposes of deciding whether to—

(i) give directions, make determinations, or exercise any contractual rights under an Academy's funding agreement (for any purpose), or

(ii) make an order under section 496, 497 or 497A(**b**) of the Education Act 1996(**c**).

(g) for the purposes of an assessment of the needs of the child or young person with respect to the provision of any statutory services for him or her being carried out by officers of an authority by virtue of arrangements made under section 5(5) of the Disabled Persons (Services, Consultation and Representation) Act 1986(**d**);

(h) for the purposes of a local authority in the performance of its duties under sections 22(3)(a), 85(4)(a), 86(3)(a) and 87(3) of the Children Act 1989(**e**);

(**a**) 1974 c.7
(**b**) Section 497A was inserted into the 1996 Act by section 8 of the 1998 Act, and amended by section 60 of and Schedule 22 to the Education Act 2002 (c.32) and by section 59 of and Schedule 2 to the Apprenticeships, Skills, Children and Learning Act 2009 (c.22)
(**c**) 1996 c.56
(**d**) 1986 c.33
(**e**) 1989 c.41

9

(i) to Her Majesty's Chief Inspector of Education, Children's Services and Skills(**a**), exercising the right to inspect and take copies of an EHC plan in accordance with section 10(1)(e) of the Education Act 2005(**b**) and section 140(2)(a) of the Education and Inspections Act 2006;

(j) to the person in charge of any relevant youth accommodation for the purposes of the provision of education or training for a detained person(**c**);

(k) to a youth offending team for the purposes of the provision of education or training for a detained person.

(2) A child may consent to the disclosure of an EHC plan for the purposes of this regulation if his or her age and understanding are sufficient to allow him or her to understand the nature of that consent.

(3) If a child does not have sufficient age or understanding to allow him or her to consent to such disclosure, the child's parent may consent on the child's behalf.

(4) The arrangements for keeping a child or young person's EHC plan must be such that they ensure, so far as is reasonably practicable, that unauthorised persons do not have access to it.

(5) In this regulation, any reference to an EHC plan includes a reference to any representations, evidence, advice or information obtained in relation to an EHC plan.

Reviews and re-assessments

Circumstances in which a local authority must review an EHC plan

18.—(1) Except where paragraph (3) applies, where a child or young person is within 12 months of a transfer between phases of education, the local authority must review and amend, where necessary, the child or young person's EHC plan before—

(a) 31 March in the calendar year of the child or young person's transfer from secondary school to a post-16 institution; and

(b) 15 February in the calendar year of the child's transfer in any other case,

and where necessary amend the EHC plan so that it names the school, post-16 or other institution, or type of school or institution, which the child or young person will attend following that transfer.

(2) Where it is proposed that a young person transfers from one post-16 institution to another post-16 institution at any other time, the local authority must review and amend, where necessary, the young person's EHC plan at least five months before that transfer takes place so that it names the post-16 institution that the young person will attend following the transfer.

(3) Where a child or young person is due to transfer from a secondary school to a post-16 institution on 1 September 2015 the local authority must amend and review the EHC plan under paragraph (1)(a) before 31 May 2015.

Conduct of reviews

19. When undertaking a review of an EHC plan, a local authority must—

(a) consult the child and the child's parent or the young person, and take account of their views, wishes and feelings;

(b) consider the child or young person's progress towards achieving the outcomes specified in the EHC plan and whether these outcomes remain appropriate for the child or young person;

(c) consult the school or other institution attended by the child or young person.

(**a**) Her Majesty's Chief Inspector of Education, Children's Services and Skills is appointed under the Chief Inspector of Education, Children's Services and Skills Order 2011 (S.I. 2011/2720) which is made under section 113(1) of the Education and Inspections Act 2006 (c.40)

(**b**) 2005 c.18

(**c**) 'Relevant youth accommodation' and 'detained person' have the same meaning as in section 72(5) of the 2014 Act.

10

Review where the child or young person attends a school or other institution

20.—(1) As part of a review of a child or young person's EHC plan, the local authority must ensure that a meeting to review that EHC plan is held and in the case of a child or young person attending a school referred to in paragraph (12), can require the head teacher or principal of the school to arrange and hold that meeting.

(2) The following persons must be invited to attend the review meeting—

(a) the child's parent or the young person;

(b) the provider of the relevant early years education or the head teacher or principal of the school, post-16 or other institution attended by the child or young person;

(c) an officer of the authority who exercises the local authority's education functions in relation to children and young people with special educational needs;

(d) a health care professional identified by the responsible commissioning body to provide advice about health care provision in relation to the child or young person;

(e) an officer of the authority who exercises the local authority's social services functions in relation to children and young people with special educational needs.

(3) At least two weeks' notice of the date of the meeting must be given.

(4) The person arranging the review meeting must obtain advice and information about the child or young person from the persons referred to in paragraph (2) and must circulate it to those persons at least two weeks in advance of the review meeting.

(5) The child or young person's progress towards achieving the outcomes specified in the EHC plan must be considered at the meeting.

(6) When the child or young person is in or beyond year 9, the review meeting must consider what provision is required to assist the child or young person in preparation for adulthood and independent living.

(7) Where the child or young person attends a school referred to in paragraph (12), the local authority must ask the head teacher or principal of the school to prepare a written report on the child or young person, setting out that person's recommendations on any amendments to be made to the EHC plan, and referring to any difference between those recommendations and recommendations of others attending the meeting.

(8) Where the child or young person does not attend a school referred to in paragraph (12), the local authority must prepare a written report on the child or young person, setting out its recommendations on any amendments to be made to the EHC plan, and referring to any difference between those recommendations and recommendations of others attending the meeting.

(9) The written report must include advice and information about the child or young person obtained in accordance with paragraph (4) and must be prepared within two weeks of the review meeting, and sent to everyone referred to in paragraph (2).

(10) The local authority must then decide whether it proposes to—

(a) continue to maintain the EHC plan in its current form;

(b) amend it; or

(c) cease to maintain it,

and must notify the child's parent or the young person and the person referred to in paragraph (2)(b) within four weeks of the review meeting.

(11) If the local authority proposes to continue or to cease to maintain the child or young person's EHC plan, it must also notify the child's parent or the young person of—

(a) their right to appeal matters within the EHC plan in accordance with section 51(2)(e) of the Act;

(b) the time limits for doing so;

(c) the information concerning mediation, set out in regulation 32; and

(d) the availability of—

11

   (i) disagreement resolution services; and

   (ii) information and advice about matters relating to the special educational needs of children and young people.

(12) Schools referred to in this paragraph are—

 (a) maintained schools;

 (b) maintained nursery schools;

 (c) Academy schools;

 (d) alternative provision Academies(**a**);

 (e) pupil referral units(**b**);

 (f) non-maintained special schools(**c**);

 (g) independent educational institutions approved under section 41 of the Act.

Review of EHC plan where the child or young person does not attend a school or other institution

21.—(1) This regulation applies where a local authority carry out a review of an EHC plan and the child or young person concerned does not attend a school or other institution.

(2) The local authority must invite the following persons to a meeting as part of the review of an EHC plan—

 (a) the child's parent or the young person;

 (b) an officer of the authority who exercises the local authority's education functions in relation to children and young people with special educational needs;

 (c) a health care professional identified by the responsible commissioning body to provide advice about health care provision to the child or young person;

 (d) an officer of the authority who exercises the local authority's social services functions in relation to children and young people with special educational needs;

 (e) any other person whose attendance the local authority considers appropriate.

(3) At least two weeks' notice of the date of the meeting must be given.

(4) The local authority must obtain advice and information about the child or young person from the persons referred to in paragraph (2) and must circulate it to those persons at least two weeks in advance of the review meeting

(5) The meeting must consider the child or young person's progress towards achieving the outcomes specified in the EHC plan.

(6) When the child or young person is in or beyond year 9, the review meeting must consider what provision is required to assist the child or young person in preparation for adulthood and independent living.

(7) The local authority must prepare a report on the child or young person within two weeks of the review meeting setting out its recommendations on any amendments required to be made to the EHC plan, and should refer to any difference between those recommendations and recommendations of others attending the meeting.

(8) The written report must include advice and information about the child or young person obtained in accordance with paragraph (4) and must be prepared within two weeks of the review meeting, and sent to everyone referred to in paragraph (2).

(9) The local authority must decide whether it proposes to—

(**a**) Alternative provision Academies has the meaning given in section 1C of the Academies Act 2010 . Section 1C was inserted by section 53(7) of the 2011 Act

(**b**) Pupil Referral Units has the same meaning given in section 19 of the 1996 Act

(**c**) Non-maintained special school has the same meaning given in section 342 of the 1996 Act

12

(a) continue to maintain the EHC plan in its current form;

(b) amend it; or

(c) cease to maintain it,

and must notify the child's parent or the young person within four weeks of the review meeting.

(10) If the local authority proposes to continue or to cease to maintain the child or young person's EHC plan, it must also notify the child's parent or the young person of—

(a) their right to appeal matters within the EHC plan in accordance with section 51(2)(e) of the Act;

(b) the time limits for doing so;

(c) the information concerning mediation, set out in regulation 32; and

(d) the availability of—

(i) disagreement resolution services; and

(ii) advice and information about matters relating to the special educational needs of children and young people.

Amending an EHC plan following a review

22.—(1) Where the local authority is considering amending an EHC plan following a review it must comply with the requirements of regulations 11, and 12, and with sections 33 of the Act, and with sections 39 and 40 of the Act (as appropriate).

(2) Where the local authority is considering amending an EHC plan following a review it must—

(a) send the child's parent or the young person a copy of the EHC plan together with a notice specifying the proposed amendments, together with copies of any evidence which supports those amendments;

(b) provide the child's parent or the young person with notice of their right request the authority to secure that a particular school is or other institution is named in the plan under section 38(2)(b)(ii)

(c) give them at least 15 days, beginning with the day on which the draft plan was served, in which to—

(i) make representations about the content of the draft plan;

(ii) request that a particular school or other institution be named in the plan;

(iii) request a meeting with an officer of the local authority, if they wish to make representations orally.

(d) advise them where they can find information about the schools and colleges that are available for the child or young person to attend.

(3) Where the local authority decides to amend the EHC plan following representations from the child's parent or the young person, it must send the finalised EHC plan to—

(a) the child's parent or to the young person;

(b) the governing body, proprietor or principal of any school or other institution named in the EHC plan; and

(c) to the responsible commissioning body

as soon as practicable, and in any event within 8 weeks of the local authority sending a copy of the EHC plan in accordance with paragraph (2)(a).

(4) Where the local authority decides not to amend the EHC plan, it must notify the child's parent or the young person of its decision and its reasons for this as soon as practicable and in any event within 8 weeks of the local authority sending a copy of the EHC plan in accordance with paragraph (2)(a).

13

(5) When sending a the finalised EHC plan to the child's parent or the young person in accordance with paragraph (3), or notifying them in accordance with paragraph (4) the local authority must also notify them of—

(a) their right to appeal matters within the EHC plan in accordance with section 51(2)(c) or 51(2)(e) of the Act (as appropriate);

(b) the time limits for doing so;

(c) the information concerning mediation, set out in regulation 32; and

(d) the availability of—

(i) disagreement resolution services; and

(ii) advice and information about matters relating to the special educational needs of children and young people.

Other circumstances in which a local authority must secure a re-assessment

23. A local authority must secure a re-assessment of a child or young person's EHC Plan where it receives a request to do so from the responsible commissioning body for that child or young person.

Circumstances in which it is not necessary to re-assess educational, health care and social care provision

24. Where a local authority receives a request to re-assess a child or young person in accordance with section 44(2) of the Act it does not need to do so where—

(a) it has carried out an assessment or re-assessment within the period of six months prior to that request, or

(b) it is not necessary for the authority to make a further assessment.

Notification of decision whether it is necessary to re-assess educational, health care and social care provision

25.—(1) The local authority must notify the child's parent or the young person whether or not it is necessary to reassess the child or young person within 15 days of receiving the request to re-assess.

(2) Where the local authority does not need to re-assess the child or young person the notification under paragraph (1) must also notify them of—

(a) their right to appeal matters within the EHC plan in accordance with section 51(2)(d) of the Act;

(b) the time limits for doing so;

(c) the information concerning mediation, set out in regulation 32; and

(d) the availability of—

(i) disagreement resolution services; and

(ii) advice and information about matters relating to the special educational needs of children and young people.

Securing a re-assessment of educational, health care and social care provision

26.—(1) When securing a re-assessment of educational, health care and social care provision in a child or young person's EHC plan a local authority must comply with the requirements of regulations 6 and 7.

(2) Regulations 8 and 9 also apply to re-assessments.

14

Amending or replacing an EHC plan following a re-assessment

27.—(1) Where the local authority decides to amend or replace an EHC plan following a reassessment it must comply with the requirements of regulations 11, 12, 13(1) and 14, and with sections 33 and 38 of the Act and with section 39 or 40 of the Act (as appropriate).

(2) The local authority must send a copy of the finalised EHC plan in accordance with section 39(8) or 40(5) of the Act (as appropriate) as soon as practicable, and in any event within 14 weeks of the notification under regulation 25(1)or of deciding it is necessary to reassess under section 44(3) to—

(a) the child's parent or the young person;

(b) the governing body, proprietor or principal of any school or other institution named in the plan; and

(c) the relevant responsible commissioning body.

(3) The local authority need not comply with the time limit referred to in paragraph (2) if it is impractical to do so because—

(a) the authority has requested advice from the head teacher or principal of a school or post-16 institution during a period beginning one week before any date on which that school or institution was closed for a continuous period of not less than 4 weeks from that date and ending one week before the date on which it re-opens;

(b) the authority has requested advice from the person identified as having responsibility for special educational needs (if any) in relation to, or other person responsible for, a child's education at a provider of relevant early years education during a period beginning one week before any date on which that provider was closed for a continuous period of not less than 4 weeks from that date and ending one week before the date on which it re-opens;

(c) exceptional personal circumstances affect the child or his parent, or the young person during that time period; or

(d) the child or his parent, or the young person, are absent from the area of the authority for a continuous period of not less than 4 weeks, during that time period.

(4) (a) Where the local authority carries out a reassessment, it must review the EHC plan within 12 months of the date on which a copy of the finalised plan is sent to the child's parent or the young person in accordance with the requirements in Regulation 14; and

(b) in each subsequent period of 12 months starting with the date on which the plan was last reviewed.

Amending an EHC plan without a review or reassessment

28. If, at any time, a local authority proposes to amend an EHC plan, it shall proceed as if the proposed amendment were an amendment proposed after a review.

Ceasing to maintain an EHC plan

Circumstances in which a local authority may not cease to maintain an EHC plan where the person is under the age of 18

29.—(1) A local authority may not cease to maintain an EHC plan for a child or young person under the age of 18 unless it determines that it is no longer necessary for special educational provision to be made for the child or young person in accordance with an EHC plan.

(2) Where a child or young person under the age of 18 is not receiving education or training, the local authority must review the EHC plan in accordance with regulations 18 and 19 and amend it in accordance with regulation 22 where appropriate, to ensure that the young person continues to receive education or training.

15

Circumstances in which a local authority may not cease to maintain an EHC plan where the person is aged 18 or over

30.—(1) When a young person aged 18 or over ceases to attend the educational institution specified in his or her EHC plan, so is no longer receiving education or training, a local authority may not cease to maintain that EHC plan, unless it has reviewed that EHC plan in accordance with regulations 18 and 19 and ascertained that the young person does not wish to return to education or training, either at the educational institution specified in the EHC plan, or otherwise, or determined that returning to education or training would not be appropriate for the young person.

(2) Where following the review, the local authority ascertains that the young person wishes to return to education or training either at the educational institution specified in the EHC plan, or at another educational institution, and determines that it is appropriate for the young person to do so, it must amend the young person's EHC plan as it thinks necessary in accordance with regulation 22.

Procedure for determining whether to cease to maintain EHC plan

31.—(1) Where a local authority is considering ceasing to maintain a child or young person's EHC plan it must—

(a) inform the child's parent or the young person that it is considering ceasing to maintain the child or young person's EHC plan; and

(b) consult the child's parent or the young person;

(c) consult the head teacher, principal or equivalent person at the educational institution that is named in the EHC plan.

(2) Where, following that consultation the local authority determines to cease to maintain the child or young person's EHC plan, it must notify the child's parent or the young person, the institution named in the child or young person's EHC plan and the responsible commissioning body of that decision.

(3) When notifying the child's parent or the young person of its decision to cease to maintain the EHC plan, it must also notify them of—

(a) their right to appeal that decision;

(b) the time limits for doing so;

(c) the information concerning mediation, set out in regulation 32; and

(d) the availability of—

(i) disagreement resolution services; and

(ii) advice and information about matters relating to the special educational needs of children and young people.

Mediation

Information to be included in notices sent by a local authority

32. Where a notice sent by a local authority must include the information set out in this regulation, that information is—

(a) the right of the child's parent or young person to request mediation under section 53 or 54 of the Act;

(b) the requirement to obtain a certificate in accordance with section 55(4) or (5) ("a mediation certificate") before any appeal can be made to the First-tier Tribunal(**a**);

(**a**) The First-tier Tribunal was established under section 3 of the Tribunals, Courts and Enforcement Act 2007 (c.15)

16

(c) contact details for the mediation adviser that the child's parent or young person should contact to obtain that certificate;

(d) the timescales for requesting mediation;

(e) the requirement to inform the local authority—

　　(i) if the parent or young person wishes to pursue mediation,

　　(ii) the mediation issues(a), and

　　(iii) where the mediation issues are or include the fact that no health care provision, or no health care provision, of a particular kind is specified in the EHC plan, the health care provision that the child's parent or young person wishes to be specified in the EHC plan;

(f) contact details for any person acting on behalf of the local authority whom the child's parent or young person should contact if they wish to pursue mediation.

Requirement to consider mediation

33. Where a parent or young person is required to obtain a mediation certificate, he or she must contact the mediation adviser within 2 months after written notice of the local authority's decision was sent, and inform the mediation adviser that he or she wishes to appeal and inform the mediation adviser whether they wish to pursue mediation.

Where a parent or young person does not wish to or fails to pursue mediation

34.—(1) Where a parent or young person who is required to obtain a mediation certificate informs the mediation adviser that he or she does not wish to pursue mediation, the mediation adviser must issue a mediation certificate under section 55(4) within 3 working days of being informed by the parent or young person.

(2) The mediation adviser may not issue such a certificate if the parent or young person did not contact the mediation adviser within 2 months of the date of the notice issued by the local authority.

(3) A parent or young person may seek leave to appeal to the First-tier Tribunal not withstanding that he or she is required to obtain a mediation certificate and a mediation adviser has not issued a certificate to him or her, where the parent or young person has failed to comply with Regulation – 33 and the time for doing so has elapsed.

Mediation – health care issues

35.—(1) This regulation applies where a parent or young person has informed the local authority that he or she wishes to pursue mediation and the mediation issues relate solely or in part to the healthcare provision specified in the EHC plan, or the fact that no health care or no health care of a particular kind is specified in the EHC plan.

(2) The local authority must, within 3 working days, from the date of being informed that the child's parent or the young person wishes to pursue mediation, notify each relevant commissioning body of—

(a) the mediation issues; and

(b) where the mediation issues are, or include, the fact that no health care provision, or no health care provision of a particular kind, is specified in the EHC plan, the health care provision that the child's parent or young person has informed the local authority he or she wishes to be specified in the plan.

(3) Where the mediation issues relate solely to health care provision, the responsible commissioning body (or, where there is more than one, the responsible commissioning bodies

---

(a) Mediation issues has the same meaning as in section 53(1)(b) of the Act

17

acting jointly) must arrange for mediation between it (or them) and the child's parent or young person within 30 days from the date on which it (or they) receive notification from the local authority under paragraph (2).

(4) Where the mediation issues do not relate solely to health care provision, the local authority must arrange for mediation between it, each responsible commissioning body and the parent or young person within 30 days from the date on which it was informed by the parent or young person that he or she wished to pursue mediation.

Mediation – no health care issues

36.—(1) This regulation applies where a parent or young person has informed the local authority that he or she wishes to pursue mediation and the mediation issues do not relate to health care provision.

(2) The local authority must arrange for mediation between it and the child's parent or young person, within 30 days from the date of on which it was informed by the child's parent or young person that he or she wished to pursue mediation.

Arrangements for mediation

37.—(1) The body (or bodies) arranging the mediation must ensure that it is attended by persons who have authority to resolve the mediation issues.

(2) That body must inform the child's parent or the young person of the date and place of the mediation at least 5 working days prior to the mediation unless the child's parent or the young person consents to this period of time being reduced.

Attendance at the mediation

38.—(1) The following persons may attend the mediation—

(a) the parties to the mediation;

(b) any advocate or other supporter that the child's parent or the young person wishes to attend the mediation;

(c) where the child's parent is a party to the mediation, the child (with the agreement of the parent and the mediator);

(d) where the young person's alternative person(a) is a party to the mediation, the young person (with the agreement of the alternative person and the mediator);

(e) any other person, with the consent of all of the parties to the mediation, or where there is no such agreement, with the consent of the mediator.

(2) Where the child's parent is a party to the mediation, the mediator must take reasonable steps to ascertain the views of the child about the mediation issues.

(3) Where the young person's alternative person is a party to the mediation, the mediator must take reasonable steps to ascertain the views of the young person about the mediation issues.

Mediation certificate under section 55(5)

39.—(1) Where mediation is pursued before making an appeal to the First-tier Tribunal, the mediation adviser must issue a certificate under section 55(5) to the parent or young person within 3 working days of the conclusion of the mediation.

(2) Where mediation is pursued before making an appeal to the First-tier Tribunal and the local authority is unable to arrange for mediation within the period specified in regulation 35(4) or 36(2), the local authority must notify the mediation adviser of this fact as soon as possible after it realises that it is unable to arrange for mediation within that period.

(a) Alternative person has the meaning given in Regulation 64

18

(3) Where paragraph (2) applies, it is deemed that the child's parent or the young person has participated in mediation, and the mediation adviser will issue a certificate under section 55(5) within 3 working days of being notified of this by the local authority, whether or not the child's parent or the young person later participates in mediation.

Training, qualifications and experience of mediators

40. Mediators must have sufficient knowledge of the legislation relating to special educational needs, health and social care to be able to conduct the mediation.

Expenses

41.—(1) Subject to paragraph (2), the body arranging the mediation shall pay the following expenses in connection with the child's parent or young person attending mediation—

Table 1

Item	Description
Travel Costs	Standard class public transport fares for the parent and their child or the young person.
	A mileage rate of 25p per mile for travel by car or motorcycle.
	Taxi fares.
Repayment for loss of earnings	Loss of earnings up to £45.
Registered child or young person care expenses	Engagement of a registered child or adult carer at £5.35 per hour, per child or young person.
Overnight expenses	Expenses up to £81 per night for inner London or £71 per night for elsewhere or £21 per night if the stay is with family or friends.

(2) The body arranging the mediation may require either or both of the following conditions before making payment of a claim for expenses under paragraph (1)—

  (a) payment is made with the prior agreement of the body arranging the mediation;

  (b) payment is made upon receipt of satisfactory supporting evidence of the expenses claimed.

Steps to be taken by a local authority

42.—(1) This regulation applies where mediation has taken place and the parties to the mediation reach an agreement, to be recorded in writing ("the mediation agreement").

(2) Where the mediation issues in the mediation agreement are those on which the child's parent or young person has a right to appeal to the First-tier Tribunal, the local authority shall comply with the time limits set out in regulation 44, as if the mediation agreement were an order of the First-tier Tribunal.

(3) Where the mediation agreement requires the local authority or responsible commissioning body to do something in relation to which the child's parent or young person has no right of appeal to the First-tier Tribunal, the local authority or responsible commissioning body must do that thing within two weeks of the date of the mediation agreement.

(4) Where the local authority was not a party to the mediation, the responsible commissioning body must notify the local authority of the mediation agreement within 1 week of the date of that agreement.

19

(5) The timescales referred to in paragraphs (2) and (3) do not apply where the parties to the mediation agree in writing to a different timescale.

Appeals

Powers of the First-tier Tribunal

43.—(1) Before determining any appeal, the First-tier Tribunal may, with the agreement of the parties, correct any deficiencies in the EHC Plan which relate to the special educational needs or special educational provision for the child or the young person.

(2) When determining an appeal the powers of the First-tier Tribunal include the power to—

(a) dismiss the appeal;

(b) order the local authority to arrange an assessment of the child or young person under section 36 or a reassessment under section 44(2) where the local authority has refused to do so, where the appeal made under section 51(2)(a) or (d);

(c) order the local authority to make and maintain an EHC Plan where the local authority has refused to do so, where the appeal is made under section 51(2)(b);

(d) refer the case back to the local authority for them to reconsider whether, having regard to any observations made by the First-tier Tribunal, it is necessary for the local authority to determine the special educational provision for the child or young person, where the appeal is made under section 51(2)(b);

(e) order the local authority to continue to maintain the EHC Plan in its existing form where the local authority has refused to do so, where the appeal is made under section 51(2)(c), (e) or (f);

(f) order the local authority to continue to maintain the EHC Plan with amendments where the appeal is made under section 51(2)(c) or (e) so far as that relates to either the assessment of special educational needs or the special educational provision and make any other consequential amendments as the First-tier Tribunal thinks fit;

(g) order the local authority to substitute in the EHC Plan the school or other institution or the type of school or other institution specified in the EHC plan, where the appeal concerns, the specific school or other institution, or the type of school or other institution named in the EHC Plan, where the appeal is made under section 51(2)(c)(iii) or (iv);

(h) where appropriate, when making an order in accordance with paragraph (g) this may include naming—

(i) a special school or institution approved under section 41 where a mainstream school or mainstream post-16 institution is specified in the EHC Plan; or

(ii) a mainstream school or mainstream post-16 institution where a special school or institution approved under section 41 is specified in the EHC Plan.

Compliance with the orders of the First-tier Tribunal

44.—(1) Subject to paragraph (3) or any direction made by the First-tier Tribunal, if the First-tier Tribunal makes an order requiring a local authority to take any action, the local authority shall take that action within the period specified in paragraph (2).

(2) Where the order—

(a) dismisses an appeal against a determination to cease an EHC Plan, the local authority shall cease to maintain the EHC Plan immediately;

(b) requires a local authority to make an assessment or reassessment, the local authority shall within 2 weeks of the order being made notify the child's parent or the young person that it shall make the assessment or reassessment and shall—

(i) where, following the assessment or reassessment, the local authority decides that it is not necessary for special educational provision to be made for the child or the young person, in accordance with an EHC plan, notify the child's parent or the young

20

person of its decision, giving reasons for it as soon as practicable, and in any event within 10 weeks of the date of the First-tier Tribunal's order; or

(ii) where, following the assessment or reassessment, it decides that it is necessary for special educational provision to be made for the child or the young person, in accordance with an EHC plan, it must send the finalised plan to those specified in regulation 13(2) as soon as practicable and in any event within 14 weeks of the date of the First-tier Tribunal's order;

(c) requires a local authority to make and maintain an EHC Plan, the local authority shall—

(i) issue a draft EHC Plan within 5 weeks of the order being made; and

(ii) send a copy of the finalised EHC plan to the child's parent or young person under Regulation 14, within 11 weeks of the order being made.

(d) refers the case back to the local authority for it to reconsider, the local authority shall do so within 2 weeks of the order being made and shall either send a copy of the draft EHC Plan as required under Regulation 13 or give notice as required under Regulation 5 of any decision not to maintain an EHC Plan;

(e) requires a local authority to amend the special educational provision specified in an EHC Plan, the local authority shall issue the amended EHC Plan within 5 weeks of the order being made;

(f) requires the local authority to amend the name of the school or other institution or the type of school or other institution specified in the EHC plan, the local authority shall issue the amended EHC plan within 2 weeks of the order being made;

(g) requires the local authority to continue to maintain an EHC Plan in its existing form, the local authority shall continue to maintain the EHC Plan; and

(h) to continue and amend an EHC Plan, the local authority shall continue to maintain the EHC Plan and amend the EHC Plan within 5 weeks of the order being made.

(3) The local authority need not comply with the time limits specified in paragraph (2)(b) and (c) if it is impractical to do so because—

(a) exceptional personal circumstances affect the child or their parent, or the young person during that period of time;

(b) the child or their parent or the young person is absent from the area of the authority for a continuous period of 2 weeks or more during that period of time; or

(c) any of the circumstances referred to in regulation 13(3) apply.

Unopposed appeals

45.—(1) This regulation applies where the child's parent or young person has appealed to the First-tier Tribunal and the local authority notifies the First-tier Tribunal that it will not oppose the appeal before it submits a response.

(2) The appeal is to be treated as if it was determined in favour of the appellant and the First-tier Tribunal is not required to make an order.

(3) Where the appeal concerned a request for a local authority to make an assessment under section 36 or a review or reassessment under section 44, the local authority shall carry out that assessment, review or reassessment within 4 weeks of the local authority's notification to the First-tier Tribunal.

(4) Where the appeal concerns the contents of the EHC Plan, then the local authority shall issue the amended EHC Plan within 4 weeks of the local authority's notification to the First-tier Tribunal.

(5) Where the appeal concerns the name of the school or other institution, or type of school or other institution to be named in the EHC plan, the local authority shall issue the amended EHC plan within 2 weeks of the local authority's notification to the First–tier Tribunal.

21

(6) Where the appeal concerns the refusal of the local authority to make an EHC Plan, then the local authority will arrange to make an EHC Plan within 5 weeks of the local authority's notification to the First-tier Tribunal.

(7) The local authority need not comply with the time limits specified in paragraphs (3), (4) or (6) if it is impractical to do so because—

    (a) exceptional personal circumstances affect the child or their parent or the young person during the relevant period;

    (b) the child or their parent or the young person are absent from the area of the local authority for a continuous period of not less than 2 weeks during the relevant period; or

    (c) any of the circumstances referred to in regulation 13(3) apply.

Miscellaneous provisions

Academic year

46.—(1) For the purposes of section 46 of the Act, an academic year is the period of twelve months which ends—

    (a) in relation to a young person attending an institution within the further education sector on 31st July;

    (b) in relation to a young person receiving apprenticeship training, on the date that that apprenticeship training finishes, or on the day before the young person attains the age of 26 if earlier;

    (c) in all other cases, on the day that the young person's course of education or training is scheduled to end, or on the day before the young person attains the age of 26 if earlier.

(2) In this regulation 'apprenticeship training' has the same meaning as in section 83(5) of the Apprenticeships, Skills, Children and Learning Act 2009(**a**).

Disclosure of EHC plans in relation to higher education

47. When a young person is intending to undertake a course of higher education, the local authority must disclose a copy of that young person's EHC plan to—

    (a) any person in connection with the young person's application for a disabled student's allowance in accordance with chapter 3 of part 5 of the Education (Student Support) Regulations 2011(**b**); and

    (b) the principal (or equivalent position) of the institution at which it has been confirmed that the young person has a place to undertake a course of higher education,

within 15 working days of being asked to do so by the young person.

Remaining in a special school or special post-16 institution without an EHC plan

48.—(1) Where a child or young person has been admitted to a special school or special post-16 institution for the purposes of an EHC needs assessment, he or she may remain at that school or post-16 institution—

    (a) for a period of ten school or institution days after the local authority serves a notice under section 36(9) of the Act informing the child's parent or the young person that it does not propose to make an EHC plan; or

    (b) until an EHC plan is finalised.

(**a**) 2009 c.22
(**b**) S.I.2011/1986

22

(2) In this regulation "school or institution day" means a day on which the school or post-16 institution is open to admit students.

PART 3

Duties on schools

Special Educational Needs Co-ordinators

Prescribed qualifications and experience of SENCOs

49.—(1) The appropriate authority of a relevant school must ensure that the SENCO appointed under section 67(2) of the Act meets all of the requirements in either paragraph (2) or (3).

(2) The requirements in this paragraph are that the SENCO—

(a) is a qualified teacher;

(b) if required to complete an induction period under regulations made under section 135A of the Education Act 2002(**a**), has satisfactorily completed such an induction period; and

(c) is working as a teacher at the school.

(3) The requirement in this paragraph is that the SENCO is the head teacher or acting head teacher (or equivalent in the case of an Academy school) of the school.

(4) Where a person becomes the SENCO at a relevant school after 1st September 2009, and has not previously been the SENCO at that or any other relevant school for a total period of more than twelve months, the appropriate authority of the school must ensure that, if the person is the SENCO at the school at any time after the third anniversary of the date on which that person becomes a SENCO, that person holds the qualification, mentioned in paragraph (5).

(5) The qualification referred to in paragraph (4) is a postgraduate qualification in special educational needs co-ordination, for the time being known as "The National Award for Special Educational Needs Co-ordination", awarded by a recognised body.

(6) For the purposes of paragraph (5), a recognised body is a body designated by the Secretary of State by order made under section 216(1) of the Education Reform Act 1988(**b**);

Appropriate authority functions and duties relating to the SENCO

50.—(1) The appropriate authority of a relevant school must determine the role of the SENCO in relation to the leadership and management of the school.

(2) The appropriate authority of a relevant school must determine the functions of the SENCO in addition to those under section 67(2) of the Act and monitor the effectiveness of the SENCO in undertaking those responsibilities.

(3) The functions referred to in paragraph (1) may include the carrying out, or arranging for the carrying out, of the following tasks—

(a) in relation to each of the registered pupils who the SENCO considers may have special educational needs, informing a parent of the pupil that this may be the case as soon as is reasonably practicable;

(b) in relation to each of the registered pupils who have special educational needs—

(i) identifying the pupil's special educational needs, and co-ordinating the making of special educational provision which meets those needs,

(ii) monitoring the effectiveness of any special educational provision made,

(iii) securing relevant services for the pupil where necessary,

---

(**a**) 2002 c.32. Section 135A was inserted by section 9 of the Education Act 2011 (c.21).
(**b**) 1988 c.40

23

    (iv) ensuring that records of the pupil's special educational needs and the special educational provision made are maintained and kept up to date,

    (v) liaising with and providing information to a parent of the pupil on a regular basis about that pupil's special educational needs and the special educational provision being made,

    (vi) ensuring that, where the pupil transfers to another school or educational institution, all relevant information about the pupil's special educational needs and the special educational provision made is conveyed to the appropriate authority or (as the case may be) the proprietor of that school or institution, and

    (vii) promoting the pupil's inclusion in the school community and access to the school's curriculum, facilities and extra-curricular activities;

(c) selecting, supervising and training learning support assistants who work with pupils with special educational needs;

(d) advising teachers at the school about differentiated teaching methods appropriate for individual pupils with special educational needs;

(e) contributing to in-service training for teachers at the school to assist them to carry out the tasks referred to in paragraph (b); and

(f) preparing and reviewing the information required to be published by the appropriate authority pursuant to regulation 51, the objectives of the appropriate authority in making provision for special educational needs, and the special educational needs policy referred to in paragraph 3 of Schedule 1 to these Regulations.

(4) For the purposes of paragraph (2)(b)(iii) "relevant services" means—

(a) special educational provision, or advice or assistance in relation to such provision or its management; and

(b) the assessment of special educational needs, or advice or assistance in relation to such needs or in relation to the management of pupils with such needs.

SEN information report

Prescribed information that must be included in SEN information report

51. For the purpose of section 69(3)(a) of the Act the SEN information which the governing body or proprietor of every maintained school, maintained nursery school and Academy school (other than a special school that is established in a hospital) must include in a report containing SEN information is set out in Schedule 1.

Manner of publication of report

52. The governing body or proprietor of the school must publish on the school's website its report containing SEN information.

PART 4

Local Offer

Information to be included in the local offer

53. A local authority must include the information in Schedule 2 when it publishes its local offer.

Consultation

54.—(1) When preparing and reviewing its local offer, a local authority must consult the following persons in its area—

24

   (a) children and young people with special educational needs and the parents of children with special educational needs;

   (b) children and young people with a disability, and the parents of children with a disability;

   (c) the governing bodies of maintained schools and maintained nursery schools;

   (d) the proprietors of Academies(a);

   (e) the governing bodies, proprietors or principals of post-16 institutions;

   (f) the governing bodies of non-maintained special schools;

   (g) the management committees of pupil referral units;

   (h) the advisory boards of children's centres;

   (i) the providers of relevant early years education;

   (j) the youth offending teams that the authority thinks have functions in relation to children or young people for whom it is responsible;

   (k) any other person that makes special educational provision for a child or young person for whom it is responsible and those who provide advice in relation to making that provision;

   (l) persons who make provision to assist children and young people in preparation for adulthood and independent living;

   (m) its officers who—

      (i) exercise the authority's functions relating to education or training;

      (ii) exercise the authority's social services functions for children or young people with special educational needs or a disability;

      (iii) so far as they are not officers within paragraph (i) or (ii), exercise the authority's functions relating to provision to assist children and young people in preparation for adulthood and independent living; and

   (n) such other persons as it thinks appropriate.

(2) When preparing and reviewing its local offer, a local authority must also consult—

   (a) the National Health Service Commissioning Board;

   (b) any clinical commissioning group—

      (i) whose area coincides with, or falls wholly or partly within, the local authority's area, or

      (ii) which exercises functions in relation to children or young people for whom the authority is responsible;

   (c) any NHS trust or NHS foundation trust which provides services in the authority's area, or which exercises functions in relation to children or young people for whom the authority is responsible;

   (d) any local Health Board which exercises functions in relation to children or young people for whom the authority is responsible;

   (e) any health and wellbeing board established under section 194 of the Health and Social Care Act 2012(b) which exercises functions in relation to children or young people for whom the authority is responsible.

(3) When preparing and reviewing its local offer, a local authority must also consult any bodies specified in paragraphs (1)(b) to (k) and (m) that are not in the local authority's area, but which the local authority thinks are or are likely to either—

   (a) be attended by children or young people for whom it is responsible; or

   (b) have functions in relation to children or young people for whom it is responsible.

(a) An academy has the same meaning as in section 1(10) of the Academies Act 2010
(b) 2012 c.7

25

Involvement of children, their parents and young people in preparation and review of local offer.

55. A local authority must consult children and young people with special educational needs or a disability and the parents of children with special educational needs or a disability in their area about—

(a) the services children and young people with special educational needs or a disability require;

(b) how the information in the local offer is to be set out when published;

(c) how the information in the local offer will be available for those people without access to the Internet;

(d) how the information in the local offer will be accessible to those with special educational needs or a disability;

(e) how they can provide comments on the local offer.

Publication of comments on the local offer

56.—(1) A local authority must seek from children and young people with special educational needs or a disability, and the parents of children with special educational needs or a disability comments on—

(a) the content of its local offer, including the quality of the provision that is included and any provision that is not included;

(b) the accessibility of the information contained in its local offer; and

(c) how the local offer has been developed or reviewed, including how those children, parents and young people have been involved in the development and review of the local offer.

(2) Subject to paragraph (3), a local authority must publish comments received by or on behalf of those people in accordance with paragraph (1), and its response to those comments (including details of any action the authority intends to take) on its website, with the local offer.

(3) Comments received and the local authority's response must be published at least annually, and must be in a form that does not enable any individual to be identified.

(4) The local authority is not required to publish or respond to any comments which—

(a) it considers to be vexatious; or

(b) relate to services provided to a particular individual.

Manner of publication

57. A local authority must—

(a) publish its local offer by placing it on their website;

(b) publish its arrangements for enabling—

(i) people without access to the Internet; and

(ii) different groups, including people with special educational needs or a disability,

to obtain a copy of the offer; and

(c) publish how those people identified in paragraph (b) can provide comments on the local offer.

26

PART 5

Approval of independent special schools and special post-16 institutions

Types of special post-16 institution that may be approved

58. The Secretary of State may approve a special post-16 institution under section 41 of the Act where it is not—

(a) an institution within the further education sector;

(b) a 16 to19 Academy(**a**);

(c) maintained by a local authority.

Matters to be taken into account in deciding to give approval

59.—(1) The Secretary of State may take into account the following matters when deciding whether to give approval to a special post 16 institution, an independent educational institution or an independent school—

(a) evidence relating to the financial viability of the institution;

(b) the proportion of children and young people attending the institution who have an EHC plan (or a statement of special educational needs or learning difficulty assessment); and

(c) reports relating to the institution by Her Majesty's Chief Inspector of Education, Children's Services and Skills, the Care Quality Commission(**b**), and any inspectorate which inspects independent schools in accordance with an agreement with the Secretary of State or which is approved by the Secretary of State under section 106 of the Education and Skills Act 2008(**c**).

(2) Where reports referred to in paragraph 1(c) are not available, the Secretary of State may consider such other evidence as the Secretary of State considers appropriate in relation to the quality of the educational provision at the institution or school concerned.

Matters to be taken into account in deciding to withdraw approval

60. The Secretary of State may take into account the following matters when deciding whether to withdraw approval—

(a) the matters identified in regulation 59(1); and

(b) any serious concerns about the institution received from a local authority or a child or young person attending the institution or from any other person.

Procedure when the Secretary of State decides to withdraw approval

61.—(1) When the Secretary of State decides to withdraw the approval of an institution, the Secretary of State must notify the proprietor of the institution of that decision.

(2) The Secretary of State must also notify all local authorities in England of that decision.

(3) The decision will take effect 28 days after that notification is given, and shall remove the institution from the list published in accordance with regulation 62 on the date that the decision takes effect.

(a) 16 to19 Academy has the same meaning as section 1B of the Academies Act 2010. Section 1B was inserted by section 53(7) of the 2011 Act
(b) The Care Quality Commission was established under section 1 of the Health and Social Care Act 2008 (c.14)
(c) 2008 c.25

27

SPECIAL EDUCATIONAL NEEDS AND DISABILITY REGULATIONS 2014

Publication of list of approved institutions

62. The Secretary of State must publish a list of all institutions that have been approved, and have not had that approval withdrawn, on the Internet.

PART 6

Parents and young people lacking capacity

Where a child's parent lacks capacity

63. In a case where a child's parent lacks capacity at the relevant time references in—

(a) Part 3 of the Act, and

(b) these regulations, except the references in regulation 6(1)(b)(iv) and paragraph 15(b) of Schedule 2,

to a child's parent or the parent of a detained person who is a child are to be read as references to a representative of the parent.

Where a young person lacks capacity

64.—(1) In a case where a young person lacks capacity at the relevant time—

(a) references to a young person in the provisions of Part 3 of the Act listed in Part 1 of Schedule 3 are to be read as references to both the young person and the alternative person;

(b) references to a young person or a detained person who is a young person in the provisions of Part 3 of the Act listed in Part 2 of Schedule 3 are to be read as references to the alternative person instead of the young person; and

(c) references to a young person in these regulations listed in Part 3 of Schedule 3 are to be read as references to both the young person and the alternative person; and

(d) references to a young person in these regulations listed in Part 4 of Schedule 3 are to be read as references to the alternative person instead of the young person.

(2) For the purposes of this regulation, "the alternative person" means—

(a) a representative of the young person;

(b) the young person's parent, where the young person does not have a representative;

(c) a representative of the young person's parent, where the young person's parent also lacks capacity at the relevant time and the young person does not have a representative.

Mental Capacity Act 2005

65. Regulations 63 and 64 have effect in spite of section 27(1)(g) of the Mental Capacity Act 2005(**a**).

Edward Timpson
Parliamentary Under Secretary of State
Department for Education

4th June 2014

(a) 2005 c.9 Section 27(1)(g) does not permit decisions on discharging parental responsibilities in matters not relating to a child's property to be made on a person's behalf.

28

SCHEDULE 1 Regulation 51

Information to be included in the SEN information report

1. The kinds of special educational needs for which provision is made at the school.

2. Information, in relation to mainstream schools and maintained nursery schools, about the school's policies for the identification and assessment of pupils with special educational needs.

3. Information about the school's policies for making provision for pupils with special educational needs whether or not pupils have EHC Plans, including—

    (a) how the school evaluates the effectiveness of its provision for such pupils;

    (b) the school's arrangements for assessing and reviewing the progress of pupils with special educational needs;

    (c) the school's approach to teaching pupils with special educational needs;

    (d) how the school adapts the curriculum and learning environment for pupils with special educational needs;

    (e) additional support for learning that is available to pupils with special educational needs;

    (f) how the school enables pupils with special educational needs to engage in the activities of the school (including physical activities) together with children who do not have special educational needs; and

    (g) support that is available for improving the emotional, mental and social development of pupils with special educational needs.

4. In relation to mainstream schools and maintained nursery schools, the name and contact details of the SEN co-ordinator.

5. Information about the expertise and training of staff in relation to children and young people with special educational needs and about how specialist expertise will be secured.

6. Information about how equipment and facilities to support children and young people with special educational needs will be secured.

7. The arrangements for consulting parents of children with special educational needs about, and involving such parents in, the education of their child.

8. The arrangements for consulting young people with special educational needs about, and involving them in, their education.

9. Any arrangements made by the governing body or the proprietor relating to the treatment of complaints from parents of pupils with special educational needs concerning the provision made at the school.

10. How the governing body involves other bodies, including health and social services bodies, local authority support services and voluntary organisations, in meeting the needs of pupils with special educational needs and in supporting the families of such pupils

11. The contact details of support services for the parents of pupils with special educational needs, including those for arrangements made in accordance with section 32.

12. The school's arrangements for supporting pupils with special educational needs in a transfer between phases of education or in preparation for adulthood and independent living.

13. Information on where the local authority's local offer is published.

29

SCHEDULE 2   Regulation 53

Information to be published by a local authority in its local offer

1. The special educational provision and training provision which the local authority expects to be available in its area for children and young people in its area who have special educational needs or a disability by—

(a) providers of relevant early years education;

(b) maintained schools, including provision made available in any separate unit;

(c) Academies, including provision made available in any separate unit;

(d) non-maintained special schools;

(e) post-16 institutions;

(f) institutions approved under section 41 of the Act;

(g) pupil referral units; and

(h) persons commissioned by the local authority to support children and young people with special educational needs or a disability.

2. The special educational provision and training provision the local authority expects to be made outside its area by persons specified in sub-paragraphs (a) to (g) of paragraph 1 for children and young people in its area with special educational needs or a disability.

3. The information in paragraphs 1 and 2 must include information about—

(a) the special educational provision and training provision provided for children and young people with special educational needs or a disability by mainstream schools and mainstream post-16 institutions including any support provided in relation to learning or the curriculum;

(b) the special educational provision and training provision provided by special schools and special post-16 institutions, and those approved under section 41 of the Act;

(c) the special educational provision and training provision secured by the local authority in mainstream schools, mainstream post-16 institutions, pupil referral units and alternative provision Academies for children and young people with special educational needs or a disability; and

(d) the arrangements the local authority has for funding children and young people with special educational needs including any agreements about how any of the persons specified in paragraph 1 will use any budget that has been delegated to that person by the local authority.

4. The arrangements the persons specified in paragraphs 1 and 2 have for—

(a) identifying the particular special educational needs of children and young people;

(b) consulting with parents of children with special educational needs or a disability and with young people with special educational needs or a disability;

(c) securing the services, provision and equipment required by children and young people with special educational needs or a disability; and

(d) supporting children and young people with special educational needs or a disability in a transfer between phases of education and transfers from one post-16 institution to another, and in preparation for adulthood and independent living.

5. Information, in relation to the persons specified in paragraphs 1 and 2, about-

(a) their approach to teaching of children and young people with special educational needs;

(b) how they adapt the curriculum and the learning environment for children and young people with special educational needs or a disability;

(c) the additional learning support available to children and young people with special educational needs;

(d) how the progress towards any of the outcomes identified for children and young people with special educational needs will be assessed and reviewed, including information about how those children, their parents and young people will take part in any assessment and review;

(e) how the effectiveness of special educational provision and training provision will be assessed and evaluated, including information about how children, their parents and young people will take part in any assessment and evaluation;

(f) how facilities that are available can be accessed by children and young people with special educational needs or a disability;

(g) what activities (including physical activities) are available for children and young people with special educational needs or a disability in addition to the curriculum;

(h) what support is available for children and young people with special educational needs or a disability;

(i) how expertise in supporting children and young people with special educational needs or a disability is secured for teaching staff and others working with those children and young people;

(j) how the emotional, mental and social development of children and young people with special educational needs or a disability will be supported and improved.

6. Where further information about the bodies specified in paragraphs 1 and 2, including the information required by section 69 of the Act, can be obtained.

7. Where the strategy prepared by the local authority under paragraph 1 of Schedule 10 to the Equality Act 2010(**a**) can be obtained.

8. Special educational provision and training provision the local authority expects to be made in relation to young people with special educational needs or a disability who have entered into an apprenticeship agreement within the meaning of section 32(1) of the Apprenticeships, Skills, Children and Learning Act 2009.

9. Special educational provision and training provision the local authority expects to be made by providers of training in its area, and outside its area for young people in its area with special educational needs or a disability.

10. Provision available in the local authority's area to assist children and young people with special educational needs or a disability in preparation for adulthood and independent living.

11. Information about support available to young people with special educational needs or a disability receiving higher education, including any disabled student's allowance available under chapter 3 of Part 5 of the Education (Student Support) Regulations 2011(**b**).

12. Health care provision for children and young people with special educational needs or a disability that is additional to or different from that which is available to all children and young people in the area, including—

(a) services for relevant early years providers, schools and post-16 institutions to assist them in supporting children and young people with medical conditions, and

(b) arrangements for making those services which are available to all children and young people in the area accessible to children and young people with special educational needs or a disability.

(a) 2010 c.15
(b) SI 2011/1986, as amended by the Education (Student Fees, Awards and Support) (Amendment) Regulations 2012[SI 2012/1628] and Education (Student Support and European University Institute) (Amendment) Regulations 2013[SI 2013/1728]

31

13. Social care provision for children and young people with special educational needs or a disability and their families including—

    (a) services provided in accordance with section 17 of the Children Act 1989;

    (b) the arrangements for supporting young people when moving from receiving services for children to receiving services for adults;

    (c) support for young people in planning and obtaining support to assist with independent living;

    (d) information and advice services made available in accordance with section 4 of the Care Act 2014(**a**).

14. Transport arrangements for children and young people with special educational needs or a disability to get to and from school or post-16 institution, or other institution in which they are receiving special educational provision or training provision including—

    (a) arrangements for specialist transport;

    (b) arrangements for free or subsidised transport;

    (c) support available in relation to the cost of transport, whether from the local authority or otherwise.

15. Sources of information, advice and support in the local authority's area for children and young people with special educational needs or a disability and their families including information—

    (a) provided in accordance with section 32 of the Act;

    (b) about forums for parents and carers of children and young people with special educational needs or a disability;

    (c) about support groups for children and young people with special educational needs or a disability and their families;

    (d) about childcare for children with special educational needs or a disability;

    (e) about leisure activities for children and young people with special educational needs or a disability and their families;

    (f) about persons who can provide further support, information and advice for children and young people with special educational needs or a disability and their families.

16. The procedure for making a complaint about provision mentioned in section 30(2) of the Act.

17. The procedure for making a complaint about any provision or service set out in the local offer.

18. Information about any criteria that must be satisfied before any provision or service set out in the local offer can be provided.

19. Information about how to request an EHC needs assessment, and the availability of personal budgets.

20. Information on where the list of institutions approved under section 41 of the Act is published.

21. Arrangements for notifying parents and young people of their right to appeal a decision of the local authority to the Tribunal.

22. Arrangements for mediation made in accordance with section 53 or 54 of the Act.

(**a**) 2014 c.23

32

23. Arrangements for the resolution of disagreements made in accordance with section 57 of the Act.

SCHEDULE 3

PART 1   Regulation 64(1)(a)

References to a young person in the Act that are to be read as references to both a young person and an alternative person

The provisions referred to in regulation 64(1)(a) are—

section 19(a), (b), (c) and (d) (first reference);

section 27(3)(a) and (b);

section 30(6)(a)(i) and (ii);

section 30(8)(d)(i) and (ii);

section 32(1) (first reference) and (2) (first reference);

section 32(3)(c).

PART 2   Regulation 64(1)(b)

References to a young person in the Act that are to be read as references to an alternative person

The provisions referred to in regulation 64(1)(b) are—

section 33(2)(a);

section 34(5)(c) and (7)(c);

section 36(1) (second reference), (4), (5) (second reference), (7) (opening words and paragraph (b)) and (9) (opening words);

section 38(1) (second reference), (2)(a) and (b), and (5);

section 39(8)(a);

section 40(5)(a);

section 42(5);

section 44(2)(a) and (6);

section 49(1) (second reference), (2) (second reference), (3)(d) and (4)(a);

section 51(1) and (3) (opening words);

section 52(2), (3) and (4) ;

section 53(1)(a), (3)(a) and (4)(a)(i);

section 54(1)(a) and (2)(a);

section 55(1), (3), (4) (opening words and (b)) and (5) (both references);

section 56(1)(f);

section 57(2)(b), (3)(b), (5)(a) and (8)(b);

section 61(3);

section 68(2) (first reference);

section 70(5) (paragraph (b) of the definition of "appropriate person").

33

PART 3

Regulation 64(1)(c)

References to a young person in the Act that are to be read as references to both a young person and an alternative person

The provisions referred to in regulation 64(1)(c) are—

regulation 5(4)(c) and (d);

regulation 7(a), (b), (d) and (e);

regulation 8(2)(a) and (b);

regulation 10(4)(c) and (d);

regulation 12(1)(a);

regulation 17(1)(c) (second reference);

regulation 19(a);

regulation 27(3)(c) and (d)

regulation 41(1) (opening words); and the description accompanying 'Travel Costs'

regulation 44(3)(a) and (b);

regulation 45(7)(a) and (b);

regulation 54(1)(a) and (b)

regulation 55(opening words);

regulation 56(1) (opening words) and (c);

Schedule 2 paragraph 5(d) (second reference) and (e)

PART 4

Regulation 64(1)(d)

References to a young person in the Act that are to be read as references to an alternative person

The provisions referred to in regulation 64(1)(d) are—

regulation 3 (opening words);

regulation 4(1) (opening words);

regulation 5(1) (opening words) and (3);

regulation 6(1)(a) and (h), (3)(a) and (b) and (4);

regulation 9;

regulation 10 (3);

regulation 13(1) and (2)(a);

regulation 14(2);

regulation 15(3)(b);

regulation 17(1) (second reference in opening words);

regulation 20(2)(a), (10), and (11)(second reference in opening words)

regulation 21(2)(a), (9), and (10)(second reference in opening words);

regulation 22(2)(a) and (b), (3)(opening words and (a)), (4) and (5) (opening words);

regulation 25(1) (first reference);

regulation 27(2)(a);

34

regulation 31(1)(a) (first reference) and (b), (2) (second reference) and (3) (opening words);

regulation 32;

regulation 33;

regulation 34;

regulation 35;

regulation 36;

regulation 37;

regulation 38(1)(b);

regulation 39;

regulation 44 (2)(b)(opening words)(i) (second reference); and (2)(c)(ii);

regulation 45(1);

Schedule 2 paragraph 4(b).

EXPLANATORY NOTE

(This note is not part of the Regulations)

These Regulations supplement the procedural framework assessing a child or young person with special educational needs, and the procedure for making, reviewing, amending and ceasing to maintain an EHC plan, set out in Part 3 of the Children and Families Act 2014 ("the Act"). They require local authorities to notify the child's parent or the young person of decisions within certain timescales, as well as notifying them of any right to appeal such decision. *(regulations 3 to 31)*.

The Regulations include details of mediation, both where mediation has to be considered before issuing an appeal in the First-tier Tribunal, and where mediation is desired in any other case, and the action local authority and commissioning bodies must take as a result of the mediation *(regulations 32 to 42)*.

The Regulations also set out the powers of the First-tier Tribunal and the timescales in which local authorities must comply with orders of the Tribunal *(regulations 43 to 45)*.

The Regulations prescribe the period of the academic year, for the purposes of continuing to maintain an EHC plan beyond a young person's 25th birthday *(regulation 46)*. They also make provision requiring a local authority to disclose an EHC plan to a person in connection with an assessment for a disabled student's allowance in connection with undertaking higher education, and to the higher education institution itself, at the request of the young person *(regulation 47)*. They set out the time period in which a child or young person may remain at a special school or post-16 institution when admitted for the purposes of an assessment *(regulation 48)*.

The Regulations set out the qualifications and experience that SENCOs must have *(regulation 49)* and details of functions in relation to those SENCOs *(regulation 50)*. They also set out details of the information to be included in a school's SEN information report and requirements for publication *(regulations 51 and 52 and schedule 1)*.

Provision is made in relation to the local offer. The Regulations set out details of what must be included in the local offer *(regulation 53 and Schedule 2)* and who the local authority must consult about the local offer *(regulations 54 and 55)*, as well as requirements in relation to publication *(regulations 56 and 57)*.

The Regulations also make provision in relation to approving schools and post-16 institutions under section 41. They set out the type of special post-16 institution that can be approved, and matters to be taken into account when approving such institutions and independent educational institutions and independent schools. They also set out the matters to be taken into account and the

35

procedure when withdrawing approval, and require the list of approved institutions to be published (*regulations 58-62*).

Part 6 of the Regulations deals with parents and young people who lack mental capacity to take the decisions or actions required. For the purposes of the Act, a person lacks capacity when they lack capacity within the meaning of the Mental Capacity Act 2005, that is when they lack mental, and not legal capacity. The Regulations provide that where a child's parent lacks capacity all references to a child's parent in Part 3 of the Act and all references in these Regulations (except two which are identified in regulation 63) are to be read as a reference to the representative of the parent (*regulation 63*). The Regulations also provide that, where a young person lacks capacity, the references to a young person in provisions in the Act identified in Part 1 of Schedule 3 to the Regulations are to be read as if they referred to both the young person and his alternative person; the references to a young person in provisions in the Act identified in Part 2 of Schedule 3 are to be read as if they referred to the young person's alternative person instead of the young person; the references to a young person in the provisions in these Regulations identified in Part 3 of Schedule 3 are to be read as if they referred to both the young person and to his alternative person; and the references to a young person in the provisions in these Regulations identified in Part 4 of Schedule 3 are to be read as if they referred to the young person's alternative person instead of to the young person (*regulation 65 and Schedule 3*).

The provisions identified in Parts 1 and 3 of Schedule 3 are those provisions in which, in relation to a child rather than a young person, both the child and the child's parent are involved in the decision or action. The provisions identified in Parts 2 and 4 of Schedule 3 are those provisions in which, in relation to a child rather than a young person, only the child's parent is involved.

The Regulations also make clear that the provisions concerning mental capacity have effect in spite of section 27(1)(g) of the Mental Capacity Act 2005 (*regulation 65*)

Printed and published in the UK by The Stationery Office Limited under the authority and superintendence of Carol Tullo, Controller of Her Majesty's Stationery Office and Queen's Printer of Acts of Parliament.

UK2014061015 06/2014 19585

http://www.legislation.gov.uk/id/uksi/2014/1530

THE FIRST-TIER TRIBUNAL PROCEDURE RULES

STATUTORY INSTRUMENTS

2008 No. 2699 (L. 16)

TRIBUNALS AND INQUIRIES, ENGLAND AND WALES

The Tribunal Procedure (First-tier Tribunal)
(Health, Education and Social Care Chamber) Rules 2008

ISBN 978-0-11-084619-4

CORRECTION

Page 3, in the preamble, first paragraph, line one: "...in accordance with paragraph 28(1) of the Tribunals, Courts and ..." should read, "...in accordance with paragraph 28(1) of Schedule 5 to the Tribunals, Courts and ...".

September 2009

PRINTED IN THE UNITED KINGDOM BY THE STATIONERY OFFICE LIMITED
under the authority and superintendence of Carol Tullo, Controller of Her Majesty's Stationery Office
and Queen's Printer of Acts of Parliament

STATUTORY INSTRUMENTS

2008 No. 2699 (L. 16)

TRIBUNALS AND INQUIRIES, ENGLAND AND WALES

The Tribunal Procedure (First-tier Tribunal)
(Health, Education and Social Care Chamber) Rules 2008

Made - - - -	*9th October 2008*
Laid before Parliament	*15th October 2008*
Coming into force - -	*3rd November 2008*

CONTENTS

PART 1
Introduction

PART 2
General powers and provisions

PART 3
Proceedings before the Tribunal other than in mental health cases
CHAPTER 1
Before the hearing

CHAPTER 2
Hearings

CHAPTER 3
Decisions

PART 4
Proceedings before the Tribunal in mental health cases
CHAPTER 1
Before the hearing

CHAPTER 2
Hearings

CHAPTER 3
Decisions

2

PART 5

Correcting, setting aside, reviewing and appealing Tribunal decisions

After consulting in accordance with paragraph 28(1) of the Tribunals, Courts and Enforcement Act 2007(**a**), the Tribunal Procedure Committee has made the following Rules in exercise of the power conferred by sections 9(3), 22 and 29(3) and (4) of, and Schedule 5 to, that Act.

The Lord Chancellor has allowed the Rules in accordance with paragraph 28(3) of Schedule 5 to the Tribunals, Courts and Enforcement Act 2007.

PART 1

Introduction

Citation, commencement, application and interpretation

1.—(1) These Rules may be cited as the Tribunal Procedure (First-tier Tribunal) (Health, Education and Social Care Chamber) Rules 2008 and come into force on 3rd November 2008.

(2) These Rules apply to proceedings before the Tribunal which have been assigned to the Health, Education and Social Care Chamber by the First-tier Tribunal and Upper Tribunal (Chambers) Order 2008(**b**).

(3) In these Rules—

"the 2007 Act" means the Tribunals, Courts and Enforcement Act 2007;

"applicant" means a person who—

(a) starts Tribunal proceedings, whether by making an application, an appeal, a claim or a reference;

(b) makes an application to the Tribunal for leave to start such proceedings; or

(c) is substituted as an applicant under rule 9(1) (substitution and addition of parties);

"childcare provider" means a person who is a childminder or provides day care as defined in section 79A of the Children Act 1989(**c**), or a person who provides childcare as defined in section 18 of the Childcare Act 2006(**d**);

(**a**) 2007 c.15.
(**b**) S.I. 2008/2684.
(**c**) 1989 c.41. Section 79A was inserted by section 79(1) of the Care Standards Act 2000 (c.14).
(**d**) 2006 c.21.

3

"disability discrimination in schools case" means proceedings concerning disability discrimination in the education of a child or related matters;

"dispose of proceedings" includes, unless indicated otherwise, disposing of a part of the proceedings;

"document" means anything in which information is recorded in any form, and an obligation under these Rules or any practice direction or direction to provide or allow access to a document or a copy of a document for any purpose means, unless the Tribunal directs otherwise, an obligation to provide or allow access to such document or copy in a legible form or in a form which can be readily made into a legible form;

"Health, Education and Social Care Chamber" means the Health, Education and Social Care Chamber of the First-tier Tribunal established by the First-tier Tribunal and Upper Tribunal (Chambers) Order 2008;

"hearing" means an oral hearing and includes a hearing conducted in whole or in part by video link, telephone or other means of instantaneous two-way electronic communication;

"legal representative" means an authorised advocate or authorised litigator as defined by section 119(1) of the Courts and Legal Services Act 1990(**a**);

"mental health case" means proceedings brought under the Mental Health Act 1983(**b**) or paragraph 5(2) of the Schedule to the Repatriation of Prisoners Act 1984(**c**);

"nearest relative" has the meaning set out in section 26 of the Mental Health Act 1983;

"party" means—

(a) in a mental health case, the patient, the responsible authority, the Secretary of State (if the patient is a restricted patient or in a reference under rule 32(8) (seeking approval under section 86 of the Mental Health Act 1983)), and any other person who starts a mental health case by making an application;

(b) in any other case, a person who is an applicant or respondent in proceedings before the Tribunal or, if the proceedings have been concluded, a person who was an applicant or respondent when the Tribunal finally disposed of all issues in the proceedings;

"patient" means the person who is the subject of a mental health case;

"practice direction" means a direction given under section 23 of the 2007 Act;

"respondent" means—

(a) in an appeal against an order made by a justice of the peace under section 79K of the Children Act 1989(**d**), section 20 of the Care Standards Act 2000(**e**) or section 72 of the Childcare Act 2006, the person who applied to the justice of the peace for the order;

(b) in an appeal against any other decision, the person who made the decision;

(c) in proceedings on a claim under section 28I of the Disability Discrimination Act 1995(**f**), the body responsible for the school as determined in accordance with paragraph 1 of Schedule 4A to that Act or, if the claim concerns the residual duties of a local education authority under section 28F of that Act, that local education authority;

(d) in proceedings on an application under section 4(2) of the Protection of Children Act 1999(**g**) or section 86(2) of the Care Standards Act 2000, the Secretary of State; or

(e) a person substituted or added as a respondent under rule 9 (substitution and addition of parties);

"responsible authority" means—

(**a**) 1990 c.41.
(**b**) 1983 c.20.
(**c**) 1984 c.47.
(**d**) 1989 c.41. Section 79K was inserted by section 79(1) of the Care Standards Act 2000 (c.14).
(**e**) 2000 c.14.
(**f**) 1995 c.50. Section 28F was inserted by section 16 of the Special Educational Needs and Disability Act 2001 (c.10), section 28I was inserted by section 18 of that Act, and Schedule 4A was inserted by section 11(2) of, and Schedule 2 to, that Act.
(**g**) 1999 c.14.

4

(a) in relation to a patient detained under the Mental Health Act 1983 in a hospital within the meaning of Part 2 of that Act, the managers (as defined in section 145 of that Act);

(b) in relation to a patient subject to guardianship, the responsible local social services authority (as defined in section 34(3) of the Mental Health Act 1983);

(c) in relation to a community patient, the managers of the responsible hospital (as defined in section 145 of the Mental Health Act 1983);

(d) in relation to a patient subject to after-care under supervision, the Primary Care Trust or Local Health Board which has the duty to provide after-care for the patient.

"restricted patient" has the meaning set out in section 79(1) of the Mental Health Act 1983;

"special educational needs case" means proceedings concerning the education of a child who has or may have special educational needs;

"Suspension Regulations" means regulations which provide for a right of appeal against a decision to suspend, or not to lift the suspension of, a person's registration as a childcare provider;

"Tribunal" means the First-tier Tribunal;

"working day" means any day except a Saturday or Sunday, Christmas Day, Good Friday or a bank holiday under section 1 of the Banking and Financial Dealings Act 1971(**a**).

Overriding objective and parties' obligation to co-operate with the Tribunal

2.—(1) The overriding objective of these Rules is to enable the Tribunal to deal with cases fairly and justly.

(2) Dealing with a case fairly and justly includes—

(a) dealing with the case in ways which are proportionate to the importance of the case, the complexity of the issues, the anticipated costs and the resources of the parties;

(b) avoiding unnecessary formality and seeking flexibility in the proceedings;

(c) ensuring, so far as practicable, that the parties are able to participate fully in the proceedings;

(d) using any special expertise of the Tribunal effectively; and

(e) avoiding delay, so far as compatible with proper consideration of the issues.

(3) The Tribunal must seek to give effect to the overriding objective when it—

(a) exercises any power under these Rules; or

(b) interprets any rule or practice direction.

(4) Parties must—

(a) help the Tribunal to further the overriding objective; and

(b) co-operate with the Tribunal generally.

Alternative dispute resolution and arbitration

3.—(1) The Tribunal should seek, where appropriate—

(a) to bring to the attention of the parties the availability of any appropriate alternative procedure for the resolution of the dispute; and

(b) if the parties wish and provided that it is compatible with the overriding objective, to facilitate the use of the procedure.

(2) Part 1 of the Arbitration Act 1996(**b**) does not apply to proceedings before the Tribunal.

(**a**) 1971 c.80.
(**b**) 1996 c.23.

PART 2

General powers and provisions

Delegation to staff

4.—(1) Staff appointed under section 40(1) of the 2007 Act (tribunal staff and services) may, with the approval of the Senior President of Tribunals, carry out functions of a judicial nature permitted or required to be done by the Tribunal.

(2) The approval referred to at paragraph (1) may apply generally to the carrying out of specified functions by members of staff of a specified description in specified circumstances.

(3) Within 14 days after the date on which the Tribunal sends notice of a decision made by a member of staff under paragraph (1) to a party, that party may apply in writing to the Tribunal for that decision to be considered afresh by a judge.

Case management powers

5.—(1) Subject to the provisions of the 2007 Act and any other enactment, the Tribunal may regulate its own procedure.

(2) The Tribunal may give a direction in relation to the conduct or disposal of proceedings at any time, including a direction amending, suspending or setting aside an earlier direction.

(3) In particular, and without restricting the general powers in paragraphs (1) and (2), the Tribunal may—

    (a) extend or shorten the time for complying with any rule, practice direction or direction, unless such extension or shortening would conflict with a provision of another enactment containing a time limit(**a**);

    (b) consolidate or hear together two or more sets of proceedings or parts of proceedings raising common issues, or treat a case as a lead case;

    (c) permit or require a party to amend a document;

    (d) permit or require a party or another person to provide documents, information or submissions to the Tribunal or a party;

    (e) deal with an issue in the proceedings as a preliminary issue;

    (f) hold a hearing to consider any matter, including a case management issue;

    (g) decide the form of any hearing;

    (h) adjourn or postpone a hearing;

    (i) require a party to produce a bundle for a hearing;

    (j) stay proceedings;

    (k) transfer proceedings to another court or tribunal if that other court or tribunal has jurisdiction in relation to the proceedings and—

        (i) because of a change of circumstances since the proceedings were started, the Tribunal no longer has jurisdiction in relation to the proceedings; or

        (ii) the Tribunal considers that the other court or tribunal is a more appropriate forum for the determination of the case; or

    (l) suspend the effect of its own decision pending the determination by the Tribunal or the Upper Tribunal of an application for permission to appeal against, and any appeal or review of, that decision.

(**a**) Provisions in primary legislation which contain time limits include: sections 66(1) and (2), 68(2) (subject to any order made under section 68A), 69(1), (2) and (4), 70, 71(2) (subject to any order made under section 71(3)) and 75(1) and (2) of the Mental Health Act 1983; sections 21(2) and 86(5) of the Care Standards Act 2000; section 166(2) of the Education Act 2002 (c.32); and section 32(2) of the Health and Social Care Act 2008 (c.14).

Procedure for applying for and giving directions

6.—(1) The Tribunal may give a direction on the application of one or more of the parties or on its own initiative.

(2) An application for a direction may be made—

(a) by sending or delivering a written application to the Tribunal; or

(b) orally during the course of a hearing.

(3) An application for a direction must include the reason for making that application.

(4) Unless the Tribunal considers that there is good reason not to do so, the Tribunal must send written notice of any direction to every party and to any other person affected by the direction.

(5) If a party, or any other person given notice of the direction under paragraph (4), wishes to challenge a direction which the Tribunal has given, they may do so by applying for another direction which amends, suspends or sets aside the first direction.

Failure to comply with rules etc.

7.—(1) An irregularity resulting from a failure to comply with any requirement in these Rules, a practice direction or a direction, does not of itself render void the proceedings or any step taken in the proceedings.

(2) If a party has failed to comply with a requirement in these Rules, a practice direction or a direction, the Tribunal may take such action as it considers just, which may include—

(a) waiving the requirement;

(b) requiring the failure to be remedied;

(c) exercising its power under rule 8 (striking out a party's case);

(d) exercising its power under paragraph (3); or

(e) except in mental health cases, restricting a party's participation in the proceedings.

(3) The Tribunal may refer to the Upper Tribunal, and ask the Upper Tribunal to exercise its power under section 25 of the 2007 Act in relation to, any failure by a person to comply with a requirement imposed by the Tribunal—

(a) to attend at any place for the purpose of giving evidence;

(b) otherwise to make themselves available to give evidence;

(c) to swear an oath in connection with the giving of evidence;

(d) to give evidence as a witness;

(e) to produce a document; or

(f) to facilitate the inspection of a document or any other thing (including any premises).

Striking out a party's case

8.—(1) With the exception of paragraph (3), this rule does not apply to mental health cases.

(2) The proceedings, or the appropriate part of them, will automatically be struck out if the applicant has failed to comply with a direction that stated that failure by the applicant to comply with the direction would lead to the striking out of the proceedings or that part of them.

(3) The Tribunal must strike out the whole or a part of the proceedings if the Tribunal—

(a) does not have jurisdiction in relation to the proceedings or that part of them; and

(b) does not exercise its power under rule 5(3)(k)(i) (transfer to another court or tribunal) in relation to the proceedings or that part of them.

(4) The Tribunal may strike out the whole or a part of the proceedings if—

7

(a) the applicant has failed to comply with a direction which stated that failure by the applicant to comply with the direction could lead to the striking out of the proceedings or part of them;

(b) the applicant has failed to co-operate with the Tribunal to such an extent that the Tribunal cannot deal with the proceedings fairly and justly; or

(c) the Tribunal considers there is no reasonable prospect of the applicant's case, or part of it, succeeding.

(5) The Tribunal may not strike out the whole or a part of the proceedings under paragraph (3) or (4)(b) or (c) without first giving the applicant an opportunity to make representations in relation to the proposed striking out.

(6) If the proceedings, or part of them, have been struck out under paragraph (2) or (4)(a), the applicant may apply for the proceedings, or part of them, to be reinstated.

(7) An application under paragraph (6) must be made in writing and received by the Tribunal within 28 days after the date on which the Tribunal sent notification of the striking out to that party.

(8) This rule applies to a respondent as it applies to an applicant except that—

(a) a reference to the striking out of the proceedings is to be read as a reference to the barring of the respondent from taking further part in the proceedings; and

(b) a reference to an application for the reinstatement of proceedings which have been struck out is to be read as a reference to an application for the lifting of the bar on the respondent from taking further part in the proceedings.

(9) If a respondent has been barred from taking further part in proceedings under this rule and that bar has not been lifted, the Tribunal need not consider any response or other submission made by that respondent.

Substitution and addition of parties

9.—(1) The Tribunal may give a direction substituting a party if—

(a) the wrong person has been named as a party; or

(b) the substitution has become necessary because of a change in circumstances since the start of proceedings.

(2) The Tribunal may give a direction adding a person to the proceedings as a respondent.

(3) If the Tribunal gives a direction under paragraph (1) or (2) it may give such consequential directions as it considers appropriate.

Orders for costs

10.—(1) Subject to paragraph (2), the Tribunal may make an order in respect of costs only—

(a) under section 29(4) of the 2007 Act (wasted costs); or

(b) if the Tribunal considers that a party or its representative has acted unreasonably in bringing, defending or conducting the proceedings.

(2) The Tribunal may not make an order under paragraph (1)(b) in mental health cases.

(3) The Tribunal may make an order in respect of costs on an application or on its own initiative.

(4) A person making an application for an order under this rule must—

(a) send or deliver a written application to the Tribunal and to the person against whom it is proposed that the order be made; and

(b) send or deliver a schedule of the costs claimed with the application.

(5) An application for an order under paragraph (1) may be made at any time during the proceedings but may not be made later than 14 days after the date on which the Tribunal sends the decision notice recording the decision which finally disposes of all issues in the proceedings.

8

(6) The Tribunal may not make an order under paragraph (1) against a person (the "paying person") without first—

(a) giving that person an opportunity to make representations; and

(b) if the paying person is an individual, considering that person's financial means.

(7) The amount of costs to be paid under an order under paragraph (1) may be ascertained by—

(a) summary assessment by the Tribunal;

(b) agreement of a specified sum by the paying person and the person entitled to receive the costs ("the receiving person"); or

(c) assessment of the whole or a specified part of the costs incurred by the receiving person, if not agreed.

(8) Following an order for assessment under paragraph (7)(c), the paying person or the receiving person may apply to a county court for a detailed assessment of costs in accordance with the Civil Procedure Rules 1998(a) on the standard basis or, if specified in the order, on the indemnity basis.

Representatives

11.—(1) A party may appoint a representative (whether a legal representative or not) to represent that party in the proceedings.

(2) If a party appoints a representative, that party (or the representative if the representative is a legal representative) must send or deliver to the Tribunal and to each other party written notice of the representative's name and address.

(3) Anything permitted or required to be done by a party under these Rules, a practice direction or a direction may be done by the representative of that party, except—

(a) signing a witness statement; or

(b) signing an application notice under rule 20 (the application notice) if the representative is not a legal representative.

(4) A person who receives due notice of the appointment of a representative—

(a) must provide to the representative any document which is required to be provided to the represented party, and need not provide that document to the represented party; and

(b) may assume that the representative is and remains authorised as such until they receive written notification that this is not so from the representative or the represented party.

(5) At a hearing a party may be accompanied by another person whose name and address has not been notified under paragraph (2) but who, subject to paragraph (8) and with the permission of the Tribunal, may act as a representative or otherwise assist in presenting the party's case at the hearing.

(6) Paragraphs (2) to (4) do not apply to a person who accompanies a party under paragraph (5).

(7) In a mental health case, if the patient has not appointed a representative, the Tribunal may appoint a legal representative for the patient where—

(a) the patient has stated that they do not wish to conduct their own case or that they wish to be represented; or

(b) the patient lacks the capacity to appoint a representative but the Tribunal believes that it is in the patient's best interests for the patient to be represented.

(8) In a mental health case a party may not appoint as a representative, or be represented or assisted at a hearing by—

(a) a person liable to be detained or subject to guardianship or after-care under supervision, or who is a community patient, under the Mental Health Act 1983; or

(b) a person receiving treatment for mental disorder at the same hospital as the patient.

(a) S.I. 1998/3132.

Calculating time

12.—(1) An act required by these Rules, a practice direction or a direction to be done on or by a particular day must be done by 5pm on that day.

(2) If the time specified by these Rules, a practice direction or a direction for doing any act ends on a day other than a working day, the act is done in time if it is done on the next working day.

(3) In a special educational needs case or a disability discrimination in schools case—

    (a) if the time for starting proceedings by providing the application notice to the Tribunal under rule 20 (the application notice) ends on a day from 25th December to 1st January inclusive, or on any day in August, the application notice is provided in time if it is provided to the Tribunal on the first working day after 1st January or 31st August, as appropriate; and

    (b) the days from 25th December to 1st January inclusive and any day in August must not be counted when calculating the time by which any other act must be done.

(4) Paragraph (3)(b) does not apply where the Tribunal directs that an act must be done by or on a specified date.

Sending and delivery of documents

13.—(1) Any document to be provided to the Tribunal under these Rules, a practice direction or a direction must be—

    (a) sent by pre-paid post or delivered by hand to the address specified for the proceedings;

    (b) sent by fax to the number specified for the proceedings; or

    (c) sent or delivered by such other method as the Tribunal may permit or direct.

(2) Subject to paragraph (3), if a party provides a fax number, email address or other details for the electronic transmission of documents to them, that party must accept delivery of documents by that method.

(3) If a party informs the Tribunal and all other parties that a particular form of communication, other than pre-paid post or delivery by hand, should not be used to provide documents to that party, that form of communication must not be so used.

(4) If the Tribunal or a party sends a document to a party or the Tribunal by email or any other electronic means of communication, the recipient may request that the sender provide a hard copy of the document to the recipient. The recipient must make such a request as soon as reasonably practicable after receiving the document electronically.

(5) The Tribunal and each party may assume that the address provided by a party or its representative is and remains the address to which documents should be sent or delivered until receiving written notification to the contrary.

Use of documents and information

14.—(1) The Tribunal may make an order prohibiting the disclosure or publication of—

    (a) specified documents or information relating to the proceedings; or

    (b) any matter likely to lead members of the public to identify any person whom the Tribunal considers should not be identified.

(2) The Tribunal may give a direction prohibiting the disclosure of a document or information to a person if—

    (a) the Tribunal is satisfied that such disclosure would be likely to cause that person or some other person serious harm; and

    (b) the Tribunal is satisfied, having regard to the interests of justice, that it is proportionate to give such a direction.

10

(3) If a party ("the first party") considers that the Tribunal should give a direction under paragraph (2) prohibiting the disclosure of a document or information to another party ("the second party"), the first party must—

(a) exclude the relevant document or information from any documents that will be provided to the second party; and

(b) provide to the Tribunal the excluded document or information, and the reason for its exclusion, so that the Tribunal may decide whether the document or information should be disclosed to the second party or should be the subject of a direction under paragraph (2).

(4) The Tribunal must conduct proceedings as appropriate in order to give effect to a direction given under paragraph (2).

(5) If the Tribunal gives a direction under paragraph (2) which prevents disclosure to a party who has appointed a representative, the Tribunal may give a direction that the documents or information be disclosed to that representative if the Tribunal is satisfied that—

(a) disclosure to the representative would be in the interests of the party; and

(b) the representative will act in accordance with paragraph (6).

(6) Documents or information disclosed to a representative in accordance with a direction under paragraph (5) must not be disclosed either directly or indirectly to any other person without the Tribunal's consent.

(7) Unless the Tribunal gives a direction to the contrary, information about mental health cases and the names of any persons concerned in such cases must not be made public.

Evidence and submissions

15.—(1) Without restriction on the general powers in rule 5(1) and (2) (case management powers), the Tribunal may give directions as to—

(a) issues on which it requires evidence or submissions;

(b) the nature of the evidence or submissions it requires;

(c) whether the parties are permitted or required to provide expert evidence, and if so whether the parties must jointly appoint a single expert to provide such evidence;

(d) any limit on the number of witnesses whose evidence a party may put forward, whether in relation to a particular issue or generally;

(e) the manner in which any evidence or submissions are to be provided, which may include a direction for them to be given—

(i) orally at a hearing; or

(ii) by written submissions or witness statement; and

(f) the time at which any evidence or submissions are to be provided.

(2) The Tribunal may—

(a) admit evidence whether or not—

(i) the evidence would be admissible in a civil trial in England and Wales; or

(ii) the evidence was available to a previous decision maker; or

(b) exclude evidence that would otherwise be admissible where—

(i) the evidence was not provided within the time allowed by a direction or a practice direction;

(ii) the evidence was otherwise provided in a manner that did not comply with a direction or a practice direction; or

(iii) it would otherwise be unfair to admit the evidence.

(3) The Tribunal may consent to a witness giving, or require any witness to give, evidence on oath, and may administer an oath for that purpose.

11

(4) In a special educational needs case the Tribunal may require—

    (a) the parents of the child, or any other person with care of the child or parental responsibility for the child (as defined in section 3 of the Children Act 1989), to make the child available for examination or assessment by a suitably qualified professional person; or

    (b) the person responsible for a school or educational setting to allow a suitably qualified professional person to have access to the school or educational setting for the purpose of assessing the child or the provision made, or to be made, for the child.

(5) The Tribunal may consider a failure by a party to comply with a requirement made under paragraph (4), in the absence of any good reason for such failure, as a failure to co-operate with the Tribunal, which could lead to a result which is adverse to that party's case.

Summoning of witnesses and orders to answer questions or produce documents

16.—(1) On the application of a party or on its own initiative, the Tribunal may—

    (a) by summons require any person to attend as a witness at a hearing at the time and place specified in the summons; or

    (b) order any person to answer any questions or produce any documents in that person's possession or control which relate to any issue in the proceedings.

(2) A summons under paragraph (1)(a) must—

    (a) give the person required to attend 14 days' notice of the hearing, or such shorter period as the Tribunal may direct; and

    (b) where the person is not a party, make provision for the person's necessary expenses of attendance to be paid, and state who is to pay them.

(3) No person may be compelled to give any evidence or produce any document that the person could not be compelled to give or produce on a trial of an action in a court of law.

(4) A summons or order under this rule must—

    (a) state that the person on whom the requirement is imposed may apply to the Tribunal to vary or set aside the summons or order, if they have not had an opportunity to object to it; and

    (b) state the consequences of failure to comply with the summons or order.

Withdrawal

17.—(1) Subject to paragraphs (2) and (3), a party may give notice of the withdrawal of its case, or any part of it—

    (a) at any time before a hearing to consider the disposal of the proceedings (or, if the Tribunal disposes of the proceedings without a hearing, before that disposal), by sending or delivering to the Tribunal a written notice of withdrawal; or

    (b) orally at a hearing.

(2) Notice of withdrawal will not take effect unless the Tribunal consents to the withdrawal except—

    (a) in proceedings concerning the suitability of a person to work with children or vulnerable adults; or

    (b) in proceedings started by a reference under section 67 or 71(1) of the Mental Health Act 1983.

(3) A party which started a mental health case by making a reference to the Tribunal under section 68, 71(2) or 75(1) of the Mental Health Act 1983 may not withdraw its case.

(4) A party which has withdrawn its case may apply to the Tribunal for the case to be reinstated.

(5) An application under paragraph (4) must be made in writing and be received by the Tribunal within 28 days after—

12

(a) the date on which the Tribunal received the notice under paragraph (1)(a); or

(b) the date of the hearing at which the case was withdrawn orally under paragraph (1)(b).

(6) The Tribunal must notify each party in writing of a withdrawal under this rule.

PART 3

Proceedings before the Tribunal other than in mental health cases

CHAPTER 1

Before the hearing

Application of Part 3

18. This Part does not apply to mental health cases.

Application for leave

19.—(1) This rule applies to applications for leave to bring proceedings under—

(a) section 4(1)(b) of the Protection of Children Act 1999(**a**) (appeal against a decision not to remove the applicant from the list kept under section 1 of that Act);

(b) section 4(2) of the Protection of Children Act 1999 (application to have the issue of the applicant's inclusion in the list kept under section 1 of that Act determined by the Tribunal);

(c) section 86(1)(b) of the Care Standards Act 2000(**b**) (appeal against a decision not to remove the applicant from the list kept under section 81 of that Act);

(d) section 86(2) of the Care Standards Act 2000 (application to have the issue of the applicant's inclusion in the list kept under section 81 of that Act determined by the Tribunal); and

(e) section 32 of the Criminal Justice and Court Services Act 2000(**c**) (application to have the issue of the continuation of a disqualification order determined by the Tribunal).

(2) An application to the Tribunal for leave must—

(a) give full reasons why the applicant considers that the Tribunal should give leave; and

(b) comply with paragraphs (1) to (4) of rule 20 (the application notice) as if the application for leave were an application notice.

(3) The Tribunal may make any directions it considers appropriate before determining the application for leave.

(4) The Tribunal must—

(a) notify the applicant of its decision in relation to the application for leave; and

(b) if it gives leave, give directions as to the future conduct of the proceedings.

The application notice

20.—(1) If rule 19 (application for leave) does not apply, an applicant must start proceedings before the Tribunal by sending or delivering an application notice to the Tribunal so that it is received—

(a) if a time for providing the application notice is specified in the Schedule to these Rules (time limits for providing application notices and responses), within that time; or

---

(**a**) 1999 c.14.
(**b**) 2000 c.14.
(**c**) 2000 c.43.

(b) otherwise, within 28 days after notice of the act or decision to which the proceedings relate was sent to the applicant.

(2) The application notice must be signed by the applicant and must include—

(a) the name and address of the applicant;

(b) the name and address of the applicant's representative (if any);

(c) an address where documents for the applicant may be sent or delivered;

(d) the name and address of any respondent;

(e) details of the decision or act, or failure to decide or act, to which the proceedings relate;

(f) the result the applicant is seeking;

(g) the grounds on which the applicant relies; and

(h) any further information or documents required by an applicable practice direction.

(3) The applicant must send with the application notice a copy of any written record of any decision under challenge, and any statement of reasons for that decision that the applicant has or can reasonably obtain.

(4) If the applicant provides the application notice to the Tribunal later than the time required by paragraph (1) or by any extension of time under rule 5(3)(a) (power to extend time)—

(a) the application notice must include a request for an extension of time and the reason why the application notice was not provided in time; and

(b) unless the Tribunal extends time for the application notice under rule 5(3)(a) (power to extend time) the Tribunal must not admit the application notice.

(5) In proceedings under Suspension Regulations, the applicant must send or deliver a copy of the application notice and any accompanying documents to the respondent at the same time as it provides the application notice to the Tribunal.

(6) In proceedings other than proceedings under paragraph (5), when the Tribunal receives the application notice it must send a copy of the application notice and any accompanying documents to each other party.

The response

21.—(1) When a respondent receives a copy of the application notice, the respondent must send or deliver to the Tribunal a response so that it is received—

(a) if a time for providing the response is specified in the Schedule to these Rules (time limits for providing application notices and responses), within that time;

(b) otherwise, within 21 days after the date on which the respondent received the application notice.

(2) The response must include—

(a) the name and address of the respondent;

(b) the name and address of the respondent's representative (if any);

(c) an address where documents for the respondent may be sent or delivered;

(d) a statement as to whether the respondent opposes the applicant's case and, if so, any grounds for such opposition which are not contained in another document provided with the response;

(e) in a special educational needs case, the views of the child about the issues raised by the proceedings, or the reason why the respondent has not ascertained those views; and

(f) any further information or documents required by an applicable practice direction or direction.

(3) The response may include a statement as to whether the respondent would be content for the case to be dealt with without a hearing if the Tribunal considers it appropriate.

14

(4) If the respondent provides the response to the Tribunal later than the time required by paragraph (1) or by any extension of time under rule 5(3)(a) (power to extend time), the response must include a request for an extension of time and the reason why the response was not provided in time.

(5) The respondent must send or deliver a copy of the response and any accompanying documents to each other party at the same time as it provides the response to the Tribunal.

Order that a school be regarded as not registered pending determination of an appeal

22.—(1) This rule sets out the procedure for the making of an order under section 166(5) of the Education Act 2002(**a**) that a school is to be regarded as not registered for the purposes of section 159 of that Act until the Tribunal determines an appeal under section 165(2) of that Act (decision to remove an independent school from the register).

(2) In this rule—

    (a) "the applicant" means the applicant bringing the appeal under section 165(2) of the Education Act 2002; and

    (b) "the respondent" means the respondent to that appeal.

(3) The respondent must make any application for an order under this rule in writing and must send or deliver it to the Tribunal and the applicant so that it is received within 28 days after the date on which the respondent received a copy of the application notice starting the appeal.

(4) An application under paragraph (3) must—

    (a) be signed by the respondent and dated;

    (b) state the grounds for the application;

    (c) state the nature of the evidence that will be provided in support of the application and the names of the witnesses who will give that evidence;

    (d) specify any working days in the following 30 days when the respondent or a witness named under sub-paragraph (c) would not be available to attend a hearing, and provide reasons why they would not be available; and

    (e) include, so far as practicable, any documentary evidence (including witness statements) that the respondent intends to rely on.

(5) The applicant must send or deliver a written response to the application under paragraph (3) to the Tribunal and the respondent so that it is received within 16 days after the date on which the respondent sent that application to the applicant under paragraph (3).

(6) The response must—

    (a) acknowledge receipt of the application and any documentary evidence included with it;

    (b) state whether the applicant requests that the application be decided at a hearing, and if so—

        (i) state the nature of the evidence that will be provided in support of the applicant's case and the names of the witnesses who will give that evidence; and

        (ii) specify any working days in the following 16 days when the applicant or a witness named under sub-paragraph (b)(i) would not be available to attend a hearing, and provide reasons why they would not be available; and

    (c) include, so far as practicable, any documentary evidence (including witness statements) that the applicant intends to rely on.

(7) If the applicant fails to comply with paragraph (5) the applicant will not be entitled to take any further part in the proceedings in relation to the application.

(8) If the applicant complies with paragraph (5) and requests that the application be decided at a hearing, the Tribunal must hold a hearing to consider the application.

(**a**) 2002 c.32.

(9) Any hearing to consider the making of an order must be held as soon as reasonably practicable, and if the respondent has applied for such an order any such hearing must be held no later than the earlier of—

(a) 14 days after the date on which the Tribunal received the applicant's response to the application; or

(b) 30 days after the date on which the respondent sent the application to the applicant.

(10) If the Tribunal is considering whether to make an order on its own initiative, the Tribunal—

(a) may not do so without giving the applicant an opportunity to make representations at a hearing in relation to the making of the order;

(b) must give directions as to the provision to the Tribunal by the parties of documents or evidence that the parties wish to be taken into account.

CHAPTER 2

Hearings

Decision with or without a hearing

23.—(1) Subject to paragraphs (2) and (3), the Tribunal must hold a hearing before making a decision which disposes of proceedings unless—

(a) each party has consented to the matter being decided without a hearing; and

(b) the Tribunal considers that it is able to decide the matter without the hearing.

(2) This rule does not apply to a decision under Part 5.

(3) The Tribunal may dispose of proceedings without a hearing under rule 8 (striking out a party's case).

Entitlement to attend a hearing

24. Subject to rules 22(7) (exclusion of applicant from proceedings to consider an order under section 166(5) of the Education Act 2002) and 26(5) (exclusion of a person from a hearing)—

(a) each party is entitled to attend a hearing; and

(b) in a special educational needs case, or a disability discrimination in schools case, the child is entitled to attend a hearing, and the Tribunal may permit the child to give evidence and to address the Tribunal.

Notice of hearings

25.—(1) The Tribunal must give each party entitled to attend a hearing reasonable notice of the time and place of the hearing (including any adjourned or postponed hearing) and any changes to the time and place of the hearing.

(2) The period of notice under paragraph (1) must be at least 14 days, except that—

(a) in proceedings under Suspension Regulations the period of notice must be at least 3 working days;

(b) the period of notice in respect of a hearing to consider the making of an order under section 166(5) of the Education Act 2002 must be at least 7 days; and

(c) the Tribunal may give shorter notice—

(i) with the parties' consent; or

(ii) in urgent or exceptional circumstances.

Public and private hearings

26.—(1) Subject to the following paragraphs, all hearings must be held in public.

16

(2) Hearings in special educational needs cases and disability discrimination in schools cases must be held in private unless the Tribunal considers that it is in the interests of justice for a hearing to be held in public.

(3) Subject to paragraph (2), the Tribunal may give a direction that a hearing, or part of it, is to be held in private.

(4) Where a hearing, or part of it, is to be held in private, the Tribunal may determine who is permitted to attend the hearing or part of it.

(5) The Tribunal may give a direction excluding from any hearing, or part of it—

(a) any person whose conduct the Tribunal considers is disrupting or is likely to disrupt the hearing;

(b) any person whose presence the Tribunal considers is likely to prevent another person from giving evidence or making submissions freely;

(c) any person who the Tribunal considers should be excluded in order to give effect to a direction under rule 14(2) (withholding information likely to cause harm);

(d) any person where the purpose of the hearing would be defeated by the attendance of that person; or

(e) in a special educational needs case or a disability discrimination in schools case, the child, if the Tribunal considers that the child's presence at the hearing would be adverse to the child's interests.

(6) The Tribunal may give a direction excluding a witness from a hearing until that witness gives evidence.

Hearings in a party's absence

27. If a party fails to attend a hearing the Tribunal may proceed with the hearing if the Tribunal—

(a) is satisfied that the party has been notified of the hearing or that reasonable steps have been taken to notify the party of the hearing; and

(b) considers that it is in the interests of justice to proceed with the hearing.

Power to pay allowances

28. The Secretary of State may pay such allowances for the purpose of or in connection with the attendance of persons at hearings as the Secretary of State may determine.

CHAPTER 3

Decisions

Consent orders

29.—(1) The Tribunal may, at the request of the parties but only if it considers it appropriate, make a consent order disposing of the proceedings and making such other appropriate provision as the parties have agreed.

(2) Notwithstanding any other provision of these Rules, the Tribunal need not hold a hearing before making an order under paragraph (1), or provide reasons for the order.

Decisions

30.—(1) The Tribunal may give a decision orally at a hearing.

(2) Subject to rule 14(2) (withholding information likely to cause harm), the Tribunal must provide to each party as soon as reasonably practicable after making a decision which finally disposes of all issues in the proceedings (except a decision under Part 5)—

(a) a decision notice stating the Tribunal's decision;

17

(b) written reasons for the decision; and

(c) notification of any rights of review or appeal against the decision and the time within which, and the manner in which, such rights of review or appeal may be exercised.

(3) In proceedings under Suspension Regulations, the documents and information referred to in paragraph (2) must be provided at the hearing or sent within 3 working days after the hearing.

(4) The Tribunal may provide written reasons for any decision to which paragraph (2) does not apply.

PART 4

Proceedings before the Tribunal in mental health cases

CHAPTER 1

Before the hearing

Application of Part 4

31. This Part applies only to mental health cases.

Procedure in mental health cases

32.—(1) An application or reference must be—

(a) made in writing;

(b) signed (in the case of an application, by the applicant or any person authorised by the applicant to do so); and

(c) sent or delivered to the Tribunal so that it is received within the time specified in the Mental Health Act 1983 or the Repatriation of Prisoners Act 1984.

(2) An application must, if possible, include—

(a) the name and address of the patient;

(b) if the application is made by the patient's nearest relative, the name, address and relationship to the patient of the patient's nearest relative;

(c) the provision under which the patient is detained, liable to be detained, subject to guardianship, a community patient or subject to after-care under supervision;

(d) whether the person making the application has appointed a representative or intends to do so, and the name and address of any representative appointed;

(e) the name and address of the responsible authority in relation to the patient.

(3) Subject to rule 14(2) (withholding evidence likely to cause harm), when the Tribunal receives a document from any party it must send a copy of that document to each other party.

(4) If the patient is a conditionally discharged patient (as defined in the Mental Health Act 1983) the Secretary of State must send or deliver a statement containing the information and documents required by the relevant practice direction to the Tribunal so that it is received by the Tribunal as soon as practicable and in any event within 6 weeks after the Secretary of State received a copy of the application or a request from the Tribunal.

(5) In proceedings under section 66(1)(a) of the Mental Health Act 1983 (application for admission for assessment), on the earlier of receipt of the copy of the application or a request from the Tribunal, the responsible authority must send or deliver to the Tribunal—

(a) the application for admission;

(b) the medical recommendations on which the application is founded;

18

(c) such of the information specified in the relevant practice direction as is within the knowledge of the responsible authority and can reasonably be provided in the time available; and

(d) such of the documents specified in the relevant practice direction as can reasonably be provided in the time available.

(6) If paragraph (4) or (5) does not apply, the responsible authority must send or deliver a statement containing the information and documents required by the relevant practice direction to the Tribunal so that it is received by the Tribunal as soon as practicable and in any event within 3 weeks after the responsible authority received a copy of the application or reference.

(7) If the patient is a restricted patient the responsible authority must also send the statement under paragraph (6) to the Secretary of State, and the Secretary of State must send a statement of any further relevant information to the Tribunal as soon as practicable and in any event—

(a) in proceedings under section 75(1) of the Mental Health Act 1983, within 2 weeks after the Secretary of State received the relevant authority's statement; or

(b) otherwise, within 3 weeks after the Secretary of State received the relevant authority's statement.

(8) If the Secretary of State wishes to seek the approval of the Tribunal under section 86(3) of the Mental Health Act 1983, the Secretary of State must refer the patient's case to the Tribunal and the provisions of these Rules applicable to references under that Act apply to the proceedings.

Notice of proceedings to interested persons

33. When the Tribunal receives the information required by rule 32(4), (5) or (6) (procedure in mental health cases) the Tribunal must give notice of the proceedings—

(a) where the patient is subject to the guardianship of a private guardian, to the guardian;

(b) where there is an extant order of the Court of Protection, to that court;

(c) subject to a patient with capacity to do so requesting otherwise, where any person other than the applicant is named by the authority as exercising the functions of the nearest relative, to that person;

(d) where a health authority, Primary Care Trust, National Health Service trust or NHS foundation trust has a right to discharge the patient under the provisions of section 23(3) of the Mental Health Act 1983, to that authority or trust; and

(e) to any other person who, in the opinion of the Tribunal, should have an opportunity of being heard.

Medical examination of the patient

34.—(1) Before a hearing to consider the disposal of a mental health case, an appropriate member of the Tribunal must, so far as practicable—

(a) examine the patient; and

(b) take such other steps as that member considers necessary to form an opinion of the patient's mental condition.

(2) For the purposes of paragraph (1) that member may—

(a) examine the patient in private;

(b) examine records relating to the detention or treatment of the patient and any after-care services;

(c) take notes and copies of records for use in connection with the proceedings.

19

CHAPTER 2

Hearings

No disposal of proceedings without a hearing

35.—(1) The Tribunal must not dispose of proceedings without a hearing.

(2) This rule does not apply to a decision under Part 5.

Entitlement to attend a hearing

36.—(1) Subject to rule 38(4) (exclusion of a person from a hearing), each party to proceedings is entitled to attend a hearing.

(2) Any person notified of the proceedings under rule 33 (notice of proceedings to interested persons) may—

- (a) attend and take part in a hearing to such extent as the Tribunal considers proper; or
- (b) provide written submissions to the Tribunal.

Time and place of hearings

37.—(1) In proceedings under section 66(1)(a) of the Mental Health Act 1983 the hearing of the case must start within 7 days after the date on which the Tribunal received the application notice.

(2) In proceedings under section 75(1) of that Act, the hearing of the case must start at least 5 weeks but no more than 8 weeks after the date on which the Tribunal received the reference.

(3) The Tribunal must give reasonable notice of the time and place of the hearing (including any adjourned or postponed hearing), and any changes to the time and place of the hearing, to—

- (a) each party entitled to attend a hearing; and
- (b) any person who has been notified of the proceedings under rule 33 (notice of proceedings to interested persons).

(4) The period of notice under paragraph (3) must be at least 14 days, except that—

- (a) in proceedings under section 66(1)(a) of the Mental Health Act 1983 the period must be at least 3 working days; and
- (b) the Tribunal may give shorter notice—
  - (i) with the parties' consent; or
  - (ii) in urgent or exceptional circumstances.

Public and private hearings

38.—(1) All hearings must be held in private unless the Tribunal considers that it is in the interests of justice for the hearing to be held in public.

(2) If a hearing is held in public, the Tribunal may give a direction that part of the hearing is to be held in private.

(3) Where a hearing, or part of it, is to be held in private, the Tribunal may determine who is permitted to attend the hearing or part of it.

(4) The Tribunal may give a direction excluding from any hearing, or part of it—

- (a) any person whose conduct the Tribunal considers is disrupting or is likely to disrupt the hearing;
- (b) any person whose presence the Tribunal considers is likely to prevent another person from giving evidence or making submissions freely;
- (c) any person who the Tribunal considers should be excluded in order to give effect to a direction under rule 14(2) (withholding information likely to cause harm); or

20

(d) any person where the purpose of the hearing would be defeated by the attendance of that person.

(5) The Tribunal may give a direction excluding a witness from a hearing until that witness gives evidence.

Hearings in a party's absence

39.—(1) Subject to paragraph (2), if a party fails to attend a hearing the Tribunal may proceed with the hearing if the Tribunal—

    (a) is satisfied that the party has been notified of the hearing or that reasonable steps have been taken to notify the party of the hearing; and

    (b) considers that it is in the interests of justice to proceed with the hearing.

(2) The Tribunal may not proceed with a hearing in the absence of the patient unless—

    (a) the requirements of rule 34 (medical examination of the patient) have been satisfied; and

    (b) the Tribunal is satisfied that—

        (i) the patient has decided not to attend the hearing; or

        (ii) the patient is unable to attend the hearing for reasons of ill health.

Power to pay allowances

40. The Tribunal may pay allowances in respect of travelling expenses, subsistence and loss of earnings to—

    (a) any person who attends a hearing as an applicant or a witness;

    (b) a patient who attends a hearing otherwise than as the applicant or a witness; and

    (c) any person (other than a legal representative) who attends as the representative of an applicant.

CHAPTER 3

Decisions

Decisions

41.—(1) The Tribunal may give a decision orally at a hearing.

(2) Subject to rule 14(2) (withholding information likely to cause harm), the Tribunal must provide to each party as soon as reasonably practicable after making a decision which finally disposes of all issues in the proceedings (except a decision under Part 5)—

    (a) a decision notice stating the Tribunal's decision;

    (b) written reasons for the decision; and

    (c) notification of any right of appeal against the decision and the time within which, and the manner in which, such right of appeal may be exercised.

(3) The documents and information referred to in paragraph (2) must—

    (a) in proceedings under section 66(1)(a) of the Mental Health Act 1983, be provided at the hearing or sent within 3 working days after the hearing; and

    (b) in other cases, be provided at the hearing or sent within 7 days after the hearing.

(4) The Tribunal may provide written reasons for any decision to which paragraph (2) does not apply.

Provisional decisions

42. For the purposes of this Part and Parts 1, 2 and 5, a decision with recommendations under section 72(3)(a) or (3A)(a) of the Mental Health Act 1983(a) or a deferred direction for conditional discharge under section 73(7) of that Act is a decision which disposes of the proceedings.

PART 5

Correcting, setting aside, reviewing and appealing Tribunal decisions

Interpretation

43. In this Part—

"appeal" means the exercise of a right of appeal on a point of law under section 11 of the 2007 Act; and

"review" means the review of a decision by the Tribunal under section 9 of the 2007 Act.

Clerical mistakes and accidental slips or omissions

44. The Tribunal may at any time correct any clerical mistake or other accidental slip or omission in a decision, direction or any document produced by it, by—

(a) sending notification of the amended decision or direction, or a copy of the amended document, to all parties; and

(b) making any necessary amendment to any information published in relation to the decision, direction or document.

Setting aside a decision which disposes of proceedings

45.—(1) The Tribunal may set aside a decision which disposes of proceedings, or part of such a decision, and re-make the decision or the relevant part of it, if—

(a) the Tribunal considers that it is in the interests of justice to do so; and

(b) one or more of the conditions in paragraph (2) are satisfied.

(2) The conditions are—

(a) a document relating to the proceedings was not sent to, or was not received at an appropriate time by, a party or a party's representative;

(b) a document relating to the proceedings was not sent to the Tribunal at an appropriate time;

(c) a party, or a party's representative, was not present at a hearing related to the proceedings; or

(d) there has been some other procedural irregularity in the proceedings.

(3) A party applying for a decision, or part of a decision, to be set aside under paragraph (1) must make a written application to the Tribunal so that it is received no later than 28 days after the date on which the Tribunal sent notice of the decision to the party.

Application for permission to appeal

46.—(1) A person seeking permission to appeal must make a written application to the Tribunal for permission to appeal.

(a) 1983 c.20. Section 72(3A) was inserted by section 1(2) to, and paragraph 10(1) and (2) of Schedule 1 to, the Mental Health (Patients in the Community) Act 1995 (c.52), and is substituted by section 32(4) of, and paragraphs 1 and 21(1) and (4) of Schedule 3 to, the Mental Health Act 2007 (c.12).

22

(2) An application under paragraph (1) must be sent or delivered to the Tribunal so that it is received no later than 28 days after the latest of the dates that the Tribunal sends to the person making the application—

(a) written reasons for the decision;

(b) notification of amended reasons for, or correction of, the decision following a review; or

(c) notification that an application for the decision to be set aside has been unsuccessful.

(3) The date in paragraph (2)(c) applies only if the application for the decision to be set aside was made within the time stipulated in rule 45 (setting aside a decision which disposes of proceedings) or any extension of that time granted by the Tribunal.

(4) If the person seeking permission to appeal sends or delivers the application to the Tribunal later than the time required by paragraph (2) or by any extension of time under rule 5(3)(a) (power to extend time)—

(a) the application must include a request for an extension of time and the reason why the application was not provided in time; and

(b) unless the Tribunal extends time for the application under rule 5(3)(a) (power to extend time) the Tribunal must not admit the application.

(5) An application under paragraph (1) must—

(a) identify the decision of the Tribunal to which it relates;

(b) identify the alleged error or errors of law in the decision; and

(c) state the result the party making the application is seeking.

Tribunal's consideration of application for permission to appeal

47.—(1) On receiving an application for permission to appeal the Tribunal must first consider, taking into account the overriding objective in rule 2, whether to review the decision in accordance with rule 49 (review of a decision).

(2) If the Tribunal decides not to review the decision, or reviews the decision and decides to take no action in relation to the decision, or part of it, the Tribunal must consider whether to give permission to appeal in relation to the decision or that part of it.

(3) The Tribunal must send a record of its decision to the parties as soon as practicable.

(4) If the Tribunal refuses permission to appeal it must send with the record of its decision—

(a) a statement of its reasons for such refusal; and

(b) notification of the right to make an application to the Upper Tribunal for permission to appeal and the time within which, and the method by which, such application must be made.

(5) The Tribunal may give permission to appeal on limited grounds, but must comply with paragraph (4) in relation to any grounds on which it has refused permission.

Application for review in special educational needs cases

48.—(1) This rule applies to decisions which dispose of proceedings in special educational needs cases, but not to decisions under this Part.

(2) A party may make a written application to the Tribunal for a review of a decision if circumstances relevant to the decision have changed since the decision was made.

(3) An application under paragraph (2) must be sent or delivered to the Tribunal so that it is received within 28 days after the date on which the Tribunal sent the decision notice recording the Tribunal's decision to the party making the application.

(4) If a party sends or delivers an application to the Tribunal later than the time required by paragraph (3) or by any extension of time under rule 5(3)(a) (power to extend time)—

(a) the application must include a request for an extension of time and the reason why the application was not provided in time; and

(b) unless the Tribunal extends time for the application under rule 5(3)(a) (power to extend time) the Tribunal must not admit the application.

Review of a decision

49.—(1) The Tribunal may only undertake a review of a decision—

(a) pursuant to rule 47(1) (review on an application for permission to appeal) if it is satisfied that there was an error of law in the decision; or

(b) pursuant to rule 48 (application for review in special educational needs cases).

(2) The Tribunal must notify the parties in writing of the outcome of any review, and of any right of appeal in relation to the outcome.

(3) If the Tribunal takes any action in relation to a decision following a review without first giving every party an opportunity to make representations, the notice under paragraph (2) must state that any party that did not have an opportunity to make representations may apply for such action to be set aside and for the decision to be reviewed again.

Power to treat an application as a different type of application

50. The Tribunal may treat an application for a decision to be corrected, set aside or reviewed, or for permission to appeal against a decision, as an application for any other one of those things.

Patrick Elias
Phillip Brook Smith Q.C
Lesley Clare
Douglas J. May Q.C.
Newton of Braintree
M.J. Reed
Mark Rowland
Nicholas Warren

I allow these Rules
Signed by authority of the Lord Chancellor

Bridget Prentice
Parliamentary Under Secretary of State
9th October 2008   Ministry of Justice

24

SCHEDULE
Rules 20(1)(a) and 21(1)(a)

Time limits for providing application notices and responses

Type of proceedings	Time for application notice	Time for response
Under Suspension Regulations (suspension of registration as a childcare provider)	10 working days after written notice of the decision was sent to the applicant	3 working days after the respondent received the application notice
Under section 79M of the Children Act 1989(a), except against a notice under section 79L(1)(a) of that Act (notice of intention to refuse an application for registration for childminding or providing day care) Under paragraph 10 of Schedule 26 to the School Standards and Framework Act 1998(b) (appeal against a decision of the Chief Inspector for Wales) Under section 68 of the Care Standards Act 2000 (appeal against a decision of the Council) except an appeal against a refusal under section 58 of that Act (refusal of an application to be included on a register of social workers) Under section 74(1)(b) to (e) and (2) of the Childcare Act 2006 (appeal against steps taken by the Chief Inspector except refusal of application for registration or against a prescribed determination)	28 days after written notice of the decision was sent to the applicant	20 working days after the respondent received the application notice
Under section 21 of the Care Standards Act 2000 (refusal or cancellation of registration, or variation of conditions of registration, by registration authority or by order of a justice of the peace) Under section 32 of the Health and Social Care Act 2008(c) (appeal against a decision of the Care Quality Commission or an order of a justice of the peace cancelling registration) Health and Social Care Act 2008 Under section 166 of the Education Act 2002 (appeal against steps taken by the registration authority)	28 day time limits are set out in section 21(2) of the Care Standards Act 2000, section 166(2) of the Education Act 2002 and section 32(2) of the Health and Social Care Act 2008	20 working days after the respondent received the application notice

(a) 1989 c.41. Sections 79L and 79M were inserted by section 79(1) of the Care Standards Act 2000 (c.14).
(b) 1998 c.31.
(c) 2008 c.14.

25

Under section 65A of the Children Act 1989(a) (refusal to give consent for a person who is disqualified from fostering a child privately to carry on, be otherwise concerned in the management of, have any financial interest in, or be employed in, a children's home)	3 months after written notice of the decision was sent to the applicant	20 days after the respondent received the application notice
Under section 79M of the Children Act 1989 against a notice under 79L(1)(a) of that Act (notice of intention to refuse an application for registration for childminding or for providing day care)		
Under section 4 of the Protection of Children Act 1999 (inclusion of a person on a list of individuals who are considered unsuitable to work with children, a refusal to remove a person from such list, or determination of inclusion on the list where a person has been provisionally included on the list for more than 9 months)		
Under section 68 of the Care Standards Act 2000 where the appeal is against a refusal under section 58 of that Act (refusal of an application to be included on a register of social workers)		
Under section 86 of the Care Standards Act 2000 (inclusion of a person on a list of individuals who are considered unsuitable to work with vulnerable adults, a refusal to remove a person from such list, or determination of inclusion on the list where a person has been provisionally included on the list for more than 9 months)		
Under the Education (Prohibition from Teaching or Working with Children) Regulations 2003(b) (decision to give a direction, or a refusal to revoke a direction, prohibiting or restricting a person from working in education or in a job which brings them regularly into contact with children)		
Under section 74(1)(a) of the Childcare Act 2006 (refusal of registration as a childcare provider)		
Under regulations made under section 28X of the National Health Service Act 1977(c) (decision contingently to remove a person from a list maintained by a Primary Care Trust or Local Health Board of persons authorised to perform primary medical, dental or ophthalmic services, or local pharmaceutical services)	(a) for the first application in relation to a decision, 3 months after the decision was made; (b) for any further application in respect of the same decision, 6 months after the Tribunal	21 days after the respondent received the application notice

---

(a) 1989 c.41. Section 65A was inserted by section 116 of, and paragraph 14(1) and (14) of Schedule 4 to, the Care Standards Act 2000 (c.14).
(b) S.I. 2003/1184.
(c) 1977 c.49. Section 28X was inserted by section 179(1) of the Health and Social Care (Community Health and Standards) Act 2003 (c.43). It was repealed by section 6 of, and Schedule 4 to, the National Health Service (Consequential Provisions) Act 2006 (c.43) subject to savings provisions in paragraph 1 of Schedule 2 to that Act.

26

	made its last determination in relation to that decision; (c) for any further application in respect of the same decision where the parties apply jointly to the Tribunal with a view to seeking— (i) the same variation of conditions, (ii) the same imposition of different conditions, or (iii) for the contingent removal to be revoked, 1 month after the Tribunal made its last determination in relation to that decision.	
Under Part 4 of and Schedule 27 to the Education Act 1996(a) (provision of education to a child with special educational needs)	2 months after written notice of the decision was sent to the applicant	30 working days after the respondent received the application notice
Under section 28I of the Disability Discrimination Act 1995(b) (disability discrimination in the education of a child)	6 months after the decision or act complained of	30 working days after the respondent received the application notice

(a) 1996 c.56.
(b) 1995 c.50. Section 28I was inserted by section 18 of the Special Educational Needs and Disability Act 2001 (c.10).

27

EXPLANATORY NOTE

(This note is not part of the Rules)

Part 1 of the Tribunals, Courts and Enforcement Act 2007 (c.15) establishes a new tribunal structure comprising a First-tier Tribunal and an Upper Tribunal. Appeal functions of existing tribunals are being transferred to this structure and assigned to chambers within the new tribunals. These Rules govern the practice and procedure to be followed in the First-tier Tribunal in proceedings which have been allocated to the Health, Education and Social Care Chamber by the First-tier Tribunal and Upper Tribunal (Chambers) Order 2008(a).

Part 1 contains provisions for interpreting and applying the Rules and sets out the overriding objective of the Rules.

Part 2 contains general powers and provisions including the Tribunal's general case management powers, the giving of directions, the power to strike out a party's case, the service of documents and rules about evidence, submissions and witnesses.

Part 3 contains provisions on starting proceedings and on responses and replies in cases other than mental health cases. It also makes provision for hearings and for decisions made by the Tribunal in those cases.

Part 4 contains provisions on starting proceedings and on statements by authorities in mental health cases. It also makes provision for hearings and for decisions made by the Tribunal in those cases.

Part 5 deals with correcting, setting aside, reviewing and appealing against Tribunal decisions.

(a) S.I. 2008/2684.

£5.00

E3141   10/2008   183141T   19585

APPENDIX 5

TABLE OF CASES

A. v Kirklees metropolitan Borough Council [2001] ELR 657 (CA)

B. v Hounslow London Borough Council and Vassie [2000] Ed CR 680

Bromley London Borough Council v Special Educational Needs Tribunal [1999] ELR 260 (CA)

Buckinghamshire County Council v H.W. (SEN) [2013] UKUT 0470 (AAC)

Bury MBC v S.U. [2011] ELR 14 (AAC)

C. v Lambeth London Borough Council and Another [1999] ELR 350 (QBD)

CCC v London Borough of Tower Hamlets [2011] UKUT 393 (AAC)

Chapple v Suffolk County Council [2011] EWCA Civ 870 (CA)

C.M. v London Borough of Bexley [2011] UKUT 215 (AAC)

Cooke v Secretary of State for Social Security [2002] 3 All ER 279 (CA)

E. v Newham London Borough Council and the Special Educational Needs Tribunal [2003] ELR 286 (CA)

E. v Rotherham Metropolitan Borough Council [2002] ELR 266 (Admin.)

E.H. v Kent County Council [2011] EWCA Civ 709 (CA)

Fairpo v Humberside County Council [1997] 1 FLR 339 (QBD)

Flannery and Another v Halifax Estate Agencies Ltd [2000] 1 WLR 377 (CA)

F.S. (Re. T.) v London Borough of Bromley [2013] UKUT 529 (AAC)

G. v Wakefield Metropolitan District Council and Another [1998] 96 LGR 69 (QBD)

H. v Kent County Council and the Special Education Needs Tribunal [2000] ELR 660

Haining v Warrington Borough Council [2014] EWCA Civ 398 (CA)

Hampshire County Council v R. & SENDIST [2009] EWHC 626 (Admin.)

Harrow Council v A.M. [2013] UKUT 0157 (AAC)

H.J. v London Borough of Brent [2010] UKUT 15 (AAC)

J. Goodwin v The Patent Office [1999] IRLR 4 (EAT)

K. v London Borough of Hillingdon [2011] UKUT 71 (AAC)

L. v Clarke & Somerset County Council [1998] ELR 129 (QBD)

Levene v Inland Revenue Commissioners [1928] AC 217 (HL)

Lucy v Royal Borough of Kensington and Chelsea [1997] EWHC 23 (QBD)

Paterson v Metropolitan Police Commissioner [2007] ICR 1522 (EAT)

R. (B.) v Vale of Glamorgan County Council [2001] ELR 529 (CA)

European cases

GUIDANCE FOR WITNESSES WHO SEEK TO GIVE EXPERT EVIDENCE IN SEND

First-tier Tribunal HESC: Special Educational Needs and Disability

Appeals and Claims

This guidance is intended to be a statement of what the Tribunal is reasonably entitled to expect of expert witnesses who give written evidence and/or attend hearings to give evidence.

The general principle in all appeals and claims is that all witnesses are expected to assist the tribunal by giving full, frank and honest evidence in a fair, impartial and independent way, regardless of whether they are employed by, or paid by, one of the parties.

SEND appeals and claims often involve evidence from witnesses who claim expertise in a particular area. They may be individuals directly employed by a local authority or other agency or directly commissioned by a party. This guidance contains a set of principles based on the detailed advice available in various codes of practice and guidance and is not intended to be a replacement for those. There is a list of such documents at the end of this guidance to which witnesses should refer.

The Tribunal may regard failure by a party to comply with a requirement (known as a direction) without good reason, as a failure to co-operate with the Tribunal. Since this could lead to all or part of a party's case being struck out, or less weight being attached to part of the evidence, it is clearly important professionals do their utmost to cooperate with each other and comply with any reasonable requests for information.

The Tribunal does not have strict rules of evidence, but the following key points are important and apply to all appeals or claims:

1. Opinion evidence will be accorded little weight before the tribunal unless provided by a witness who has expertise in the relevant area

2. Experts are witnesses with particular qualifications, knowledge and/or skills, which may enable them to give an opinion as long as it is based upon their area of expertise. They do not need to be medically or scientifically qualified but must have specialist knowledge acquired by education or experience.

3. All witnesses should assist the tribunal in accordance with the overriding objective. Parties have a duty to cooperate with the Tribunal, and therefore all witnesses should put this duty first, before any obligation to a person or body instructing them or who pays them.

GENERAL PRINCIPLES

1. Knowledge and understanding

Expert witnesses depending upon the circumstances should be able to demonstrate:

a. Knowledge of the Tribunal's process and their role in it

b. Knowledge of the Code of Practice

c. An understanding of the issues in the case

d. Compliance with all relevant professional codes of conduct and best practice

e. Up to date knowledge of their particular area of expertise

2. Communication and Liaison

The Tribunal's case management process is designed to ensure experts share information and evidence as soon as it is available and identify any need for further expert evidence as quickly as possible.

Good communication and regular liaison between all parties is an essential part of an effective case. It is in the child's interests, and beneficial to all those involved, for experts to communicate from the outset in an open and transparent process. Therefore witnesses should recognise the importance of the overriding objective, taking reasonable steps to ensure all those involved in the case can communicate properly and effectively with each other as early as possible and co-operate to share knowledge and expertise with colleagues for the child's benefit.

3. Evidence

3.1 THE APPROACH TO INFORMATION-GATHERING, ASSESSMENT, PRESENTATION OF FACTS, CONCLUSIONS AND THE GIVING OF EVIDENCE MUST BE BASED ON:

a. ethical, sound, evidence-based standards and principles.

b. instructions, where given, that are clear and unambiguous.

c. precise factual and objective information that clearly identifies what is within their own knowledge and what is not, and the basis for that information.

d. an accurate identification of needs that is in the child's interests and is not influenced by any pressure from a party's wishes or time constraints, and which is not resource-led.

e. consideration of any previous or planned assessment relevant to their area of knowledge and practice to prevent the possibility of test score invalidation.

f. advice that is justifiable and supported by evidence based on the child's needs and considers any material facts that affect that advice either way.

g. the specification and quantification of any recommendations about provision unless there are clearly stated reasons for not doing so.

h. the identification of any hypothesis (as opposed to fact or opinion)

3.2 REPORTS/STATEMENTS

In writing a report, for whatever initial purpose, all expert witnesses must abide by any individual professional code of conduct. They should give details of their qualifications and experience where relevant and include any other information required by their codes of conduct.

In particular, reports must be based on the principles of knowledge and understanding set out above, and be restricted to areas where they have relevant expertise.

Expert Reports should:

a. state the purpose for which they were originally written

b. set out the substance of all material instructions (whether written or oral) and facts supplied that are relevant to the conclusions and opinions expressed

c. give details of any literature or other research material relied on

d. describe the assessment process and process of differential diagnosis, highlighting factual assumptions, deductions from those assumptions, and any unusual, contradictory or inconsistent features of the case;

e. state, with their qualifications, the name of anyone who carried out any test, examination or interview which the expert has used for the report and whether or not that has been carried out under the expert's supervision. State whether other experts have been consulted, at what stage in the process, what information was shared and how did this inform the views expressed

f. include all relevant information whether this supports one party's case or not, including confidence in quoted test scores

g. identify, narrow and agree any issues where possible

h. make it clear if there is not enough information on which to reach a conclusion on a particular issue or point, regardless of any pressure to commit to a certainty

i. identify any relevant facts not requiring an expert explanation in order to understand or interpret the observation, comprehension and description given, as well as any such facts that do require an explanation e.g. properly conducted examinations or appropriate tests.

j. highlight any hypotheses or an opinion based on peer-reviewed and tested technique, research and experience accepted as a consensus in the scientific community; Include other relevant background information whether case-specific, or arising from personal observations, or field-specific arising from relevant literature or research

k. explain relevant technical subjects, or the meaning and application of applicable technical terms where helpful.

l. indicate whether an opinion is provisional or qualified, stating the qualification and the reason for it, and identifying what further information is required to give an opinion without qualification;

m. summarise the range of opinion on any question/issue to be addressed, highlighting and analysing an "unknown cause" (whether on the facts of the case e.g. too little information to form a scientific opinion, or due to limited experience, lack of research, peer review or support in the field of their expertise;

n. summarise opinions expressed with sound reasons for them

o. give a clear summary of the recommendations made and be clearly dated and signed.

Reports should also contain the following statements:

"I understand that my overriding duty is to assist the tribunal in matters within my expertise, and that this duty overrides any obligation to those instructing me or their Clients. I confirm I have complied with that duty and will continue to do so"

"I confirm that I have made clear which facts and matters referred to in this report are within my own knowledge and which are not. Those that are within my own knowledge I confirm to be true. The opinions I have expressed represent my true and complete opinions on the matters to which they refer."

3.3 LETTERS OF INSTRUCTION

The tribunal is entitled to expect that any letter from a representative to an expert should

a. set out the context in which the expert's opinion is sought (including any diverse ethnic, cultural, religious or linguistic contexts)

b. define carefully the specific questions the expert is required to answer.

c. provide clear, focused and direct questions within the ambit of the expert's area of expertise

d. list the documentation provided

e. send any new documentation when it is filed and regular updates to the list of documents provided

f. identify the relevant lay and professional people concerned with the appeal or claim and any other expert instructed and inform the expert of his/her right to talk to the other professionals provided an accurate record is made of the discussion

3.4 ADMISSIBILITY OF EVIDENCE

Where the relationship between the expert and the party calling him or her or any placement being recommended is such that a reasonable observer might think it was capable of affecting the view of the expert so as to make them unduly favourable to that party, it is for the tribunal to decide what weight to attach to his or her evidence.

Witnesses who are directly employed by a party or a public body are not prevented from giving evidence.[1] If an expert witness can demonstrate independence, that is a matter which will be taken into account in considering the weight of the evidence given overall. The tribunal uses its specialist expertise in deciding issues[2] and evaluating all the evidence at the hearing.[3] It will indicate in its decision whether it accepts the evidence of a particular witness and why it does so in preference to that of another such witness, but it is not required to give detailed reasons for so doing.[4]

Judge John Aitken
Deputy Chamber President
February 2010

---

1 See the case of *Factortame* at para 74: the Court pointed out that the MAFF experts were civil servants, but that there could be no suggestions that their positions rendered their giving evidence contrary to public policy.

2 See R (L) v London Borough of Waltham Forest and Another [2003] EWHC2907 (Admin).

3 See F Primary School v Mr & Mrs T and SENDIST [2006] EWHC 1250 Admin.

4 R (H) v West Sussex County Council [2006] EWHC 1275.

INDEX